ROBERT BEYER is Managing Partner˙ of Touche, Ross, Bailey & Smart. He is a C.P.A. of New York, Wisconsin, Illinois, and Michigan and is a national director of the National Association of Accountants. Mr. Beyer was previously a lecturer at the University of Wisconsin and the Harvard Graduate School of Business, and conducted seminars for the University of Wisconsin Management Institute and the American Management Association.

PROFITABILITY ACCOUNTING FOR PLANNING AND CONTROL

ROBERT BEYER, C.P.A.
MANAGING PARTNER,
TOUCHE, ROSS, BAILEY & SMART

THE RONALD PRESS COMPANY • NEW YORK

Library of Congress Catalog Card Number: 63–18550

To my wife, Monica, without whose inspiration and patience this book would never have been possible.

Preface

As competitive and technological pressures relentlessly impelled modern business toward greater growth, complexity, and diversity, management was forced to rely more and more on information systems for the planning and control of operations. Unfortunately, this at first resulted in the more or less independent and often divergent development of various internal information systems, both within the accounting area and between it and other areas such as marketing, production, and engineering. Some years ago, farsighted businessmen began to be aware of conflicts in the signals from these various systems and of the general inadequacy of available information. They and their advisers then began investing time and money in efforts to modernize internal lines of communication.

It was such efforts that resulted in Profitability Accounting. The term *Profitability Accounting* refers to a philosophy of unified business accounting, aimed at simultaneously satisfying both custodial and managerial accounting needs, and to a management information system that carries out the philosophy through the integration of all of the modern accounting techniques. The system produces managerial accounting information without sacrificing consistent application of the principles of custodial accounting.

One of the principal features of Profitability Accounting is the provision of a means for systematic profit planning whereby individual plans may be integrated, converted into forecast profit, reappraised, and, if desirable, revised. Management's attention is focused on potentially unsatisfactory performance which it may be able to avoid by realistic revision of initial plans. In addition, the system furnishes control over performance through the reporting of accounting information by responsibility and in terms

of the deviations from plan that require attention. This includes
the effect on profits of deviations from planned sales prices, volumes, and mix as well as from standard and budgeted cost allowances at the current volume levels.

This is a practical working system. Individually tailored versions of the basic structure are functioning successfully in a wide
variety of manufacturing and service industries. This structure
not only permits integration of all accounting into a single management information system but also puts the accountant in a
position to capitalize on the advent of Electronic Data Processing
and to play a constructive role in the continuing development of
more advanced business systems.

No preface to this book would be complete without an expression of my sincere appreciation for the efforts of Joseph F. Buchan
and Donald J. Trawicki, who assisted me throughout the writing
of the book, the formulation of the ideas, and the development of
illustrations, and to Irvan Featherstone, who is largely responsible
for Chapter 6. I also wish to thank Mrs. Peace Donohue, who
typed the entire manuscript, and Mrs. Barbara Dow, who prepared most of the exhibits in final form. All of these people are
with Touche, Ross, Bailey & Smart. Finally, I wish to thank Pro-
fessor J. B. Bower, of the University of Wisconsin, who reviewed
the manuscript.

ROBERT BEYER

New York, New York
    July 1963

Contents

PROFITABILITY ACCOUNTING FOR PLANNING AND CONTROL

Chapter 1

Increased Emphasis on Management Information Systems

A NEW APPROACH TO ACCOUNTING

In the latter half of the 1950's and the early 1960's, the term *Profitability Accounting* came into increasing use to identify both a philosophy of accounting and a system for carrying out the philosophy.[1] The philosophy can be stated simply: A single unified accounting structure should satisfy simultaneously the objectives of financial (or custodial) accounting and those of managerial accounting. The system is complex, involving the integration of all the modern, profit-oriented, accounting techniques into a single, decision-impelling, management information system.

During this period, Profitability Accounting systems were installed and effectively utilized by small and large companies in a wide variety of industries. These included banks, television stations, construction, foundries, machine shops, fabrication and assembly, process manufacturing, and job shops. During the same period, very similar systems were installed in a number of companies which did not use the term *Profitability Accounting*.[2]

This book is devoted to description of the various accounting techniques which are employed under Profitability Accounting and of the way in which they are integrated into a comprehensive management information system. This first chapter, however, is devoted basically to a discussion of the pressures on business and the advances in technology which led to the increased emphasis on, and the rapid evolution of, management information systems during the period mentioned above. This discussion is preceded by a brief description of the principles and the accounting techniques embodied in Profitability Accounting.

A BRIEF INTRODUCTION
TO PROFITABILITY ACCOUNTING

A variety of management experiences over the years, involving the problems of planning, making decisions, and controlling cor-

---

[1] Robert Beyer, "Meaningful Costs for Management Action," *Harvard Business Review*, Sept.–Oct. 1960.

[2] Harry P. Kelley, "A System Integrating Direct Costing, Standard Costs, Flexible Budgets, and Return on Investment," *Business Budgeting*, June 1959. Marshall K. Evans, "Profit Planning," *Harvard Business Review*, July–Aug. 1959.

porate performance based on the information from the financial-accounting and satellite accounting systems, led to the specification of some principles which seemed essential to the design of a more satisfactory system for accounting information. These principles can be summarized as follows:

Comprehensiveness. The system in any one company should incorporate all of the accounting techniques which are available to supply management with any quantitative information which is useful. Insofar as possible, the conceptual design of the general system should encompass all of the techniques which may be useful in any company.

Consistency. The various satellite accounting systems should be sufficiently integrated so that there is no actual or apparent conflict in the information they provide to management.

Flexibility. The system should be designed so that it can be adapted to future changes in the organization structure and in the data processing procedures and techniques.

Practicability. The system must be designed so as to balance the utility of information against the effort required to obtain it and to be within the operating capabilities of the available personnel and equipment.

The process of designing a system which embodies these principles includes analyzing all of the kinds of accounting data in a company and determining the smallest elements in which the data are initially available. The process also includes a determination of the various kinds and levels of plans, decisions, and performance measures for which accounting data can be of use. Then, by a process of selective synthesis, a system can be designed which combines the elemental data in various ways so as to provide information tailored to each level and type of management need.

The system which results from this process should incorporate the basic concepts of managerial accounting which have evolved and been proved sound during the first half of the twentieth century. These include:

Profit Planning. This is the concept of laying out a detailed, quantitative plan for the performance of each organizational component within the company, usually for a year. The plans are tied together in such a way that each deviation from planned performance can be expressed in terms of its effect on corporate profit.

Responsibility Accounting. This is the concept of fitting the accounting structure to the organization structure so that performance measures can be compiled and reported in groupings which reflect individual responsibilities.

Exception Reporting. This is the concept of focusing reporting effort and managerial attention on the exceptions from planned performance which require action rather than on the bulk of the activity which is performed according to plan. This is exemplified by variance reporting and analysis.

Profit Contribution Accounting. This is the concept of segregating revenues and costs which vary directly with product volume from those that do not. The resultant variable cost per unit does not vary with volume. The contribution from revenue less variable costs is shown before deducting the remaining costs to arrive at net profit.

The system should also make use of all of the bodies of accounting techniques which have been developed more or less independently in response to the various informational needs of management. These include:

Standard costs of material and direct labor which can be used both to measure performance and cost products

Flexible budgets for performance control and product costing in the overhead areas

Return on investment analysis to measure the profitability of the resources employed in various activities of the business and the desirability of alternative capital investments

Management reports which show product profitability and organizational performance, in the amount of detail appropriate to the level and function of the particular manager

A Major Contribution—Integration

Perhaps the most important contribution of Profitability Accounting is the integration of the concepts and techniques listed above into a single consistent and comprehensive system. The diagram in Exhibit 1–1 is an attempt to illustrate both the importance and the complexity of such integration. It illustrates

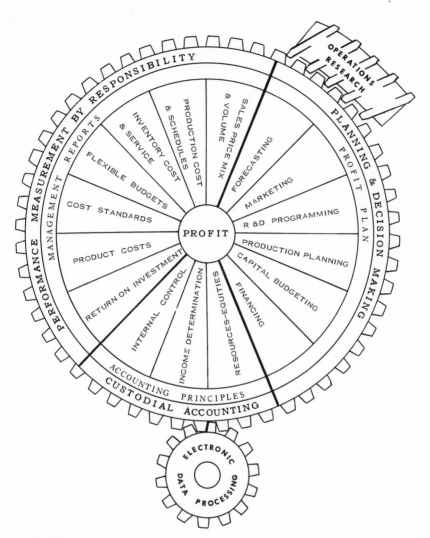

Exhibit 1–1. The functions and techniques which require integration in a management information system.

the three different kinds of accounting objectives which must be satisfied: custodial accounting, performance measurement, and aid to planning and decisions. These are discussed later in this chapter. It also points up the fact that Electronic Data Processing and Operations Research are affecting the accounting system in more and more companies.

Most importantly, the exhibit emphasizes the variety of managerial functions which can be assisted by various accounting techniques, which are related to profit, and which should be integrated. Thus the accounting system used to report on actual performance against planned, in such areas as the cost of production inventories and the price, volume, and mix of sales, should also assist in the evaluation of the planning decisions at the time they are being made. The same system which performs these managerial accounting functions must also meet the custodial accounting objectives of determining income in accordance with accepted accounting principles.

Before proceeding into the details of accounting technique and system design which make up Profitability Accounting, it is worth considering the conditions which led to the relatively rapid and widespread adoption of it and similar systems at a particular period in time.

FORCES INCREASING THE COMPLEXITY OF MANAGEMENT

The manager of the 1950's and 1960's worked in an increasingly complex and continually changing environment. Changes within a company because of changes in the economic environment in which the company operated were not only more rapid but also more extensive than in any previous period. The basic forces which caused these changes and complicated the job of management, although neither easily definable nor readily separable, might be grouped into three classes: technological advances, increasing size of companies, and changing social climate.

Technological Advances

Perhaps the most obvious forces at work, though not the most predictable, were the technological advances which resulted in many new and more complex products accompanied by drastic changes in production and marketing processes.

- Whole new industries such as petrochemicals, aero-space, and atomic energy grew up during the 1950's as a direct result of scientific breakthroughs.

- Developments in the field of solid state physics resulted in the vacuum tube giving way to the transistor, thus opening the entire new field of semi-conductors and speeding the widespread use of computers.
- The word "automation" came into prominent use about 1950 to describe a phenomenon in its infancy at that time. Within ten years, electronically controlled machine tools were in common use; oil refinery operations were automatically controlled by computer programs; strip steel and automobile engine blocks were produced in plants where only a few workmen watched instrument dials.

While these developments were striking, they were only fore-runners of progress to come, for scientific knowledge feeds on itself and tends to increase at a geometric rate. The rate of technological advance during the 1950's was likely to continue, if not accelerate, during the 1960's and beyond.

Increasing Size of Companies

Another force at work to increase the complexity of management was the steadily expanding size of the business entity. By acquisition, merger, or growth from within, many business firms had grown steadily larger. Where there had been only one billion dollar corporation a few years earlier, there were several by 1960. Where there had been dozens of one hundred million dollar corporations, there were hundreds. Many companies grew merely by maintaining their relative position in a steadily expanding economy, which was providing more and more goods and services for each member of an increasing population. The more successful firms grew even faster. Adoption of the divisional type of organization structure enabled many companies to grow to a size beyond that which would once have been considered administratively infeasible.

There are certain desirable functions in our economy which the very large firm can perform best. One of these functions is the reduction in the unit cost of a delivered product through the economies of mass production and mass distribution.

- The effect of the large mail order houses, supermarket chains, oil companies, and appliance manufacturers on their smaller, independent competitors, even after the passage of the Robinson-

Patman Act, is sufficient evidence of the existence of such economies.

The large company can maintain a group of specialized but diverse talents which can systematically advance the frontiers of knowledge and create whole new areas of technological employment.

- The initial development of the satellite communications system by the American Telephone and Telegraph Company is an excellent example of the contribution of big business to technological progress, entirely apart from the controversy surrounding the use of government funds.
- The research and development capabilities of International Business Machines Corporation must be given much of the credit for the rapid evolution of business data processing, although this technological advance is also a reflection of the capabilities mentioned immediately below.

The concentration of material and human resources in the large company, which provides the capacity for mass production and distribution, is usually accompanied by an accumulation of capital which makes it possible to risk the introduction of new products to a mass market. The automobile industry offers several dramatic examples of the effect of corporate size on the ability to risk the introduction of new products.

- Consider the ill-fated advent of the Tucker automobile shortly after World War II. Regardless of the potential market for his product, Tucker could not assemble and organize the necessary material and human resources for mass producing and marketing his automobile in time to capture part of this market from the established manufacturers.
- When American Motors came out with a compact car, their estimate of the market had to be correct or the company might very well have gone out of existence.
- On the other hand, the Ford Motor Company could invest approximately $250,000,000 in a wrong decision about the Edsel, without putting the company in a hopeless financial position.

Although some might disagree with the economic desirability of the particular kind of risks taken in the auto industry, it is the ability of large companies to take such risks that led to the development of synthetic diamonds, commercial jet transports, color television, electronic computers, and a host of other products. Despite the obvious desire of government to restrict the size of "big business," economic pressures and national interest tend to ensure the existence of the large company. And successful small and medium size companies will grow bigger.

This growth in the size of companies increased the managerial span both horizontally and vertically. A manager could expect to have more people reporting to him, and there were likely to be more levels of supervision between the planner and the person who implemented the plans. It is management's task to see that the benefits accruing to the company, and to the economy, from the increased size of the firm are not frittered away because of inability to manage a larger firm efficiently.

Changing Social Climate

The third force which complicated the task of management was the changing social climate which prevailed, as epitomized by the increased influence of government, unions, and public opinion on business decisions. The economic dominance which businessmen once had over their employees, and which was not always exercised wisely, was broken forever in the 1930's by the rise of strong labor unions which had public sympathy and, in consequence, government support. The increase in the economic power of unions continued steadily through the 1950's until it affected management decisions in almost every phase of every business. The union leaders did not exercise their power any more wisely than had management in an earlier era. After they had raised sub-standard wages by eliminating exorbitant profits, their continued pressure for annual pay increases in excess of the increase in real productivity could only lead to inflation or to corporate decay. Their increasing attempts in the 1950's to safeguard the existence of jobs made obsolete by advancing technology led in the same direction. Examples of the effect of increased union power on management decisions are practically endless, but a few will suffice here.

- The strength of unionism and its effect on the prevailing wage scale became major considerations in the location of new plants, stimulating a general exodus of jobs from the industrial and heavily unionized northeastern United States to the South and West, particularly in the textile, electrical, and automotive industries.

- The so-called featherbedding rules in union contracts were an important factor in the decline of most railroads under the pressure of airplane and truck competition. For example, trainmen (including the "fireman") on a modern diesel were paid for a trip according to the time that an ancient coal burner would have required to travel the same distance.
- One of the major automobile manufacturers discovered that its work standards were as much as 20% below the level of its two major competitors. A two-year program of attempting to tighten these standards to competitive levels encountered hundreds of "wildcat" strikes.
- The introduction of "automatic-load" cargo ships and palletized loads, which would enable 4 longshoremen to do the work of 40, was countered by union rules that required "the load (not the pallet) to touch the pier" and set minimums on the number of men per ship loaded.

Although there was evidence in the early 1960's that government was nearing the point of legislating some curbs on union power, the unions will continue to be an important factor in business. And government appears destined to play an increasing role in our business lives as well as in our private lives.

The federal government exercised considerable control over business practices through its various regulatory bodies such as the Securities and Exchange Commission, the Federal Trade Commission, the Federal Communications Commission, and the Pure Food and Drugs Administration. Businessmen who had become familiar with the Robinson-Patman restrictions on price differentials to customers were reminded of the dangers of price similarities between competitors by the anti-trust action against the electrical manufacturers. The government also had a significant impact on economic stability and the economic climate in general by its use of the Federal Reserve powers, taxation, and its own fiscal management and purchasing policies.

There was also increasing evidence of more direct governmental intervention in the area of economic planning, much of it brought on at the insistence of business itself, by means of special legislation involving things such as subsidies, tariffs, and quotas. Even the powers of taxation were being used less as a means of raising revenue and more as a means of directing business effort. The changing policies on depreciation allowances offer a good example of this. Nor is the government's intervention necessarily limited by existing legislation, as was dramatically illustrated in the spring of 1962 by the hastily rescinded increase in steel prices. Management was and is faced with an increasing problem of working with government to provide a stable and growing economy while maintaining sufficient freedom to perform its essential function—the efficient production of goods and services.

CHANGES IN THE MANAGERIAL FUNCTION

The role of the manager changed radically during the first half of the twentieth century. Management of a business evolved as a full time occupation requiring special skills and became increasingly distinct from ownership of the business. The basic forces mentioned above greatly reduced the likelihood that a business could be successful by merely maintaining the "status quo." The planning function was made more difficult by these forces and also more important. More and more the successful manager became one who could set goals and then take action to achieve these goals. Peter Drucker puts it well: ". . . managing goes way beyond passive reaction and adaptation. It implies responsibility for attempting to shape the economic environment, for planning, initiating and carrying through changes in that economic environment, for constantly pushing back the limitations of economic circumstances on the enterprise's freedom of action." [3]

Greater Reliance on Information Systems

In order to provide this kind of creative leadership in an increasingly complex and competitive business environment, management needs, above all else, information. The modern

[3] Peter F. Drucker, *The Practice of Management* (New York: Harper & Row, 1954), p. 11.

manager, except in the very small firm, cannot have personal experience with, or first-hand knowledge of, all that is necessary to manage his business effectively, nor can he rely upon his intuition to include and evaluate all of the complex factors which affect most of his business decisions. He must place more and more reliance on information which is developed by others, both within and without the company, and which is communicated to him by means of an efficient information system. He needs information in order to perform each of the basic tasks in the management cycle: to set the proper objectives; to establish the plans for attaining those objectives; to carry out those plans; to appraise the performance of the organization in carrying out those plans; and, finally, to feed back into revised and additional planning.

Management needs the right information, in the right form, at the right place, and at the right time. The "right" information is that which is necessary for effective performance of each function of management at its various levels. It must be accurate and pertinent to the action at hand. It must be in a form that is clearly understandable to the person who is supposed to act upon it. It must be provided to the particular persons within the organization whose actions can be improved by it, and it must be received in time to influence the action which it is supposed to assist.

The availability of increased information does not reduce the need for sound judgement in the making of all management decisions. Nor does it eliminate the need for managers to assume the responsibility for making decisions based on incomplete and inadequate information. The quality of judgement exercised in such decisions will continue to distinguish the well-managed company from the indifferently managed one, provided that the information systems in each company are of comparable quality. A properly designed information system, however, can make it possible for management judgement to be applied on a much more objective and efficient basis. It can greatly reduce the number of decisions which have to be based on inadequate information. As more information becomes available in more explicit form, the areas in which such information is not readily available become more clearly recognized at the same time as management is enabled to devote more effort to subjective judgements in these areas.

INCREASED USE OF QUANTITATIVE INFORMATION

While the increasing complexity of business forced management to rely more heavily upon information systems, parallel developments increased the availability and the utility of quantitative information. The development and refinement of accounting techniques such as standard costs, flexible budgets, and profit contribution analysis continued steadily through the first half of the twentieth century. However, developments in two other technological areas dramatically increased the emphasis on business use of quantitative information during the 1950's. These were Electronic Data Processing and Operations Research. This book is primarily devoted to the developments in the first of these three areas while the last chapter contains a discussion of the other two. The remainder of this first chapter, however, contains a brief summary of these developments, their interactions, and their effect upon the evolution of management information systems. The discussion concludes with a mention of the more highly integrated information systems which can be anticipated in the future and the impact of the trend toward these systems upon the functions of the controller.

Effect of Increased Demands upon Accounting

Accounting has been the primary source of quantitative information in business for so long that it may well be considered the "language of business." Its evolution into a complex and comprehensive body of professional disciplines has been directed primarily, however, toward the establishment of generally accepted rules which enable the over-all financial status of any business to be expressed in comparable terms. One of the best examples of a successful rule for this purpose was the adoption in the early 1900's of "full absorption costing," under which all of the manufacturing costs were assigned to products and carried through inventory into cost of sales. It helped to ensure consistency of accounting treatment among businesses and made periodic income statements more meaningful.

While financial accounting for external reporting purposes was being codified, however, management's expanding needs for internal information were reflected in increased demands for different kinds of accounting information. It wanted quantitative measures of the effects of various decisions and the performance of various sub-divisions of the company. In attempting to satisfy these increased demands, the accountant was frequently faced with two alternatives, neither of which was completely satisfactory.

He could design a basic accounting system around the financial data requirements and then attempt to satisfy the other needs for information by rearranging the data available from this system. This explains the tendency for some accountants to treat the "full absorption cost" mentioned above as a "true cost," and to supply it to management in situations where it is completely inappropriate. (See Chapter 9, for a few examples of this.)

Alternatively, the accountant could satisfy many of management's other information needs by designing a number of "satellite accounting systems" without integrating them with either the financial accounting system or each other. This explains such developments as "memorandum accounting" for standard costs and budgets, with the attendant risk that management may receive conflicting signals from their various information systems.

Because the technological restrictions which initially pressured the accountant toward the selection of one of these two alternatives are less severe than they once were, it is worthwhile to take a fresh look at the multiple objectives of the accounting function in a business. These are summarized in the next section of this chapter. This section also describes briefly the general type of business accounting structure which existed at the time when the developments in data processing technology began to affect this structure.

The Three Objectives of Accounting

All of the business accounting functions can be classified into three major conceptual categories which have significantly different objectives. Although the following classification may at first seem rather pointless from an accounting viewpoint, it is quite useful for focusing attention on the different objectives of the accounting system. It distinguishes among decisions as to what plans the business should adopt, measurement of detailed performance against these plans, and the over-all financial results of this performance.

Custodial accounting is defined as the financial accounting for the assets entrusted to the enterprise. It is basically concerned with preparation of reports and data for groups or persons other than management. This includes the preparation and presentation of reports to stockholders, as well as to creditors or governmental agencies such as the SEC or the Internal Revenue Service.

Performance accounting is the quantitative matching of performance against some plan by organizational responsibility. It includes all accounting procedures and reports which exist in order to evaluate organizational performance. Performance accounting includes the functions which some accountants call responsibility accounting, i.e., the collection of costs by organizational responsibility. It also deals, however, with quantitative data other than costs. This may include such things as product line revenue, physical workload statistics, and internal net income reports. It implies the use of standards and budgets. Its distinguishing characteristic is that it serves to measure actual performance against planned performance by responsibility.

Decision accounting is the quantitative evaluation of alternative courses of action. It includes all disciplined techniques for providing quantitative information in the form which can best assist a specific management decision at the time when the decision has to be made. This includes all of the profit planning decisions as to product pricing, make or buy, inventory policies, and choice of alternative production methods. It is the area in which business has historically depended on special analyses and memorandum accounts.

The last two of the above classes are grouped in the minds of many under the heading of "managerial accounting." Certainly the three classes are not unrelated. The decision-making and planning process within a business vitally affects the performance measurement system, may even determine it. In turn, information fed back from this measurement system should help in evaluating the plans and decisions as well as measuring performance against them. The important fact is that the accounting structure which must serve custodial accounting objectives handles most of the

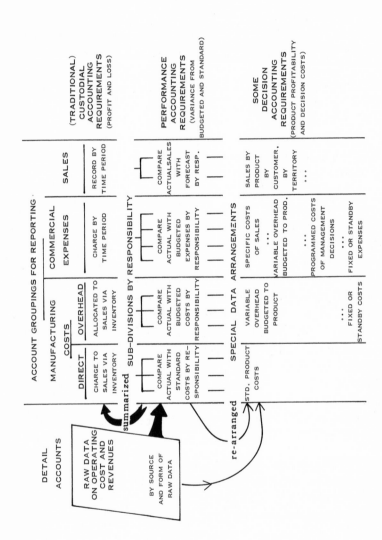

Exhibit 1-2. Influence of accounting objectives on the accounting structure.

same data used for making decisions and measuring performance. Therefore, this structure and the operation of this structure may vitally affect both decision making and performance measuring ability.

Exhibit 1–2 represents a kind of conceptual worksheet of a company's accounting structure. It indicates how the various accounting objectives affect the grouping of accounts and the use of particular accounting techniques. The exhibit does not imply that three parallel accounting systems should be maintained in a company. It does imply, however, that the basic elements of a single accounting system should be designed with a view toward satisfying the three different kinds of requirements.

As indicated in the exhibit, the traditional effect of the custodial requirements on the collection of accounting data has been to treat manufacturing costs and commercial costs separately. The former were carefully allocated between inventory and cost of sales, while the latter were charged as a period cost.

The desire for measuring individual performance in business of increasing size and complexity led to sub-grouping costs by responsibility and using standard and budgeted costs. Standard costs for direct material and labor require some effort to maintain, but they do provide useful performance variances. They are also useful for the custodial requirements of costing sales and inventory. The typical overhead standards are useful for costing sales and inventory and may be fairly inexpensive to maintain, depending upon the number of product cost centers. But they are seldom useful and may be misleading for performance measurement. The flexible budget, based on careful analysis of workload, is the commonly useful technique for performance measurement in the overhead area.

Many management decisions can be helped by segregating the variable costs which relate to the dicision. (See examples in Chapters 9, 11, and 12. Thus compilation of all of the variable costs which relate to a product may aid decisions in such areas as product pricing, make or buy, and selective selling. This may mean that some commercial expenses are included and some manufacturing costs are excluded. Separate collection of total costs resulting from the annual determination of an advertising or a research program is also a form of accounting for the variable costs of a decision, since costs which may be fixed for a year after the decision is made are variable at the time of the decision.

Exhibit 1–2 illustrates the way in which accountants have continued to expand the areas in which they could aid management by providing more and better quantitative information. It also indicates how the requirements of custodial accounting, along with the restrictions of existing data processing technology, led to the development of satellite accounting systems, outside of the formal financial accounting structure, in order to provide this information. This evolution of accounting technology was both stimulated and altered by the emergence of two other bodies of technology. The advent of the Management Sciences increased the number of special arrangements of quantitative data which could be useful to management. At the same time, the advent of Electronic Data Processing reduced the need for maintaining separate accounting systems in order to meet differing accounting objectives. Nor does the increased ability to arrange accounting data in a variety of special groupings necessarily mean an increase in accounting cross-charges and re-allocations. Rather, the raw data is more likely to be grouped in several different ways at the point of initial collection. More and more the utility of the accounting information which can be produced from a single integrated system will be limited only by the form, content, and accuracy of the raw data. The effects upon accounting of these two emerging technologies is elaborated upon briefly below.

Emergence of the Management Sciences

The 1950's saw the application to business of a body of techniques which greatly increased the pressures for more quantitative information. This new technology is variously called *Management Sciences* or *Operations Research.* These two terms and the techniques which they encompass are discussed in Chapter 12. The significance of these techniques lies in their ability to introduce greater rationality and objectivity into management's efforts to solve business problems involving complexity and uncertainty. Most of this technology is mathematically based and directed toward providing a more accurate determination of the quantitative effects of various management decisions.

The availability of the techniques increases the kinds of quantitative data which are useful in a business, as well as increasing the importance of accuracy in those data. Although the practical application of these techniques to the solution of business problems was initially limited to certain well-defined areas, considerable research and development effort was expended in a continuing expansion of the areas of application. Most of these techniques make use of accounting data and Electronic Data Processing, but, in their initial use at least, they were not integrated with the formal accounting information system. Although there were a number of good reasons for this lack of integration, including the experimental nature of much of the early work, one reason is of particular interest to accountants. Much of the accounting data required for the application of these techniques was not routinely available from the existing accounting system.

The Impact of Electronic Data Processing

Of overriding importance to the whole field of management information was the advent of Electronic Data Processing. The sheer speed and calculation capabilities of the digital computer have completely changed the nature of business information systems. These systems are now less restricted by the ability to compile, process, and provide data than by the ability of people to interpret data and act upon them. This development has been greeted with naive hope by some managers and irrational fear by others: naive hope that acquisition of a computer will automatically close the information gap in existing systems, and irrational fear that the manager will be replaced by the big computer.

The fact is that no amount of speed or capacity in gathering and processing huge amounts of data can obviate the need for designing a system which can analyze, translate, and organize these data into a form which is useful in the management process. Furthermore, unless the organization is properly structured, the availability of the "right" information does not necessarily mean that correct decisions will be made or that proper action will be taken at the various levels in the company. The information gap will exist regardless of the hardware used, until management accurately diagnoses its functional needs for information and puts into operation a system to provide that information, whether this be by manual, mechanical, or electronic methods.

The fear that managers will be replaced by electronic computers is unfounded in most instances. It is likely that the organization structures of companies will be changed by the advent of the computer and the accompanying pressures for integrated information systems, but organization structures have changed in the past. It is also likely that there will be a trend to automation in some areas of management as well as in the clerical and blue collar areas. But, at least in the foreseeable future, the automation of management will be restricted to the highly repetitive and routine decisions which can be expressed in terms of explicit and quantitative rules. The majority of managers whose duties truly require human skills beyond mere manipulation of quantitative data will be little affected. The two important characteristics of Electronic Data Processing, at least insofar as its initial effect on management information systems is concerned, can be summarized as follows:

- It enables existing information systems to be operated faster, more accurately, and perhaps at a lower cost.
- It opens up avenues of information which were previously closed because of the time and expense of handling huge volumes of data.

In connection with the latter point, Electronic Data Processing complements the Management Sciences. Without the computer many scientific techniques would not be feasible. Without the Management Sciences many of the computer installations would not be worthwhile. But Electronic Data Processing does not, of itself, provide an information system for management.

MANAGEMENT INFORMATION SYSTEMS IN THE FUTURE

The ultimate impact of Electronic Data Processing on management information systems does not end with its ability to handle larger volumes of data more rapidly and to perform more complex calculations. There is every reason to believe that Electronic Data Processing, along with the Management Sciences, new concepts of business organization, and an analysis of management's functional needs for information, will soon result in a single automated and integrated management information and control system. To it will flow all of the basic data generated in the enterprise, and from it will come information tailored to satisfy the particular needs of particular managers. In many cases this will require re-arrangement and re-interpretation of the same basic data. The system will satisfy the objectives of both custodial and managerial accounting. It will encompass quantitative, non-financial information, and eventually will include non-numerical information as well. Thus the concept of integrated information which underlies Profitability Accounting will be enlarged to encompass the Management Sciences and Electronic Data Processing techniques in a single "advanced business system." The trend toward such a system is discussed at some length in Chapter 12.

The Future Role of the Controller

Historically, most of the data processed in a company has been of an accounting nature, and the controller, as the chief accounting officer, has usually been considered the primary provider of management information. Developments in Electronic Data Processing and the Management Sciences, however, have greatly increased the use by business of non-financial information. These developments have drastically changed the scope and the nature of the information systems within a business. They have also occasioned a re-examination of the controller's function with respect to the over-all information requirements of a company. The Concept of Modern Controllership as adopted by the Controllers Institute of America is quite broad in its scope:

"1. To establish, coordinate and administer, as an integral part of management, an adequate plan for the control of operations. Such a plan would provide, to the extent required in the business, profit planning, programs for capital investing and for financing, sales forecasts, expense budgets and cost standards, together with the necessary procedures to effectuate the plan.

"2. To compare performance with operating plans and standards, and to report and interpret the results of operations to all levels of management and to the owners of the business. This function includes the formulation and administration of accounting policy and the compilation of statistical records and special reports as required.

"3. To consult with all segments of management responsible for policy or action concerning any phase of the operation of the business as it relates to the attainment of objectives and the effectiveness of policies, organization structure and procedures.

"4. To administer tax policies and procedures.

"5. To supervise or coordinate the preparation of reports to governmental agencies.

"6. To assure fiscal protection for the assets of the business through adequate internal control and proper insurance coverage.

"7. To continuously appraise economic and social forces, and governmental influences, and interpret their effect upon the business."

This concept of controllership extends well beyond the boundaries of traditional financial accounting. It can encompass the development and administration of an information network which will serve all of the needs of management, as well as those of outside interests. Such an interpretation effectively re-defines the controller's job as "Director of Management Information," but it requires the controller to extend his range of interests, activities, and responsibilities beyond his traditional accounting functions. The importance of custodial accounting will continue to shrink, relative to other aspects of the total information system, and the public accounting profession will exert increasing influence in determining policies and procedures for reporting to outsiders. Economics, mathematics, and Electronic Data Processing will assume greater significance, and men trained in these disciplines will compete for the job of "Director of Management Information." Controllers have the opportunity to lead in the evolution of the advanced business systems described in Chapter 12 and to increase the importance of their position as the provider of management information. Those controllers who do not grasp this opportunity, who limit their activities to the development of financial data and the issuance of financial statements, may well find themselves relegated to a gradually shrinking role in business affairs.

SUMMARY

The continuing growth in the size and complexity of business led to increased managerial reliance on information systems and increased demands for accounting information. The emergence of Operations Research and Electronic Data Processing in the 1950's increased both the demands and the capabilities for satisfying these demands. At the same time, these developments gave added impetus to the evolution of Profitability Accounting as both a concept and an integrated system which could meet the various requirements of custodial accounting, performance accounting, and decision accounting. The system was directed at integrating the various satellite accounting systems in such areas as standard costs and budgeting with the traditional financial accounting system. It incorporated the concepts of profit planning, responsibility accounting, exception reporting, and profit contribution accounting, and it was adopted by companies of varying sizes in a wide variety of industries.

Chapter 2

The Concepts of Profitability Accounting

THE PLANNING and control cycle, which in the broad sense is synonymous with management, consists of at least the following six functions:

1. The predetermination or planning of objectives and standards of performance
2. The measuring and recording of actual performance and results
3. The determination of variances between plans and performance
4. The reporting of results
5. The evaluation of reasons underlying variations from planned performance
6. The appropriate managerial decision and action

These functions operate in a continuous cycle which has no real starting point. Although the first four provide the information which is the basis for the last two, the action taken is fed back into the cycle in terms of new or revised plans. Effective management depends upon the accomplishment of all six functions in almost every part of the enterprise.

Profitability Accounting incorporates the first four of these functions into a management information and control system which provides a bridge between the data generated in an organization and the essential functions of management. This system is the means by which mere data are converted into valuable information for effective management action.

THE CONCEPTS

In Chapter 1, the principles underlying the development of a sound accounting information system were enumerated as comprehensiveness, consistency, flexibility, and practicability. The primary concepts or characteristics of the Profitability Accounting system, which was designed around these principles and directed toward providing the information for carrying out the management functions of planning and control, are the following:

- *Profit Planning.* The focus of Profitability Accounting is on planned profits. The system helps managerial planning by providing measures of the effect of alternative decisions on profit. It then provides for summarizing the results of the planning process into an integrated and quantitative profit plan against which actual performance can be measured and reported.

- *Responsibility Accounting.* Quantitative information is compiled within the system and reported in groupings which correspond to individual responsibilities within the organization. This information includes not only costs but also other quantitative data such as revenues and statistics.

- *Management by Exception.* The reporting system focuses most attention on the deviations from planned performance which indicate a need for management action and pays correspondingly less heed to performance which is proceeding more or less according to plan.

- *Building Block (Modular) System Design.* To meet the information needs of various functions and organizational levels within a company, similar data may have to be arranged in a variety of ways. Because of this, the data are originally grouped into "building blocks." A building block is the smallest unit of data which is required to satisfy an information need and which is economically feasible to obtain. These "blocks" are then put together in various ways to serve a variety of needs.

- *Profit Contribution and Incremental Costs.* The system does away with the need for special break-even analyses to determine the effect of production fluctuations on profit. It does this by segregating revenues and costs which vary with volume from those which do not.

- *Integration.* In Profitability Accounting, all of the information and accounting techniques which are useful in a particular company are integrated into a single comprehensive and consistent system.

The above concepts are fundamental. They prescribe an approach to providing management with the information needed for decision making which is as valid for firms engaged in distribution or service operations as it is for those engaged in manufacturing.

PROFIT PLANNING

Maximum Profit

It has long been classic economic theory that the basic objective of a business enterprise is the achievement of maximum profit. A great many businessmen agree. Yet several leading corporation consultants and highly respected business educators contend that the concept of profit maximization is "false" and "irrelevant"; [1] that it is "unrealistic" and "immoral"; [2] and furthermore that "many firms, particularly the big ones, do not operate on the principle of profit maximization in terms of costs and revenues, but rather set standards or targets of reasonable profits." [3]

The issue concerns us here only as it bears on questions which are fundamental to the practice of management and therefore affect the design of a management and control system. Under existing economic and social conditions, the average enterprise must fulfill a responsibility to the people who are employed by it, to the people whose money is invested in it, and to the community and nation in which it functions.

Existing legislation provides ample evidence of government insistence that a business be socially desirable as well as economically sound.

Even within these sociological restraints, there are relatively few businesses and businessmen whose sole objective is the maximization of short-range profits. These are usually speculators or special purpose companies formed to take advantage of a specific situation.

The average businessman must balance the maximization of short-range profits against the effect of this policy on future profits. At this point, the theory of profit maximization begins to break down as a sole guide because of the difficulty of measuring the future profits which will result from foregoing current profits. The relationship, though real, is probabilistic and difficult to define with any degree of accuracy. For example:

- In the years following the death of the OPA, after World War II, when the demand for automobiles was still high, manufacturers could have charged much higher prices than they did and still sold all of their output. Instead, they chose to hold the line and take only a reasonable profit. Their reasons for this included the avoidance of government intervention and the maintenance

---

[1] Peter F. Drucker, *The Practice of Management* (New York: Harper and Row, 1954), p. 35.

[2] Robert N. Anthony, "The Trouble with Profit Maximization," *Harvard Business Review*, Nov.–Dec. 1960.

[3] Joel Dean, *Managerial Economics* (Englewood Cliffs, N.J.: Prentice-Hall, Inc., 1951), p. 28.

of customer goodwill—reasons with definite long-range implications.

Similar problems involving subjective judgements about restricting short-range profits to ensure profitability occur constantly. For example:

- How much, if anything, should be spent on research and development of new products which will not materialize for years in the future, if ever?
- Should a new sales territory be opened even though it is not expected to pay its way for from three to five years?
- Should an employer pay severance pay in a situation not covered by an employment contract?

Planned Profit

Planning is the reconciling factor and planned profit the common denominator between the past and the future. But not only does it furnish a perspective for evaluating decisions that have long-range implications, it also furnishes a means of coordinating the actions of managers within the firm to achieve desired objectives and serves as a means of measuring and evaluating operational performance in the continuum of the firm's existence.

Planning is the foundation of Profitability Accounting, just as it must be the first step in effective management. In Profitability Accounting, profit planning provides management with quantitative analyses of the probable effect of alternate planning decisions upon profit. It is the means whereby costs, revenues, levels of operation, programs to be undertaken, physical and financial resources, and product strategies are all considered and inter-related in the planning process.

It is important that this profit planning be conducted in a formal manner to make sure that none of these factors be overlooked. A properly ogranized procedure also confers the additional benefit of allowing management to revise initial plans in an objective manner if the projected profit from these plans proves unsatisfactory.

Some of the mechanics of preparing a formal plan are described in the latter part of Chapter 7. The use of Profitability Accounting information as an aid to communication and coordination during the planning process itself is described in Chapter 9, with a number of examples of how this information must be tailored to fit particular decisions.

The profit plan which results from this process then becomes the basis for management control through the reporting of performance against plan. The plan provides a basis of measurement from a plotted course, rather than a measurement against historical and perhaps irrelevant performance. The performance reported against each element of the plan can be expressed in dollars so as to permit complete reconciliation of planned profit and actual profit by adding the amounts of individual variances.

Making a Profit Plan

Planning is a continuous function of every manager. Under Profitability Accounting, however, some elements of planning take on a very formal aspect several months before the beginning of each year. This process of profit planning involves not only the development of detailed plans but the integration of these plans into a comprehensive whole. The steps which have to be integrated in the profit-planning process include the following:

- Making detailed forecasts of sales by product line and of mix within product lines
- Setting flexible budgets for all overhead expenses in accordance with the responsibility structure of the organization
- Classifying all planned costs into their variable, standby, and programmed elements
- Determining planned product costs, using engineered or estimated specifications for material and direct labor and applying budgeted expenses to obtain the variable manufacturing overhead
- Determining incremental product costs, by adding to planned product costs any budgeted variable overhead from areas other than manufacturing
- Assigning specific costs and allocating general standby and programmed costs to product lines
- Making detailed forecasts of cash flows and the balance sheet and of assets employed by product line

The detailed plans for every aspect of operations are considered, revised, reviewed, and finally agreed upon by responsible managers. The complexity of combining these into a master plan

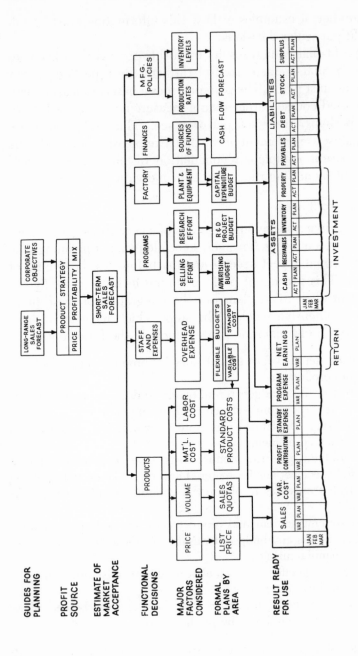

Exhibit 2–1. The profit plan—integrates subsidiary plans.

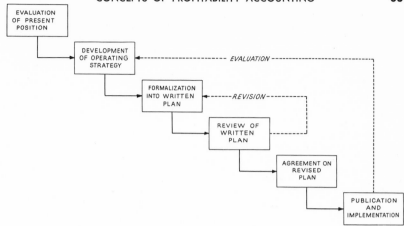

Exhibit 2–2. Profit planning—an evolutionary process.

called the profit plan is illustrated in Exhibit 2–1. Here we have
the building block principle being applied to the process of handling data so that it is possible to start with basic elements and
shape them into a summary statement of the company's operating
plans, though still retaining the flexibility which permits the basic
data to be used for a variety of other purposes. The profit plan
is then put up for review, which provides a means for re-challenge
of volume, sales mix, production planning, inventory levels, cost
allowances, and other vital management considerations. If the
outcome is unsatisfactory, the detailed plans may be revised until
a satisfactory combination can be agreed upon. This evolutionary, and perhaps cyclical, nature of the profit-planning process is
illustrated in the diagram of Exhibit 2–2.

A typical plan is presented in Exhibit 2–3. Here is a statement
in financial terms which relates plans for the coming year and
reveals the results that can be expected if the plans are followed.
The profit plan and all the detailed plans which underlie it represent the first step in the development of an integrated management control system.

RESPONSIBILITY ACCOUNTING

There comes a time in the growth of most successful enterprises when no one man has the time or talent to make all the
decisions, supervise a host of subordinates, and maintain first-hand

	Total Company	Product Lines		
		A	B	C
Gross sales	$70,637,000	$42,382,000	$13,421,000	$14,834,000
Variable costs				
Specific sales deductions:				
Trade discounts	$ 3,532,000	$ 2,826,000	$ 706,000	
Commissions	5,298,000	4,238,000		$ 1,060,000
Freight out	353,000	183,000	170,000	
Allowances	70,000	10,000	23,000	37,000
Cash discounts allowed	280,000	141,000	60,000	79,000
Direct materials	21,191,000	11,655,000	4,238,000	5,298,000
Direct labor	11,176,000	5,588,000	1,866,000	3,722,000
Variable manufacturing expense	7,065,000	4,945,000	997,000	1,123,000
Variable commercial expense	2,507,000	1,630,000	653,000	224,000
Total variable costs	$51,472,000	$31,216,000	$ 8,713,000	$11,543,000
Profit contribution	$19,165,000	$11,166,000	$ 4,708,000	$ 3,291,000
Standby expenses:				
Specific	$ 6,978,000	$ 3,023,000	$ 1,538,000	$ 2,417,000
General	3,284,000	1,616,000	922,000	746,000
	$10,262,000	$ 4,639,000	$ 2,460,000	$ 3,163,000
Programmed expenses:				
Specific	$ 2,699,000	$ 2,027,000	$ 270,000	$ 402,000
General	634,000	291,000	176,000	167,000
	$ 3,333,000	$ 2,318,000	$ 446,000	$ 569,000
Planned operating earnings	$ 5,570,000	$ 4,209,000	$ 1,802,000	$ (441,000)
Taxes on income	2,891,000			
Planned net earnings	$ 2,679,000			
Average monthly capital employed	$32,500,000			
Capital turnover rate	2.17			
Percentage return on sales	3.79%			
Percentage return on capital employed	8.24%			

Exhibit 2–3. This year's profit plan for the Vortex Manufacturing Company.

knowledge of operations by personal contact with the people who are doing the work. Then the authority and responsibility for the direction of the enterprise must be shared among a group of people in order to bring to bear the wider range of abilities and greater amount of management effort required for the success of the enterprise. The people in this group manage, plan, organize, make decisions, take action, and assume responsibility for achieving individual objectives. They must work together if the over-all objectives of the enterprise are to be attained.

The Organization Structure

The organization structure defines the relationship among the managers. Its purpose is to set forth for each the scope of his activity, responsibility, and authority and thereby contribute to effective interaction. The shape an organization structure takes in any particular company results from a variety of influences, such as the philosophy of top management, the dispersion of plants and markets, the diversity of products, and the abilities and interests of the various members of the management team. No one type of organization structure fits all companies or all phases of growth and development. However, one principle of organization is universally applicable: Internal authority and responsibility must be clearly and unequivocally assigned if management is to be effective.

Control by Responsibility

A clear assignment of responsibility is essential to an effective management information system. Business data become information only when in a form which can be used in the process of management. Profitability Accounting builds on this principle. It gathers raw data on costs, revenues, and profits; then it organizes, classifies, and develops these data into information which is tailored to the responsibility structure of the enterprise. The information and control system is built around the organization in the sense that the necessary information is brought to the proper point in a form which is most useful to management. This tailoring process serves two purposes:

1. It provides a feedback of information to the responsible manager, revealing to him the effects of his past actions and indicating to him the important areas for future consideration and attention. It specifically directs this information to the manager who can take action, the one who has authority and responsibility in the area affected.
2. It enables higher management to evaluate individual performance and take action in good time if any situation gets out of hand.

Management control, as embodied in the concept of management by responsibility, means control *by* managers as well as control *of* managers. Although it provides a means of measuring how well a manager is doing his job, it also requires that he be provided with the tools he needs. It is not a restrictive activity but a constructive one. It makes possible the delegation of authority and responsibility which is essential for the effective management of any sizeable enterprise without sacrificing over-all control.

Responsibility for Costs

Establishing responsibility for costs is not an easy task. It is particularly difficult to define responsibility in such areas as maintenance, quality control, methods, scheduling, and materials handling. For example, we run into such questions as these:

- Is maintenance in a machine shop a responsibility of the machine shop foreman, the plant manager, the maintenance foreman, or the director of engineering?
- What are the boundaries of the machine shop?
- What is the difference between fabricating and assembly?
- How is responsibility defined for shifts within a department?

In some manufacturing plants, responsibility will run by function, so that one foreman might be responsible for all welding, and welding might be done anywhere in the plant. In another case, a foreman might be in charge of all work on one class of products. Responsibility would then follow product line rather than function.

The organization chart should supply most of the information required to resolve problems of defining responsibility. In some companies which do not have a formal organization chart, it is necessary to sit down with management and draw one up. Even if a chart exists, it is often found to be inadequate, either because it does not reflect all responsibilities or because it portrays incorrectly the actual division of responsibility and authority within the organization. It may be necessary to revise the chart or the organization or both, so that lines of authority and responsibility flow cleanly. In some cases, efforts to solve other problems fail because these problems are only symptoms of a faulty organization structure.

Once organizational responsibilities for costs are determined clearly and unequivocally, two kinds of information are provided for each element of cost within each area of responsibility:

1. Planned or allowable amounts of costs are developed. Standard costs and flexible budgets are used to predetermine allowable amounts for each element of cost under varying conditions of volume. These basic data are used for other purposes as well, but in the first instance they are used to control costs by responsibility.
2. Actual costs are collected and reported by responsibility groupings.

The comparison of actual costs with allowable costs provides the responsible manager with a ready means of planning and controlling his own operation. It enables him to exercise continuous control over costs, and produces far better results than sporadic cost-cutting campaigns hastily launched in time of crisis. At the same time, it provides his superiors with a concise and comprehensive report of his performance in an important phase of his job.

Responsibility for Revenues and Profits

Nearly every manager in the organization has a direct responsibility for costs of one kind or another. Fewer managers have direct responsibility for revenues and still fewer have direct responsibility for profits. The process of establishing responsibility for revenues and profits is quite similar to that of establishing responsibility for costs. A clear-cut assignment of responsibility to a particular manager who has enough authority to exercise control is the first essential. Next, standards or goals are set which represent satisfactory performance, a step which involves a sales forecast and a profit plan. Finally, actual revenues and profits are collected by responsibility and compared to the pre-set goals.

The important distinction between the responsibility for costs and revenues and the responsibility for profits should be clearly understood. A sales manager will most certainly have responsibility for revenues, just as a foreman will have a direct responsibility for costs. In both cases, variations from planned performance will affect planned profits, but in neither case can the manager be held directly responsible for the absolute level of profits. Only a general manager who has direct responsibility for both revenues and costs, and who can influence the spread between them, has this important responsibility.

Recording Actual Performance

A carefully designed chart of accounts is essential to good managerial control. Profitability Accounting follows the principle that the chart of accounts should conform to the responsibility structure of the organization so that the data originally recorded in the accounts are grouped by responsibility insofar as possible. The application of this principle facilitates the reporting of consistent, accurate, and meaningful information for managerial planning and control.

Exhibit 2–4 is a simplified functional diagram illustrating the major aspects of the flow of data in a Profitability Accounting system. The details of this diagram, as well as those in the illustrations of the profit plan in Exhibits 2–2 and 2–3, are related to a manufacturing company, but the system is equally appropriate for a firm providing services or for one engaged in distribution.

Actual data on revenues, expenses, and operations are collected in the normal manner, as a by-product of billings to customers, recording and paying bills from suppliers, compensating employees, and other regular functions. Some of the data necessary for managerial control are non-financial in character and may include measures of such items as employee turnover or absenteeism, unit production or direct labor efficiency. Such data are easily accommodated in reports to managers.

Only the financial segment of these data, of course, enters the accounts of the enterprise. Financial data are sorted by type and by responsibility, as specified in the chart of accounts, and then recorded. Finally, the actual data are compared to plans, budgets, and standards, and expense variances are determined and recorded.

In some cases it may be desirable to charge some of the expenses of a service department, such as the tool room, to other departments which use these services in order to reflect the secondary responsibility for cost. It is never appropriate to charge the items of expense directly to the department served. All overhead expenses are first charged to the department spending the money. They may then be charged to the department using the service, and finally related to the product line. The first charge, and perhaps the second, is actually made on the books of account,

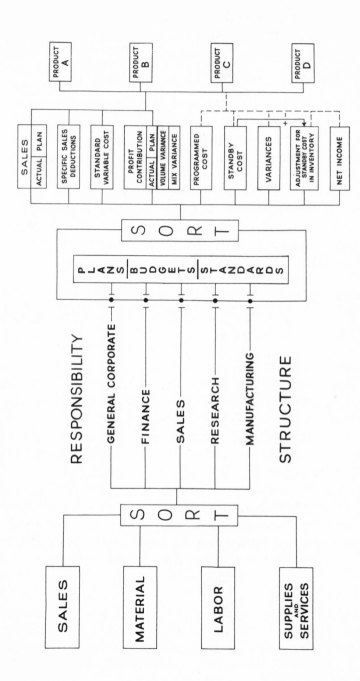

Exhibit 2–4. Profitability accounting and control.

while the third is made only on specially designed worksheets in the preparation of management reports.

MANAGEMENT REPORTING BY EXCEPTION

Once the detailed operating plans of the enterprise have been agreed upon, the recording of actual performance, if done accurately and efficiently, becomes a routine function of little concern to the operating managers. It is the exceptions or variances from planned performance which assume significance, because these are the signals for management attention. It is the *cause* of the variance, not the variance itself, that should be the focus of management attention and action. A variance signals the existence of a problem which may mean faulty performance, faulty planning, or changes in anticipated conditions.

The Variances

In Profitability Accounting, the entire difference between planned profits and actual profits is first accounted for by reporting the following four basic kinds of variances:

1. *Sales Volume Variance.* If the actual volume of sales at standard prices differs from the planned volume at these prices, then actual profit will differ from planned profit by an amount equal to the expected profit contribution which is gained or lost because of this difference in sales. This is what is meant here by "volume variance," and it should not be confused with the "volume variance" which results from over- or under-absorption of overhead under full absorption accounting.

2. *Sales Mix Variance.* If the over-all, average rate of profit contribution on the actual mix of products sold is different from the rate of profit contribution on the planned mix, actual profit will differ from planned profit by an amount equal to this difference in profit contribution rates extended by the actual sales (at standard prices). This deviation from planned profit contribution is called the sales mix variance.

3. *Sales Price Variance.* If the prices at which sales are made differ from the planned prices, actual profits will differ from planned profits to the extent of the total of these differences. If

the alteration in price is made by changing an established discount structure, the variance may be recorded as a trade discount variance and included in the total of expense variances. Where there is no discount structure, however, the price variance would automatically be included in the mix variance, unless some additional effort is expended to determine it. In the many cases where this would prove worthwhile, the price variance would then be grouped in the top earnings statement, along with volume, mix, and cost variances. Sales price variances are vital information in situations where the same products are sold at different prices. (See Exhibit 11–12, for an example of the computation of these three variances.)

4. *Cost Variances.* Any variations of actual costs from standard and budgeted allowances for cost will be directly reflected in deviations from planned profit. This includes variances from planned ratios of specific sales deductions such as cash discounts, sales commissions, and freight; departmental spending variances in material usage, labor efficiency, and overhead expense; and variations from programmed amounts of maintenance, research, and advertising expenditures. Other variances include purchase price and material yield.

The extent to which variances are further detailed may vary considerably from one company to another, depending on the kinds of problems which are most troublesome and the particular structure of responsibility in the organization. Whatever the particular situation may be, the extent to which variances are to be detailed is determined during the preliminary planning and this is readily reflected in the design of the chart of accounts and the management reports.

Management Reports

The effectiveness of Profitability Accounting as a managerial control system depends to a great extent on the quality of the reports generated by the system. It is in these reports that the integration, which is the central theme of Profitability Accounting, is most evident, and it is this integration which makes the system uniquely useful in the management of an enterprise.

The exact nature of the reports for a particular company are determined by the nature of that company; they must be tailored

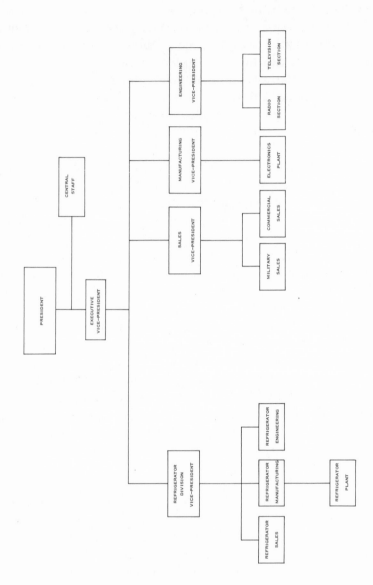

Exhibit 2–5.   Vortex Manufacturing Company organization chart.

to fit personnel, systems, policies, and organization. They must reflect the operating climate and the objectives of the business. They must reveal the problem and assist the manager in finding solutions.

The reports in Exhibits 2–6 and 2–7 are typical of those generated by a Profitability Accounting system. They are from the hypothetical Vortex Manufacturing Company, which is a multi-plant, multi-product operation. Since the management reporting structure must be tailored to the needs of the particular company, the Organization Chart is shown in Exhibit 2–5. The company manufactures refrigerators in a completely separate, integrated division, comparable to a wholly owned subsidiary, which is responsible for its own sales and its own manufacturing. The electronics division of the firm manufactures television sets and radios in another plant, using common facilities for both, and sells to military as well as industrial markets.

Exhibit 2–6 is a consolidated statement of the net earnings in April for all divisions. Such a report is furnished to top management each month. April was a good month and net earnings were $258,000 better than planned. Moreover, they are $622,000 better than planned for the year to date, and the company currently anticipates earnings of $2.03 per share for the year, representing a 7.3% return on investment. This is also much better than originally planned.

The differences between actual results and planned results are summarized in the lower left corner of the report in terms of the four variances described earlier.

1. Sales, at standard prices, are running $974,000 ahead of those anticipated for the year to date. These additional sales, of course, provide additional profit contribution—some $234,000 for the year to date. The *sales volume variance* shown at the lower left in Exhibit 2–6 is the effect on profits of a variance from planned sales volume.

2. The company is selling a mix of products that has a higher profit contribution rate than the average anticipated. The rate for the year to date is 2.2 better than planned, which is equivalent to $514,000. The *sales mix variance* shown is the effect on profits of a variance from the planned mix.

( ) = UNFAVORABLE VARIANCE   (DOLLARS IN THOUSANDS)

MONTH	GROSS SALES OVER (UNDER)	GROSS SALES ACTUAL PLAN*	STANDARD PROFIT CONTRIBUTION — AMOUNT OVER (UNDER)	STANDARD PROFIT CONTRIBUTION — AMOUNT ACTUAL PLAN*	PER CENT SALES OVER (UNDER)	PER CENT SALES ACTUAL PLAN*	SALES PRICE VARIANCES OVER (UNDER)	EXPENSES VARIANCES OVER (UNDER)	EXPENSES STANDBY PLAN	EXPENSES PROGRAMMED PLAN	OPERATING EARNINGS BEFORE TAXES OVER (UNDER)	OPERATING EARNINGS BEFORE TAXES ACTUAL PLAN*	BONUS AND PROFIT SHARING OVER (UNDER)	BONUS AND PROFIT SHARING ACTUAL PLAN*	NET EARNINGS OVER (UNDER)	NET EARNINGS ACTUAL PLAN*	EARNINGS PER SHARE ACTUAL PLAN*	MONTH
JAN	(225)	3,750	(190)	1,073	(3.2)	28.6	(59)	164	850	249	(85)	79	(17)	16	(34)	31	.02	JAN
FEB	237	5,035	205	1,432	2.8	28.4	(42)	140	852	284	303	394	21	79	143	160	.13	FEB
MAR	483	6,458	386	1,758	4.3	27.6	(10)	183	858	307	559	766	43	153	255	304	.24	MAR
APR	475	8,155	347	1,879	3.1	23.0	(50)	237	856	385	534	825	32	165	258	337	.27*	APR
MAY		5,991*		1,617*		27.0*			855	245		517*		103*		211*	.17*	MAY
JUN		6,348*		1,775*		27.8*			855	50		870*		174*		343*	.28*	JUN
JUL		6,262*		1,712*		27.4*			855	277		580*		116*		209*	.17*	JUL
AUG		7,111*		1,927*		27.2*			856	324		747*		149*		292*	.24*	AUG
SEP		6,804*		1,854*		27.2*			856	372		626*		125*		225*	.18*	SEP
OCT		5,305*		1,527*		28.9*			855	237		435*		87*		158*	.13*	OCT
NOV		5,413*		1,511*		27.9*			856	276		379*		76*		139*	.11*	NOV
DEC		5,354*		1,498*		23.1*			858	327		313*		63*		107*	.09*	DEC
YEAR TO DATE	974	23,398	748	6,142	2.2	26.2	(161)	724	3,416	1,225	1,311	2,064	79	413	622	832	.66	
ORIGINAL PLAN		71,012		18,815		26.5			10,262	3,333		5,220		1,227		1,894	1.53	
CURRENT FORECAST		71,986		19,563		27.2	(161)	724	10,262	3,333		6,531		1,306		2,516	2.03	

	THIS MONTH	YEAR TO DATE
PLANNED EARNINGS BEFORE TAXES	291	753
SALES VOLUME VARIANCE	95	234
SALES MIX VARIANCE	252	514
SALES PRICE VARIANCE	(50)	(161)
EXPENSE VARIANCE	237	724
ACTUAL EARNINGS BEFORE TAXES	825	2,064

	ORIGINAL PLAN	CURRENT FORECAST
AVERAGE CORPORATE ASSETS	34,500	34,500
CAPITAL TURNOVER	2.06	2.09
× RETURN ON SALES	2.7%	3.5%
RETURN ON ASSETS EMPLOYED	5.5%	7.3%

Exhibit 2–6.   Vortex Manufacturing Company statement of net earnings.

ASSETS

MONTH	NET WORKING CAPITAL		CASH AND SECURITIES		CURRENT ASSETS NET ACCOUNTS RECEIVABLE		INVENTORIES		NET PROPERTY, PLANT AND EQUIPMENT		TOTAL ASSETS EMPLOYED		MONTH
	Plan	Actual	Plan	Actual	Plan	Actual	Plan	Actual	Plan	Actual	Plan	Actual	
JAN	13,009	12,486	1,650	1,548	4,500	4,291	13,900	13,991	11,450	11,974	31,500	31,804	JAN
FEB	13,001	12,884	950	852	5,100	5,094	14,700	14,751	11,500	11,599	32,250	32,296	FEB
MAR	13,575	13,539	1,000	827	5,800	5,902	14,800	14,843	11,150	11,207	32,750	32,779	MAR
APR	12,948	13,737	850	973	6,000	6,072	15,000	15,179	11,650	10,897	33,500	33,121	APR
MAY	13,446		700		5,200		15,200		11,400		32,500		MAY
JUN	13,714		600		5,200		15,400		11,550		32,750		JUN
JUL	13,417		1,000		5,000		15,000		11,750		32,750		JUL
AUG	14,176		1,850		5,400		14,400		11,350		33,000		AUG
SEP	14,876		2,650		5,200		14,200		10,950		33,000		SEP
OCT	14,610		2,650		4,800		14,000		11,050		32,500		OCT
NOV	14,692		2,100		4,750		14,000		11,150		32,000		NOV
DEC	14,742		1,850		5,000		13,900		10,750		31,500		DEC

LIABILITIES AND STOCKHOLDERS' INVESTMENT

MONTH	CURRENT RATIO		TRADE ACCOUNTS PAYABLE		CURRENT LIABILITIES NOTES PAYABLE TO BANKS		ACCRUED INCOME TAXES		LONG-TERM DEBT		STOCKHOLDERS' INVESTMENT		MONTH
	Plan	Actual	Plan	Actual	Plan	Actual	Plan	Actual	Plan	Actual	Plan	Actual	
JAN	2.8	2.7	3,809	4,111	3,000	3,000	232	233	5,000	5,000	19,459	19,460	JAN
FEB	2.7	2.6	4,672	4,756	2,800	2,800	277	257	5,000	5,000	19,501	19,483	FEB
MAR	2.7	2.7	5,016	5,002	2,600	2,600	409	431	5,000	5,000	19,725	19,746	MAR
APR	2.5	2.6	5,824	5,371	2,400	2,400	678	716	5,000	5,000	19,598	19,634	APR
MAY	2.8		4,507		2,200		947		5,000		19,846		MAY
JUN	2.8		4,197		2,000		1,289		5,000		20,264		JUN
JUL	2.8		4,192		1,800		1,591		5,000		20,167		JUL
AUG	2.9		3,895		1,600		1,979		5,000		20,526		AUG
SEP	3.1		4,864		1,400		910		5,000		20,826		SEP
OCT	3.1		4,504		1,200		1,136		5,000		20,660		OCT
NOV	3.4		3,825		1,000		1,333		5,000		20,842		NOV
DEC	3.5		5,108		800		100		4,500		20,992		DEC

Exhibit 2-7. Vortex Manufacturing Company data with respect to financial condition.

3. Price concessions below the established discount structure resulted in a reduction of profits in the amount of $50,000 during the month of April, and a reduction of $161,000 for the year to date. This illustrates the *sales price variance*.

4. Expenses during the month of April were $237,000 less than the budgeted or standard amounts, and $724,000 less for the year to date. Thus the *cost variances* shown are directly reflected in variance from planned profits.

The total of the sales volume and the sales mix variances is the difference between the planned profit contribution and the actual contribution, or $748,000, as shown in Exhibit 2–6, for the year to date. When actual and planned profit contributions are computed, all sales are assumed to be at standard prices and all costs are assumed to be at the budgeted or standard levels. The net deviation from these conditions, $563,000 for the year to date, is reported in the column headed "Variances," and it is broken down between $161,000 of unfavorable sales price variance and $724,000 of favorable cost variances in the summary in the lower left corner of Exhibit 2–6. The additional statements for this company, which are included in Chapter 10, show that these sales price variances are in addition to an amount of price concessions which were programmed by management decision.

The information provided in such a statement of net earnings may suggest that current and projected economic conditions should be re-examined and perhaps original goals should be revised on the basis of this re-examination. The difference between the current forecast for the year and the original plan in Exhibit 2–6 indicates such a revision. This is an illustration of how the reports in Profitability Accounting allow early detection of deviations from plan so that they may have immediate management attention.

Exhibit 2–7 shows the balance sheet of the Vortex Manufacturing Company on a trend basis. The inventories, in this case, include an unchanging complement of standby manufacturing overhead for all 12 months of the year because it has been forecast that inventories will be approximately the same at the end of the year as they were at the beginning. If there were to be a significant change, an amount representing the change in standby costs in the inventory could be provided for as a programmed expense.

In any case, the financial statements produced for external reporting purposes in a Profitability Accounting system are the same as the statements which could have been produced by a traditional custodial accounting system applying generally accepted accounting procedures and principles. Accounting for external reporting purposes has not been lost, but, rather, managerial control has been gained.

PROFIT CONTRIBUTION AND INCREMENTAL COSTS

Failure to recognize that there is no such thing as a single "true" cost of a product or service has been the cause of much misunderstanding and many poor managerial decisions.

- In one instance, the president of a company manufacturing office furniture called in his controller and asked him: "What is the cost of our Model 60 desk?" The controller came back with a figure of $247.50 for that particular model, based on absorption of all manufacturing costs at the current level of operations, which was 50% of capacity. To this controller, $247.50 was the true cost of a Model 60 desk. However, the president was developing a bid to supply 2,500 Model 60 desks to the federal government which, if successful, would raise the level of operations to 65% of capacity. He was unaware that this unit cost, based on 50% utilization, was not the cost which applied at 65% utilization, and he was unwittingly exposed to the error of overstating his costs in submitting the bid.

This example, and others like it in Chapter 9, illustrates the fact that a cost is true only for a given purpose. The proper cost for income determination is not necessarily proper for bidding or pricing purposes or for decisions about adding or dropping a product. The point is so important that it will bear repeating:

There is no such thing as a "true" cost in an absolute sense; there is only a cost which is proper for the particular decision for which it is being used—one which will lead to logical conclusions.

Incremental Costs

For managerial decisions which recur frequently, such as those affecting short-term pricing and volume, make or buy determinations, and profit planning, the problem is to determine how much a unit of product adds to or subtracts from the net profit of the company. For this purpose, the incremental cost of a unit of that product is the proper cost. This is the cost that will be incurred if an additional unit of the product is made and sold, or that will be avoided if one unit less of the product is made and sold. The difference between the selling price of the unit of product and the incremental cost to manufacture, distribute, and sell it is the profit contribution, the amount by which the net profit of the company is affected.

In Profitability Accounting, incremental costs are equivalent to those which have been defined as the variable costs. These are the costs which will increase or decrease with the volume of activity. The variable costs include the planned specific sales deductions resulting from the sale of the product, the cost of the standard direct labor and the standard materials which go into the unit of product, and the planned variable overhead costs that are incurred as a result of its manufacture, distribution, and sale.

Standard material cost and standard direct labor cost are normally predetermined by engineering studies or estimates which are useful for cost control purposes and which also provide product cost. The planned variable overhead costs are derived from the flexible budgets of each of the responsibility units affected by the product. These flexible budgets are also designed, in the first instance, to control costs. For example, the planned variable overhead costs in the machine shop may be related to direct labor hours in the machine shop.

The work on a product in the machine shop may cause the planned variable overhead cost of that department to increase in proportion to the amount of direct labor involved in the machining of the product. The amount of the increase per unit of product in all of the departments similarly affected is the incremental or variable overhead cost of a unit of the product.

Exhibit 2–8 illustrates how the effect of volume on net profit is measured. The top line in the top graph shows the total sales for one or all products, a directly proportional increase in sales dollars for each increase in physical volume. The other straight line in this graph, with a lower rate of increase, shows variable costs, proportional to volume. The latter are the incremental costs which

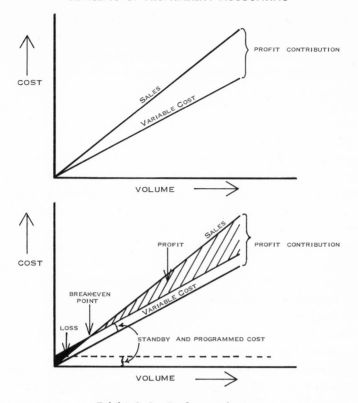

Exhibit 2–8. Profit contribution.

are incurred only as a product is manufactured, distributed, and sold. The difference between the revenue from sales and the variable cost of those sales is profit contribution, which increases with volume as long as the unit sales price exceeds the unit variable cost.

In the bottom graph, the standby and programmed costs are added. These costs are not related to volume. They are the same absolute amount at all levels of volume. Without any sales at all, the amount of the loss would be the amount of standby and programmed costs. With every added unit of sales in which the selling price is in excess of variable costs, this loss is reduced until a break-even point is reached. A break-even point is a point at which profit contribution equals the amount of standby and programmed cost. Profit contribution is, therefore, the net amount of money which a particular volume of product contributes toward first covering programmed and standby costs and then producing net profit. It is the appropriate measure of profitability for many management decisions in the areas of short-range pricing and volume, make or buy determinations, and profit planning.

Product Line Profit Contribution

Managers are continually interested in evaluating the profitability of individual product lines in order to make decisions in the areas of product planning, target pricing, and performance measurement. A product line is a grouping of products which are related for purposes of certain management decisions. They may be similar in design and go through the same manufacturing operations. They may be sold through a common distribution channel. They may be under a single , sales or manufacturing responsibility. They may face similar competitive pressures and therefore be priced as a group. They may conform to a divisional breakdown in a divisionalized organization.

Though other factors enter, the grouping chosen in any such situation is likely to be the one which promises to be the best for decision-making purposes.

Product line profitability implies product line revenue less product line cost. However, this cost may range from incremental cost to what is traditionally referred to as full cost. To meet varying needs, the building blocks of cost in Profitability Accounting provide a means for the measurement of product line profitability at various levels within this range. The appropriate measure of profitability and, therefore, the appropriate cost will differ, depending on the specific purpose involved.

The determination and accumulation of variable costs as distinguished from all other costs permit the ready calculation of profitability on at least three different levels and under various conditions of volume or mix within a product line. The first level is revenue less directly variable costs. A second level is reached by the further deduction of standby, programmed, and any variance costs which are specifically identified with a product line and which can be avoided if the product line is dropped. The general standby and programmed costs which are not incremental with units of product and not specifically related to a product line can be allocated to product lines on the basis of a concept of long-term utilization of the general services and facilities of the enterprise. The deduction of these allocated costs produces a third level of profitability which corresponds to net profit at full cost.

The appropriate measure of product line profitability for nearly any decision involving product line strategy can be obtained by the selective combination of these categories of product line costs.

BUILDING BLOCK (MODULAR) SYSTEM DESIGN

The essential criterion for a management planning and control system is its ability to deliver information in a form which is meaningful and useful in the management of the enterprise. But the same pattern of information is not appropriate for all of management's needs. That is precisely why traditional accounting has not filled the role of a comprehensive management information system. Traditional accounting is designed and operated to maintain accountability for assets and liabilities, and to determine periodic over-all corporate income in accordance with sound accounting principles. Its aim is to satisfy the information needs of shareholders, governmental agencies, and the general public. In this area it has done a creditable job. However, the same type of information is not adequate for controlling operations, costing products, planning profits, and making various managerial decisions.

In Profitability Accounting, the traditional accounting objectives of accountability and income determination are met and the varying needs of different managers in the organization are satisfied, all within a single system. This is done by means of "building blocks" or, as the computer people would say, "modular systems design." Under this principle, data are originally classified in the smallest units, or "building blocks," which can be determined in an economical manner and which are required to satisfy any of the information or control objectives. These units are then arranged and re-arranged to form a variety of information patterns.

The kind and frequency of decisions in the various areas for which information is required determine how the data are to be collected. Data are originally collected and arranged to aid directly in the most important and frequently recurring type of decision and are then re-arranged for less pressing decisions.

The application of the building block principle to the compilation of revenue data makes possible various kinds of sales forecasts and analyses: by product or product line, by customer, by salesman, by sales division, by territory, or by whatever other classification may be useful to management. Such information breakdowns and combinations are put to valuable uses in sales management, profit planning, and performance measurement.

The building block principle is perhaps of greatest value in the area of costs because the same basic data can be used for profit planning, controlling costs, and developing product costs for short-range make or buy and pricing decisions, while simultaneously satisfying the cost requirements for income determination and asset valuation. It can also be used to supply information for capital budgeting and long-range planning.

The Cost Building Blocks

In Profitability Accounting, it is recognized that the costs which a business incurs behave, or should behave, differently under varying conditions of volume. Therefore, all costs are classified into six distinct groups as follows:

1. *Specific sales deductions* are those costs incurred only if and when a sale is made. They may include planned commissions, outbound transportation, royalties, trade discounts, and cash discounts. They vary directly with volume of sales.

2. *Specification costs*, or prime costs, are the planned direct material and direct labor costs of a product. These costs are determinable from the bill of materials or blueprint, and from the process routing. They vary directly with volume of production.

3. *Variable overhead costs* are those which, it is planned, will vary with some measure of volume, but they are not necessarily associated directly with a product. They include both manufacturing and commercial costs. It is important to emphasize that these costs can vary in significantly different ways. They may vary directly with volume or they may vary in step fashion. They may vary with specific products, specific operations, or company-wide activity.

4. *Programmed costs* are those planned costs which will be incurred for some particular time period as a result of a specific management policy decision. Once this decision is made, the

costs become established for the time period, unless, and until, they can be cut back by a countermanding management decision which may be required by a change in business conditions. Typical examples of programmed costs are research and development expenditures, costs of advertising media, and abnormal training, change-over, or start-up costs.

Programmed costs are further classified as specific or general. That is, they may be specifically attributable to a product line or profit center, and would cease if that segment of the enterprise should be discontinued. Or they may apply to general corporate functions which would continue unaffected by what might happen to an individual product line or profit center.

5. *Standby costs* are planned overhead costs which would be incurred at zero volume of business, perhaps in the case of a strike, if there were full expectation that normal operations would be resumed before it became necessary to trim costs to such an extent that the basic organization would be impaired. They would include wage and salary costs of that essential nucleus of supervisory and maintenance personnel which would be retained under such "ready to serve" conditions. They would also include taxes, depreciation, and other costs. Standby costs, too, may either be general or specific to product lines or profit centers.

6. *Cost variances* are the differences from the planned amounts of cost in all of the above categories. They may result from unexpected changes in operating conditions or a deviation of actual performance from standard performance. Although they are usually unfavorable, or additional costs, they may also be a reduction from standard costs.

The first three of the above categories are variable costs. They are expected to vary with some measure of volume. The first five categories are planned costs, provided for in the financial planning of the enterprise. The sixth category, the cost variances, will arise as the result of operations. The six categories together include all of the costs of the enterprise, classified in accordance with their incidence and expected behavior.

In Profitability Accounting, each item of cost, account by account, is analyzed, and the allowable amount is determined objectively at the various possible levels of activity and under standby conditions. Setting schedules of allowable amounts for cost at the various levels of activity is, in fact, setting standards and constructing variable or flexible budgets.

INTEGRATION

One of the weaknesses of the managerial information provided in many companies arises from the fact that it is produced by a number of more or less independent systems which have evolved at various times in order to satisfy particular information needs. Thus, a system of collecting marketing data for sales-forecasting purposes may not be tied to a production and inventory control system, and neither may be tied into the accounting system. Even within the accounting area, the standard cost system and the budgeting system may be independent of each other and irreconcilable with the financial accounting for external reporting purposes. As a result, the information which is provided to managers is often incomplete, conflicting, or so structured that it is useful for only one purpose.

In Profitability Accounting, at least all of the accounting information and control techniques needed for the effective management of the enterprise are integrated into a single control system in which the different kinds of information provided for all the various purposes are comprehensive and completely consistent. Managers are not confused by conflicting and overlapping data nor frustrated by the need for special studies to obtain information for regularly recurring decisions.

This integration of the various management control tools is accomplished initially in the planning stage. It is carried through to the recording of performance, the measurement and analysis of variations from the plans, and the reports to managers. Standard costs, flexible budgets, profit planning, and return on capital employed are all integral parts of a single system. This system also provides valuable information for capital budgeting, and pricing as discussed briefly below.

Return on Capital Employed

As stated earlier in this chapter, a businessman must earn a profit adequate to cover the cost of the capital utilized and to provide for future risks, if he is to remain in business. Loosely defined, the cost of capital is the interest charged by suppliers of debt capital and the current and future dividends expected by suppliers of equity capital.

Financial management has long been concerned with the sources of capital funds, balancing the lower cost and higher risk to the enterprise of additional borrowed capital against the lower risk and higher cost of additional equity capital, with a view to improving the position of existing stockholders. The concept of rate of return on equity capital is familiar as a measure of the effectiveness of financial management in balancing the risks and costs of the various sources of capital funds.

From the point of view of operating management, however, there is another concept which is found more useful. It is the rate of return on capital employed. This concept has been a part of the control systems of such well-managed companies as duPont and General Motors for 30 or 40 years, but only recently has it been widely adopted by others.

As far as operating management's use of funds is concerned, a dollar of equity capital is indistinguishable from a dollar of debt capital. The total funds invested must produce the total profit necessary to cover the cost of capital, from whatever source, and also provide for future risks. The concept of rate of return on capital employed is a measure of the effectiveness of the utilization of funds, regardless of their source. This is the relevant measure for the operation of the enterprise, and this is the measure which is emphasized in Profitability Accounting.

Needless to say, there is no "true" rate of return on capital employed, any more than there is a "true" product cost. The true rate of return is one which is meaningful and appropriate for the use to which it is put. This fact is recognized in Profitability Accounting, and the system is flexible enough to permit the use of this concept in several ways in order to meet the needs of the enterprise.

In the use of the concept of return on capital employed to make comparisons among companies, the appropriate data to be employed may well be those which would appear in the published financial statements, since these are the only data normally available on other companies. This kind of calculation is illustrated in

Exhibit 2–6 for the Vortex Manufacturing Company. It uses the total assets of the company as the capital employed. The return is earnings after income taxes.

On the other hand, when determining the profitability of divisions or product lines for internal comparisons or evaluation of managerial performance, it may be desirable to use a more direct and detailed measure. Capital employed may be calculated to include only the assets specific to the division. However, the carrying value of the assets may be adjusted to reflect current rather than historic values. The return may be earnings before taxes and bonuses. If the product line is being measured, it may be desirable to exclude performance variances from earnings, since these are deemed to be attributable to managers, not to the product line.

Note that the two factors which make up the rate of return on capital employed—earnings as a percentage of sales and capital turnover—are separately stated. The calculation could be done directly by dividing earnings by capital employed, since the sales factor cancels out in both fractions, as is indicated below:

$$\frac{\text{Earnings}}{\text{Sales}} \times \frac{\text{Sales}}{\text{Capital Employed}} = \frac{\text{Earnings}}{\text{Capital Employed}} = \frac{\text{Rate of Return}}{\text{on Capital Employed}}$$

However, showing both fractions points up the effect of both capital turnover and the ratio of earnings to sales and shows how each influences the rate of return on capital employed.

Capital Budgeting

Rate of return determinations for capital-budgeting purposes are necessarily accomplished in special studies apart from the information reported to managers on a recurring basis, because these determinations may require estimates of future cash flows, revenues, and expenses. However, they frequently require use of past and current data as well.

Because of the manner in which information is developed in Profitability Accounting—starting with the basic building blocks— the relevant data are readily available in most cases. Make or buy decisions fall in somewhat the same category, and are often simply special problems in capital budgeting. Capital budgeting is discussed at length in Chapter 8, and make or buy problems are illustrated briefly in Chapter 9.

Pricing

Product pricing is probably the area of management in which there is the least agreement as to theory and the least consistency in practice. Yet pricing decisions are probably the most frequent and most important decisions that managers make. The considerations of price are a fundamental determinant of profitability.

Because pricing is so fundamental, there is a need for a basic price policy. The objective of such a policy is to provide effective control, disclosing the need for changes in operations which may result in the channeling of available capital into newly profitable areas.

Essentially, pricing is an instrument of long-range planning. The establishment of basic price policy and target prices under Profitability Accounting, based on the concept of rate of return on capital employed, and integrated with the entire system of financial control, will be discussed at length in Chapter 11.

There is another more immediate pricing problem, however, and this has to do with the specific price of a product at a given point in time, rather than with the basic price policy. Because of the intensive competition that exists in nearly every sector of a free enterprise economy, managers must be able to react quickly and intelligently to changes in the relationships of supply and demand. They must know what the incremental cost of a product is so that they can determine the possible effect on profit of a contemplated price adjustment and volume change.

It is in this area that Profitability Accounting is of special benefit, because basic reporting under the system is in terms of incremental costs and profit contribution, as illustrated in Exhibit 2–6. Managers no longer need special studies and lengthy calculations to translate "full costs" and "gross profits" into meaningful information for making price decisions. Managers are presented with product unit costs which are constant for any level of output and are useful separately or with the other costs which are specifically related to a product. This information is a by-product of the build-up of costs for budgetary control purposes, and is available immediately as a part of the regular accounting process under Profitability Accounting.

SUMMARY

Perhaps the most unique feature of Profitability Accounting is the manner in which the various managerial control tools are integrated into a single system. This integration is carried through all four of the essential steps in the functioning of a management information and control system: planning, recording of actual performance, determination of variance, and reporting to managers.

The concepts on which Profitability Accounting is based have been indicated as follows:

Profit planning
Responsibility accounting
Exception reporting
Profit contribution and incremental costs
Building block system design
Integration

This and the preceding chapter have been designed to provide the reader with a broad picture of what Profitability Accounting is and what it does. Subsequent chapters will present specific, detailed procedures and ideas on how to apply Profitability Accounting to a wide variety of business situations.

Chapter 3

Profitability Accounting and Direct Costing

INTRODUCTION

CHAPTERS 1 and 2 have described the basic concepts of Profitability Accounting. Now, before discussing its many valuable applications, let us see how Profitability Accounting compares in fundamental philosophy with another concept which in some respects is similar but in other respects is quite different. This second concept, increasingly popular since World War II, is known as *Direct Costing*.

Direct Costing was first discussed formally in this country by Jonathan Harris as early as 1936 in an article entitled "What Did We Earn Last Month?" In this article, Mr. Harris expressed the view that managers were being misled by the financial statements developed for them on the traditional "Absorption Costing" basis. In his opinion, profits were being overstated when production exceeded sales and understated when sales exceeded production. He held, in effect, that they were only correct when production and sales were in balance.[1]

This provocative enunciation stimulated thought but little action in the next few years. Then came the lush years of World War II. Nobody could get excited about dissertations on the reporting of profits. Business in general was profitable and the type of problem which inspired Mr. Harris' article simply was not critical at the time.

Right after the war, however, the situation changed and the article came to be widely read, for managers were again beginning to feel that something was missing in the financial information being presented to them. It was hard to find an accountants' convention or seminar which did not offer the subject of Direct Costing as part of the program.

At one of the seminars, a large and well-known company with long experience in the use of the traditional Absorption Costing method reported the incredible fact that, during months when production was heavy and sales were low, it was not unusual to find that earnings were greater than sales. This was certainly a clear reflection of the fact that something was wrong with traditional methods of reporting, and first-class evidence that management needed improved explanation and greater clarification of its operating results.

As indicated in Chapter 2, the inventory amounts computed under Profitability Accounting contain the full complement of standby manufacturing overhead. Thus, insofar as pricing inventory and reporting of over-all corporate income are concerned, Profitability Accounting produces the same results as the traditional Absorption Costing method. It is only in reporting the details underlying these results that Profitability Accounting departs from the Absorption Costing method.

Under the Direct Costing method, on the other hand, inventories are priced to contain only the variable portion of manufacturing overhead. The standby amount of such overhead is

[1] Jonathan N. Harris, "What Did We Earn Last Month?" *NAAC Bulletin*, January 15, 1936.

charged against earnings during the period in which it is incurred. This is the amount referred to by the term *period expense*. It is obvious, with changing levels of in-process and finished goods inventories, that this difference in the method of pricing inventory can be accompanied by a significant difference in the reported earnings.

In order to convey more clearly an understanding of the concepts we are comparing, let us (1) examine the postulates of income reporting, then (2) see to what extent they are satisfied under Profitability Accounting, and (3), under Direct Costing. Then let us seek conclusions with respect to the most desirable method of reporting income to managers and shareholders.

THE PURE CONCEPT OF INCOME

From a purely conceptual point of view, *income* may be defined as the amount of wealth that a company can distribute during a stated period and still be as well off at the end of the period as it was in the beginning. This is the economist's concept of income. Logically, income under this concept would be measured by the difference between the worth of an enterprise at the beginning and its worth at the end of the period, plus any wealth distributed in the interval.

Although this definition of *income* is straightforward and simply stated, it is of little practical value to the accountant. The income figure which is determined by the accountant is so widely used, and is of such importance to diverse and often conflicting interests, that the accountant has had to lay primary emphasis on objectivity. The accountant's purpose, as he sees it, is to make objective determinations of a company's income for relatively short segments of its total life.

There are, however, no objective criteria by which to measure the worth of a going enterprise at specific points in its life, as called for under the pure concept of income. An enterprise enters upon a variety of different projects and transactions at different points in time. The lives of the projects may vary in length, and some of them, indeed, may span several years. It is only when all have been concluded, at the end of the life of the enterprise, that their values can be objectively determined.

The liquidation values or replacement values of assets, which might be determined with some degree of objectivity at an interim date, are irrelevant because the worth of a going concern depends on its future earning power far more than on its tangible assets. Any estimate of future earning power is necessarily the result of a speculation rather than an objective determination.

THE MATCHING CONCEPT OF INCOME

While accountants may have agreed in principle with the economist's pure concept of income, they found that it was not practical for their purposes. Consequently, they had to substitute another concept of income which would more adequately meet their need for objectivity of measurement. They recognize the pure concept of income primarily as a point of departure.

Rather than attempt to measure and compare aggregate worths at specific points in time, the accountant has adopted the approach of determining income for a period as the difference between revenues and the costs of producing those revenues. Paton and Littleton give meaning to this idea when they describe costs as "efforts" and revenues as "accomplishments." [2]

Even this concept of income presents problems of subjective valuation, however, relating to how revenues are defined and at what point they are recognized. In an effort to minimize this problem, accountants adopted the postulate of realization usually stated as follows: "The entire income from sale arises at the moment when realization is deemed to take place."

The sales transaction is normally the act which signals realization or conversion of goods into money or its equivalent. It is the point at which revenue measures are objective because they are validated in the market place. Costs have previously been measured objectively by the market transaction in which the goods and services were originally acquired. Since realization now provides a similar measure of revenue, it is the first and most logical point at which to measure net income.

The accountant's task, then, is one of finding some reasonable basis for assigning all costs or efforts to the related revenues or

[2] W. A. Paton and A. C. Littleton, *An Introduction to Corporate Accounting Standards* (American Accounting Association), p. 14.

accomplishments in the period in which those revenues will be recognized. Stated more specifically, it is the task of keeping account of all costs through the various groupings and regroupings, until they can be matched with specific revenues in a particular period, or until it can reasonably be determined that no positive benefits will result from the cost.

ABSORPTION COSTING

To aid them in the task of periodic income determination, accountants long ago recognized the use of the product as a convenient vehicle for matching manufacturing costs with revenues. Manufacturing costs are incurred solely to make possible the creation of a product, and thus the benefits derived from these costs should be reflected in the price received when the product is sold.

Some manufacturing costs, namely, material and direct labor, are directly related to a specific unit of product and are easily associated. However, manufacturing overhead costs must also be incurred if production is to take place. Many of these costs are indirect; that is, they cannot be identified with specific units of product. They can only be allocated to products on the basis of some reasonably assumed relationship between these costs and production.

Furthermore, since these indirect overhead costs do not vary proportionately with manufacturing activity, it is necessary to forecast the volume of production over which these indirect costs are to be allocated in order to predetermine a unit cost. If the actual production is higher than forecasted volume, the extension of this unit cost times the actual volume will not equal the total overhead cost. This extension, or absorption, of costs on a per unit basis gives "absorption costing" its name. When this extended amount exceeds the actual cost, we have a condition of over-absorption.

An over-absorbed balance may be used to reduce the assumed cost of production, both of that which was sold during the period and of that which remains in inventory at the end of the period. An under-absorbed balance is usually treated as a loss in the current period.

Inventories are actually deferred product costs held in suspense. They represent cost or efforts to be matched with revenues which are realized at the time the products are sold. Plant, equipment, and prepaid expenses are examples of other manufacturing costs held in suspense. In the normal course of events, they too will be re-grouped and assigned to a product and ultimately will be matched with the revenues generated by product sales.

All other costs of the enterprise, which may be broadly categorized as selling and administrative costs, must also be matched with revenues during the period in which they contribute to revenues. These costs do not, for the most part, have as their objective the creation of the product and are not readily identifiable with it. Consequently, the product does not provide a suitable vehicle for these costs; nor does the sale of the product provide a proper signal for matching them with revenues.

Generally, with a few exceptions, accountants have been unable to find a reasonable or logical basis for the systematic association of selling and administration costs with specific revenues. There is no question but that some of these costs, incurred in a current period, relate to revenues to be recognized in subsequent periods.

Frequently, however, in the absence of an objective basis for determining the amount of costs to be deferred and the deferment period, selling and administrative costs are matched with the revenues of the period in which the costs are incurred. This procedure is an expedient which has the advantages of objectivity and conservatism. It does not imply a dilution of the matching process. In those cases where a reasonable basis for deferment of selling and administrative costs does exist, it is desirable to defer such costs for a better determination of income during the various periods.

DIRECT COSTING

Direct Costing, like Absorption Costing, is a method of determining periodic income. Under Direct Costing, all costs are classified as either direct (variable) or periodic (standby), and then further classified as manufacturing or non-manufacturing costs. The direct manufacturing costs, namely, direct material, direct labor, and the variable portion of manufacturing overhead, are assigned to products and matched with revenues from these products at the time the products are sold. All other costs are assigned to the period in which they are incurred.

Direct or Variable Costs

Direct or variable costs are defined as the incremental costs incurred in direct proportion to the amount of goods produced and sold.

Period or Standby Costs

Period or standby costs are those costs which are incurred in relatively fixed amounts per calendar period for an existing level of production capacity. Up to this capacity, period costs will not increase if volume is increased; nor will they decrease if volume is reduced.

Under the Direct Costing method, the direct costs of manufacturing and selling those products sold during a period are deducted from the revenues generated by the products. The balance is marginal income or contribution margin. This amount measures the net contribution which the revenue for the period has made toward covering the period costs of providing manufacturing and selling capacity, and providing a profit. Period costs are deducted from marginal income to arrive at earnings before taxes.

Direct Costing is popular because it is associated with isolating the variable portion of product cost. This variable cost concept is useful not only for estimating break-even points and contribution to standby overhead for purposes of profit planning but also in determining the relative profitability of products and product lines. Under Direct Costing, overhead cost items are segregated, generally in the accounts, into variable and standby categories. This also simplifies budgeting for different production levels and facilitates cost control.

The use of the variable cost concept of product cost for internal profit measurement and management decision making is not, however, peculiar to Direct Costing; nor is the segregation of costs into those classified as standby and those which are variable with volume. The same or similar techniques can be used without resorting to Direct Costing for financial accounting. The only true distinguishing characteristic of the Direct Costing method lies in the determination of net income for external reporting where all costs, except direct product costs, are charged to the period in which they are incurred.

INCOME DETERMINATION FOR EXTERNAL REPORTING

It is universally recognized that the determination and reporting of income is of vital importance to the shareholders and creditors of any enterprise. Existing and potential creditors and investors use reported income to measure economic progress in the past and apply it, along with other information, to form opinions on the prospects for the future.

Income is also the basis on which a major share of the tax burden is levied. It is a determinant of compensation under many profit-sharing and bonus plans. In a broader sense, income plays a vital role in maintaining the equilibrium and progress of our free enterprise system by directing the flow of capital to those areas where it promises to be most productive.

Each of these uses of income data is different, but all are satisfied by essentially the same kind of information. They require a calculation of over-all corporate income, which is an objective measure of the economic progress of the enterprise for the period. They require a measure of income which is consistent with that of other companies and which allows adequate comparisons from period to period within the company itself.

Historically, the determination of net income for external use has relied upon the "absorption method" of costing products, in accordance with the generally accepted interpretation of the matching concept. The measure of net income so produced satisfies the criteria by which it must be judged. It is objective, it is consistent, and it measures the realized economic progress of the enterprise for the period.

Yet the proponents of Direct Costing claim that the traditional method of income determination which has been used for so many years is wrong. They claim that only the Direct Costing method produces the correct measure of periodic net income.

The conflict between Direct Costing and traditional Absorption Costing in the determination of income for general reporting centers around the deferment of standby manufacturing costs in inventory. Over the total life of the enterprise, both methods will produce the same net income because all costs are matched with total revenues.

However, over a relatively short period such as a year, during which production and sales are not in balance, reported income under the two methods may differ substantially. In a period when production exceeds sales, and the inventories are therefore increased, the net income determined by Absorption Costing will exceed the net income determined by Direct Costing. This occurs because a part of the standby manufacturing overhead cost is deferred in inventory under Absorption Costing, while all of the standby manufacturing overhead costs are charged in the period under Direct Costing.

The Direct Costing argument is that the standby manufacturing overhead costs are the costs of standing ready to produce, not the costs of the product. To put it another way, they are the costs of being in business, not the costs of doing business. These costs arise from providing and keeping capacity for production in readiness, regardless of the extent to which it is utilized.

Since the opportunity to use this capacity expires with time, the costs of providing the capacity are also considered to expire with time. Therefore, the standby costs, it is argued, should be assigned directly to a period rather than being assigned initially to products and then matched with revenues as the goods are sold.

Advocates of Direct Costing maintain that, since gross income can be realized only through a sales transaction, net income should tend to vary with sales. Under Absorption Costing, net income for a period may be reduced by low production or increased by high production even though there is no change in sales volume. The advocates of Direct Costing conclude that this constitutes recognition of unrealized income.

Net income is a function of both revenues and costs, and it may be increased by a rise in revenues or a reduction in costs. The concept of realization, however, relates only to the timing of the recognition of revenues, and is tied to the sales transaction. Unrealized income can only occur if sales are assumed to have taken place when they have not. Since both Direct Costing and Absorption Costing use the same signal, the point of sale, for the timing of the recognition of revenue, no part of the difference between the two methods can be unrealized income.

The whole difference lies in the timing of the recognition of costs. Direct Costing ignores the difference between using fixed facilities for producing or letting them stand idle. All standby costs are charged to the current period. Absorption Costing, on the other hand, recognizes this difference. To the extent that capacity is not utilized, the standby manufacturing overhead costs are treated as losses in the current period. The implication is that the incurrence of these costs provides no benefit. To the extent that capacity is used to produce, these costs are deferred for matching with revenues when the production is sold.

CONCLUSIONS

The basic issue involved in deciding which procedure is correct revolves around whether or not the behavior of a cost is a proper criterion for the deferment of that cost. The tendency for costs to be either standby or variable in relation to changes in volume, and the effect of the variability of costs on different decisions, are certainly matters of which management should be aware. However, the economic significance of the cost is the proper criterion for determining whether or not it is deferrable, and economic significance is independent of behavior characteristics.

The cost is deferrable to a future period if it has created some comparable economic value which can reasonably be expected to contribute to the revenues of the future period. To deny this, as Direct Costing does, is to deny the concept of income determination by matching with revenues the cost of producing those revenues.

The Direct Costing procedure for handling standby manufacturing overhead costs is not, as it is so often claimed to be, a process of matching costs with revenues of the period in which the costs are incurred. Matching implies an association of one item with another. Under Direct Costing, standby manufacturing overhead costs are assigned as charges for a period, even though there may be no revenues in that period.

As a practical matter, costs are not inherently direct or period in nature. They acquire these characteristics, to a greater or lesser degree, as a result of managerial decisions with respect to organization, facilities, and control of costs. If management decides to retain certain employees, regardless of volume, their wages or salaries become period costs. If the decision is to vary the number of employees with the volume of work to be done, the same costs become direct costs. It is not difficult to see how managers might manipulate reported profits by changing their decisions as to which are the direct and which are the period costs.

But, if one assumes no intentional misrepresentation, the concepts of direct and period costs are almost as numerous as the theorists who discuss them. Thus, the proportion of overhead in inventory could vary greatly between companies in the same industry, depending upon the particular concept of direct and period cost held by management. In such circumstances, there would be no standards at all, and it would become even more difficult than it is today to compare one company with another.

Much of the confusion and conflict surrounding the disagreement between the advocates of Direct Costing and those who favor Absorption Costing exists because of a failure to consider the different uses of income data. However, each of these groups, approaching the problem of income determination from a different point of view, presents a solution which has a certain usefulness.

The advocates of Absorption Costing place great emphasis upon the matching concept as the sole criterion of income determination, and they are probably correct insofar as that objective is concerned. The advocates of Direct Costing, on the other hand, give lip service to the matching concept, but, because the segregation of variable and period costs is undoubtedly useful for a number of management decisions, they ask us to embrace this concept for income determination. It would seem, for expediency's sake, the advocates of Direct Costing contend, that a solution which is useful for management purposes is useful for all business purposes.

Herein lies one of the primary advantages of Profitability Accounting. It accepts the matching concept which is fundamental to the absorption method in connection with problems of over-all corporate net income determination. However, we are in the delightful position of being able "to have our cake and eat it too." Profitability Accounting provides the income which results under full absorption but also gives full recognition in the interim income statement to the behavior of costs by showing the marginal income less standby for the period, as under the Direct Costing method. The connecting link between the two concepts may be shown as one figure in the earnings statement, and it then reflects the change in the complement of standby cost which is included in the inventory.

Chapter 4

Responsibility Accounting for Costs and Profits

FUNCTIONS OF THE CHART OF ACCOUNTS

THE FIRST step in the development of a Profitability Accounting system is the construction of a suitable chart of accounts. The basic element in any accounting system, the chart of accounts provides the framework for the original collection and recording of all financial data and the preparation of both internal and external reports. It furnishes the structure of accountability for the assets and liabilities of the enterprise.

In Profitability Accounting, however, the chart of accounts is also important for other reasons. For example:

1. It is the means by which the information and control system is "built around" the organization structure. It determines the way in which raw data are originally recorded in groupings that relate to responsibility as set forth in the organization chart.
2. It enables reporting of incremental costs and profit contributions for internal purposes as well as the reporting of the traditional absorption costs for external purposes.
3. It provides for orderly accumulation of any costs, expenses, or revenues which may be of particular interest to managers.

These are some of the more important features of Profitability Accounting that should be reflected in an integrated chart of accounts which also provides for the normal functions of custodial accounting.

DEVELOPMENT OF THE CHART OF ACCOUNTS

In order to illustrate many of the factors to be considered and the techniques to be employed in developing the chart of accounts, frequent reference will be made to Exhibits 4–1 and 4–2, which appear at the end of this chapter. Exhibit 4–1 is the organization chart of the ABC Manufacturing Company, and Exhibit 4–2 is a typical chart of accounts which might be developed for this company.

The chart of accounts which is appropriate for any particular company depends more upon the complexity of the company's organization rather than upon its size. The ABC Manufacturing

Company might, for example, have annual sales ranging anywhere from $5,000,000 to $100,000,000 and total employment anywhere from 500 to 10,000 people. But, if the organization chart presented in Exhibit 4–1 is an accurate picture of its responsibility structure, a chart of accounts such as the one in Exhibit 4–2 is appropriate, regardless of the sales volume or the number of employees.

In designing the chart, every effort should be made to provide enough detailed accounts so that the items which go into each account are relatively homogeneous. Insofar as feasible, the data in a detail account should reflect one kind of activity, one responsibility, and one type of behavior. Such homogeneity is important for establishing good budgetary control. It also reduces the need for frequent special analysis to determine the contents of an account.

In the beginning, it is generally good practice to err on the side of over-providing accounts, some of which can later be eliminated or consolidated if they prove unnecessary.

The accounts should be given good descriptive titles so that information can be classified easily and accurately. It is often desirable to prepare a supplement to the chart of accounts containing a detailed description of each account and detailed instructions regarding its use.

Account Coding

In constructing a chart of accounts, it is important to consider the type of coding system to be used for identifying individual accounts. Over the years, many kinds of codes have been proposed and used, but the one which has gained the most widespread acceptance is a straight numerical code. To a great extent, this has resulted from the increasing use of punched card and electronic methods of data processing, which are less efficient when handling alphabetical characters or alpha-numerical combinations. Thus, in view of the increasing trend toward automated data processing, even in smaller companies, it appears that the adaptability and efficiency of the numerical coding system make it the logical choice in nearly every situation.

The underlying principle in a numerical coding system is that the position as well as the value of each digit of a particular number has a definite meaning. Thus, in Exhibit 4–2, each three-digit number is a balance sheet account. The second digit is a finer classification within the broad category. The three digits together specify a particular account. For example, any three-digit number beginning with 1 is a current asset, while a 1 followed by a 0 indicates a cash account in the current asset category. The particular number 105 specifies the petty cash account. The same principle is employed in the income and expense section. However, because of the large number of accounts required, a six-digit rather than a three-digit number is used in this particular section.

In the design of a coding system, every effort should be made to use as few digits as possible to facilitate easy understanding and application. Yet the system must be flexible enough to permit expansion or revision without having to completely re-number.

When, because of the complexity of the organization or operation of a company, it becomes necessary to use lengthy code numbers, reading can be made easier if meaningful sections of the numbers are separated by a decimal point or a dash.

Organization of the Enterprise

The chart of accounts, or for that matter the entire information and control system, however carefully designed, can correct neither weaknesses in the basic organization of the enterprise nor any shortcomings in its organization chart. These problems must already have been solved if the system is to be effective.

Certain fundamental principles of organization are generally recognized as essentials to an effective operation. "The Ten Commandments of Good Organization," issued by the American Management Association, comprise an excellent statement of such a code. The first two of these are as follows:

1. Definite and clear-cut responsibilities should be assigned to each executive.
2. Responsibility should always be coupled with corresponding authority.

The remaining eight spell out the commonsense principles of applying courteous human relations to the problems of operating through an organization structure and emphasize the importance of clearly defining any changes in the prescribed organization channels.

This is not to say that there is only one form of organization. Managers work in different ways and have varying ideas of how to assign authority and responsibility. Individualized personal or company policies can usually be incorporated within the limits of sound organization principles in such a way as to produce an effective and smooth-running management team.

Before a chart of accounts is designed, the organization of the enterprise should be analyzed to make sure that the lines of authority and responsibility are clear and unmistakable, without overlap. Likewise, the organization chart should be examined critically to make certain that it truly reflects the way the organization actually operates. Corrective action may involve a realignment of managerial duties and responsibilities, or it may require only a re-drawing of the organization chart to give formal recognition to the way the organization has actually been functioning.

Responsibility Groupings

The chart of accounts should be designed to conform to the responsibilities indicated in the organization chart so that responsibility groupings govern the original collection and recording of revenue and expense data.

For example, under manufacturing expenses (the 500,000 control) in Exhibit 4–2, the head of each department reporting to the vice-president of manufacturing is assigned an individual department number for the budgeting and recording of all the expenses of his operation. Thus, at any managerial level, the actual and planned expenses for which that manager is responsible can readily be summarized and reported.

The foreman of the machine shop would receive a report covering only his own department. The director of manufacturing could get a separate report for each department from 520 through 529; or he could receive separate reports for Departments 520, 521, and 522, and a single report covering Departments 525 through 529, since, according to the organization chart, the assistant director of manufacturing has direct responsibility for those productive departments.

Under the sales and cost of sales sections of the chart in Exhibit 4–2 (control accounts 100,000 through 300,000), provision is made for classifying sales by sales division so that revenues can be recorded and reported by the responsible unit. These sales divisions are also responsible for incurring costs. Under commercial expenses (700,000 control), each is assigned a department number for budgeting and reporting its expenses.

Thus, both the manufacturing and the commercial departments are established to include costs for which an individual is responsible. Far too often in companies, departments which were clearly the responsibility of an individual have been pulled apart —or forced together—to achieve some sort of "cost center" results. On rare occasions, a department has been excluded from manufacturing responsibility in the chart of accounts because the accountant did not wish to include its costs in the manufacturing overhead rate.

Such forcing of normal human and business relationships into artificial patterns merely for accounting convenience is apt to impair good managerial control. It can result in late and inaccurate reporting and confusion on the part of the managers as to who should take action. The prompt reporting of information by responsibility is the primary objective of a control system, and this should never be compromised. Statement classification and cost accounting problems can always be dealt with on secondary levels.

BALANCE SHEET ACCOUNTS

Development of the balance sheet section of the chart of accounts is usually quite simple and straightforward. Actually, the problem is usually one of too little detail rather than too much. For best results, accounts must be provided in enough detail so that the assets, liabilities, and equities are adequately identified for the accounting process and for subsequent classification in both external and internal financial reports. Exhibit 4–2 illustrates the degree of detail usually required to facilitate the accounting for financial reporting purposes.

The most significant problems encountered in designing the balance sheet section of the chart of accounts usually arise in connection with inventory and with the classification of assets in multiple locations.

Inventory Accounts

In Profitability Accounting, the detailed dollar accounting for inventories is usually restricted to separate accounts for the material, the labor, and the overhead content of the inventories. It is also frequently desirable to record the input of these elements into inventory in accounts which are separate from those used to record the relief of inventory for cost of goods sold. Thus, any changes in the mix of these elements over a period of time is readily noticeable and the inventory balance by element, as well as in total, is easily obtained by netting the accounts.

According to the philosophy underlying this concept, good managers do not control an inventory in terms of dollars by broad production stage, such as raw material, work in process, and finished goods. Rather, they control it through the efforts of a well-organized production-planning and -control section. This section thinks in terms of units, not dollars; in terms of availability, not custodial accountability.

The company must have confidence in the ability of the production-planning and -control section to control inventories. If this control is adequate, there should be no need for attempting to superimpose it through accounting mechanics. If the control is not adequate, accounting entries will not provide it.

The purpose of inventory accounting should be merely to account for the dollar flow through the accounts, so that the aggregate dollars in the book inventories are always properly stated, and so that the assets of the enterprise are safeguarded. Once this philosophy is accepted, it becomes apparent that the burdensome task of transferring dollars from raw materials through various work in process accounts to finished goods is generally unnecessary. Furthermore, these multiple transfer entries increase the possibilities for error.

Experience has shown that, where the "production stage" concept is employed, the book inventory may compare very well with physical inventory in the aggregate, while the sub-totals by production stage are often highly inaccurate. This is not surprising in view of the extensive clerical effort involved in recording the many transfers.

Some argue that the production stage concept of inventory accounting better enables a manager to spot imbalances and faulty practices. As far as imbalance is concerned, it is doubtful whether data on dollars by production stage are of any great use. When a manager is dealing with dollar figures running to 10 or 11 digits, it is extremely difficult for him to ascertain whether physical imbalance is present.

However, if it is doing a proper job of controlling inventories, the production-planning department should have a ready answer to that question. As for highlighting faulty inventory-accounting practices, the *four-wall* concept should be just as effective as the production stage concept, and at considerably less cost.

In certain instances, it may be desirable to maintain separate dollar value accounting for certain sections of an inventory, though this has been overdone in the past. Separate accounting may be desirable where important quantities of materials are on hand which happen to be highly volatile in price and which also happen to be of great concern to the directors and high-level managers far removed from the operating details. It may also be desirable where bulk raw material is converted into pieces in an initial operation and it is important to obtain accurate knowledge of the material lost in the conversion process.

The use of the *four-wall inventory* concept in Profitability Accounting can best be illustrated by reference to Exhibit 4–2. Beginning inventories of productive materials, direct labor, and variable manufacturing overhead—regardless of the stage in the production cycle—are recorded in Accounts 141, 142, and 143, respectively. Additions to the inventory, in the form of productive materials, direct labor costs, and variable manufacturing overhead costs, are charged to Accounts 144, 145, and 146, respectively.

The relief of inventory for goods sold is costed separately in terms of productive material, direct labor, and variable manufacturing overhead content, and these amounts are credited to Accounts 151, 152, and 153, respectively. In the usual Profitability Accounting application, a standard cost system is in operation, tied in to the books of account. Therefore, all inventory amounts would be stated at standard cost.

The accounts described above are the only accounts required to provide financial control and reporting of inventories on an incremental cost and profit contribution basis for use by internal management. In Profitability Accounting, only incremental or variable product costs are charged directly to and relieved directly from the inventory accounts. These are the costs described above.

However, the system must also provide for the recording of inventories and the determination of income on a basis which is acceptable to interested outside parties, and this means that an appropriate amount of standby manufacturing overhead cost must be included in the inventory. This is accomplished by the use of Account 155—standby manufacturing overhead. In each period, this account is charged with the amount of standby manufacturing overhead normally absorbed into inventory because of production, and is credited with the amount normally relieved from inventory because of sales.

The difference between the charges and credits is applied directly to income as a separate identifiable amount. In this way, the internal reports prepared for management on the basis of profit contribution less standby for the period are consistent with the external reports prepared on a traditional full absorption basis for use by interested outsiders.

For profit-planning purposes, if the inventory at the end of the year is expected to differ from that at the beginning of the year, a programmed income or expense item can be provided in the programmed expense control to account for the effect of the standby adjustment on reported income.

At any balance sheet date, the net total of all the inventory accounts will produce the aggregate inventory amount which can be used for financial statement purposes. If the company takes a physical inventory, the aggregate amount may be replaced by the production stage breakdown.

Divisional Accounts

In situations where a company is organized on a divisional basis, it is often desirable to set up separate accounts by division for items such as accounts receivable, inventory, property, plant and equipment, and accounts payable. Such separation is useful in assigning custodial responsibility and in developing data to measure the assets employed, the asset turnover ratio, and also the return on capital employed. If the number of divisions is small, these accounts may be accommodated within the three-digit code. For example, in Exhibit 4–2, notes and accounts receivable for Division A would be recorded in the series of Accounts 121 through 125; for Division B, from 126 through 130; and, for Division C, from 131 through 135. If the number of divisions is large, another digit may be added to the coding system.

INCOME AND EXPENSE ACCOUNTS

The design of the income and expense section of the chart of accounts is quite important because these accounts are the repositories of the data that reflect the current operation of the enterprise, and are the source of much of the information required by management.

The first accounts provided under this section are those related to the responsibility for sales within the organization. These are grouped under separate control accounts, as illustrated in Exhibit 4–2 for sales (100,000), price variances (200,000), specific sales deductions (210,000 through 260,0000), and cost of sales (310,000 through 330,000).

In the coding system used in the illustration, the first two digits designate the control account and the last four digits determine the particular detailed account. The detail coding provides for classification of data by sales division (to a maximum of 9 divisions), by customer class (to a maximum of 9 classes), and by product (to a maximum of 99 products).

Usually, the first digit or two of the detail coding is used to classify the data by sales responsibility so that actual sales and profit contribution can be compared with forecasted sales and profit contribution. In many cases, sales responsibility will be by product line or profit center, which is the classification used for preparation of periodic operating statements. Where this is not the case, an additional digit of the detail code may be used to make product line or profit center classification of the data.

Subsequent digits in the detail code can be used to provide the information required for sales analysis. The degree of detail can be increased merely by expanding the number of digits used in the coding system. However, if more than eight or ten digits are used, the coding tends to become unwieldly.

Note that the sales controls, the specific sales deduction controls, and the cost of sales controls all use the same detail coding. The normal operating statements of earnings by product line or profit center are easily prepared. Because the control accounts all have the same detail coding, a statement of profit contribution can be prepared very simply for any classification included in the code. This is accomplished by sorting the data for all controls by the classification desired and applying the appropriate variable commercial overhead cost.

Sales Accounts

The control account for sales—Account 100,000 in Exhibit 4–2 —is entitled "Gross sales less perfect goods returned at list or established prices." Returned sales should be charged to the accounts at established prices. If there are any allowances or adjustments in sales or returns, they should be recorded in a control specifically provided for this purpose, such as Account 140,000, and not netted against sales. Otherwise management can lose track of the cost of these allowances, which might be significant. If other costs related to returns are a problem, the returns may also be recorded in a separate control.

Sales Price Variances and Trade Discounts

Where products with a list or established price are being sold, there is often a question whether to record sales at list (or established) prices or at net prices. Many companies resist using list or established prices because of the additional work required to extend sales invoices at prices other than those being billed to customers. In many cases, however, it is a necessary task if management control is to be effective. Differences between list or established prices and net prices arise from two sources:

1. Price variances or concessions which are deviations from planned sales prices and which directly affect performance against planned profit

2. Trade discounts, which are a normal part of the marketing program

Price concessions affect profits directly but in no regular pattern and they are seldom planned for. Where price concessions occur, sales should be recorded at established prices and the differences between established prices and net prices should be charged as sales price variances, attributable to the appropriate sales responsibility. This variance may be captured in a separate control as illustrated in Exhibit 4–2, Account 200,000, and it should encompass the same detail codes as the sales control account.

Trade discounts, on the other hand, are planned reductions from list prices. The objective here is to isolate the impact on earnings of sales to different classes of customers, under a multiple trade discount price structure. Sales are recorded at regular list prices, and the actual trade discount is charged to the trade discount control. When the proportionate sales made to various classes of customers differ from the proportions in the forecast, there is a deviation from planned earnings.

This effect is revealed through the trade discount structure coding as trade discount variance against the profit plan. The effect is not lumped with the so-called sales mix variance, which is designed to show the effect on earnings of selling a mix of products different from the forecasted mix, irrespective of class of customer or distribution channel.

Specific Sales Deduction Accounts

Following the sales control is a series of controls (210,000 through 260,000) for the specific sales deductions. These are not overhead costs in the ordinary sense of the term. These costs are incurred directly as a result of sales, and thus they are really a reduction of gross margin. These are ordinarily shown as the responsibility of the sales manager, although they are more a measure of mix of sales than of sales effort or cost control. The usual specific sales deduction controls, illustrated in Exhibit 4–2, include cash discounts, trade discounts, sales allowances, commissions, royalties, and freight out.

Cost of Sales

The cost of sales control accounts are used to relieve the inventory and to charge against revenues the cost of products sold. In accordance with the *four-wall inventory* concept, three control accounts (310,000 through 330,000) are used to separate productive material, direct labor, and variable manufacturing overhead.

Programmed Expense Accounts

The programmed expense control account (400,000 in Exhibit 4–2) is next in order on the chart of accounts. Programmed expenses are sometimes called "project-type expenses" or "decision expenses." They occur because management has authorized the expenditure of sums of money which should not be provided for in formal overhead rates or the regularly recurring portion of departmental operating budgets. Expenses of this type may be high in one year and low, or altogether non-existent, in another year. Examples of programmed costs are major research and development programs, engineering projects, and advertising campaigns.

The detail coding of programmed expenses provides for classification by department responsible for the over-all program and by project number as well. It often happens that services called for in the program are provided by several departments within the organization. In such cases, expenses are dual-coded, and charged first to the department actually spending in order to maintain control of costs by responsibility. They are then eliminated from the departmental operating accounts and charged to the proper project number and departmental responsibility within the programmed expense control. The dual-coding is important when a productive department does work in connection with a special program. For example, any materials required would be charged directly to the program, although any variances arising from material usage would be the responsibility of the productive department.

Manufacturing Expense Accounts

The primary coding of the manufacturing expense control accounts follows the same pattern as that of the controls already discussed. Typical coding for the detailed expense accounts is illustrated on the last several pages of Exhibit 4–2. Since the responsibility structure is the determinant, the manufacturing expense control should include all departments for which the top manufacturing manager is responsible. For example, if the manager in charge of the purchasing function is responsible to the vice-president for manufacturing, the purchasing department should be included in the manufacturing expense control, regardless of whether or not it theoretically represents manufacturing expense.

If the classification of manufacturing expenses thus obtained and used for internal reporting is not acceptable for external reporting because of the effect on inventory pricing and income determination, it is a simple matter to adjust the accounts at year-end and reverse the adjustment at the beginning of the following year.

Within the control account, the non-productive departments should be segregated from the productive departments. The latter should be arranged in the order of the production flow whenever this is feasible. In a multi-plant company, it may be necessary to add a digit to the code to indicate plant as well as department number.

The detail accounts ending in 999 are departmental credit accounts for absorbing standard variable manufacturing overhead costs into the inventory accounts. The total of the entries to these accounts are summarized in the 590,000 control account in Exhibit 4–2. Note that it provides for the absorption of only the *variable* element of manufacturing overhead costs into inventory.

Variance Accounts

In Profitability Accounting, the several variances from the profit plan are handled so that, in each case, the variance is determined and accounted for simply and economically and reported in a meaningful manner. All of the variances are dealt with in one of five ways, as follows:

1. Sales volume and sales mix variances never enter into the accounts. They are determined in the course of preparing the earnings statement for management and reported as partial ex-

planations of the difference between planned earnings and actual earnings by product line. (See Exhibit 2–6, Chapter 2.)

2. Sales price variances, as pointed out earlier, are captured in a separate control account and included in the management reports. (See Exhibit 2–6, Chapter 2.)

3. In a standard cost system, direct labor and raw materials enter the inventory accounts at standard cost. Certain of the variances from standard are within the control of departmental managers. These are the material usage and scrap variances, the labor performance variance, and the labor rate variance.

4. Accounts 100 through 130 and 505 through 550 in the detail expense account section of Exhibit 4–2 are examples of these variances. They are charged as overhead costs to the responsible department and are thereby included in the manufacturing expense control. These standards are usually set in such a way that some amount of variance is unavoidable and may often be provided for in the departmental variable budgets. The amounts to be reported as variances from plan, therefore, are determined by taking only the difference between the totals of the accounts and the planned amounts of the variances. They are included in total in the management report on "summary of cost variances" (see Chapter 10) and are also included according to responsibility in more detailed reports.

5. In a standard cost system, two other variances may arise: a material purchase price variance and a yield variance. In many cases, these variances are beyond the control of managers within the organization and are excluded from the overhead accounts which are classified by responsibility. A separate control account is provided for these variances—the 600,000 control in Exhibit 4–2. In some cases, one or both of these variances may be properly reported as a departmental responsibility.

Buyers within the purchasing department may have some measure of responsibility for material price variances. If it is considered desirable, provision may be made in the detail coding for the classification of variances by buyer responsibility as well as by type of material.

Where responsibility for the yield variance is definitely assignable to one departmental supervisor, the amounts should be included in the normal overhead accounts for his department. Where the variances are not definitely assignable to one departmental supervisor, however, or where the losses and gains are outside the control of supervision altogether, they should be included in the price and yield variance control. They are thus excluded from departmental responsibility but, along with purchase price variances, are highlighted for management attention. Such attention may take the form of finding substitute materials, finding other sources of supply, or changing formula mixtures.

Commercial Expense Accounts

Commercial expense accounts are generally established with one control account for each department, in a manner similar to that used with manufacturing expense accounts. In many companies, however, particularly the smaller ones, so-called departments exist where the "manager" is actually a group leader with very little, if any, ability to control cost, and where most of the cost is of the salary and wage variety. Under such circumstances, it is generally inadvisable to report separately the costs for each commercial department. The appropriate expense accounts may be included under a broader base of responsibility. For example, cost-accounting wages may be included as a detail expense account under the controller's department, because the cost supervisor has little authority over them.

The commercial expense control utilizes the same set of detail expense account codes as the manufacturing expense control, but with different control and departmental codes.

Detail Expense Accounts

A typical set of detail expense accounts is illustrated in Exhibit 4-2. Of course, not all of the detail accounts are applicable to all departments. It is generally advisable to prepare a worksheet type of control form, listing all the detail accounts vertically and all the departments horizontally, with a check mark to indicate each account which applies to each department. Some of these accounts are common to every company, but many others are peculiar to a single organization. In every situation, the expense incurred by a company should be analyzed. The expense accounts should be set up in such detail that expenses are accurately described for control by managers and for external reporting.

There are two unusual types among the detail expense accounts used in Profitability Accounting. They are the direct labor accounts and the variable overhead transfer account.

The direct labor detail expense accounts, 001 to 004, are memorandum accounts only. Standard direct labor is charged to inventory, and any labor variances are charged to the 100 series of accounts. However, the direct labor is recorded first in this series of memorandum accounts by department. Thus it is available for use as a measure of activity in determining allowable amounts for many items of overhead cost and also as a basis for the absorption of variable overhead into inventory. Not every company or department can use direct labor as a basis for measuring activity or absorbing variable manufacturing expense, but, where this is feasible, the direct labor memorandum account is a useful device.

Overhead transfer accounts are provided to permit the transfer of overhead when necessary. Normally, it is not advisable to make arbitrary allocations of cost from overhead departments to productive departments, but, in those cases where it is done as a matter of policy, accounts may be provided for this purpose in the 800 series.

The transfer accounts are intended for a situation where charges are made by one department to another for actual services requisitioned. In such case, the charge is made to a specific account which describes the nature of the charge, such as "Repairs to Machinery." This account would contain charges to the machine shop from the maintenance department. The credit to maintenance would be to a separate account, such as "Departmental expense transferred (credit)." Credits are never made directly against the account in which the charge was previously recorded.

Note that the expense accounts are not segregated into product and period expenses, nor into fixed, semi-variable, and variable categories. Any account may contain both variable and standby elements. The original recording of expenses is designed to collect the particular type of expense by responsibility for incurring it.

Exhibits 4–1 and 4–2 and the discussion in this chapter are directed primarily toward manufacturing enterprises because the manufacturing process generally presents the greatest variety and complexity of problems in designing a chart of accounts. However, the same principles of chart design and construction are equally applicable to a sales or to a service organization. Only the detailed and some of the specialized accounts such as the *four-wall inventory* accounts and the manufacturing expense absorbed accounts would not be appropriate.

SUMMARY

A properly designed chart of accounts provides the basic framework for the operation of a Profitability Accounting system. It facilitates control by responsibility and the reporting of incremental costs and profit contribution as well as the accumulation of other vital information for managers. Straight numerical account coding is usually the simplest and most efficient, especially where some form of automated data processing is to be employed.

The organization of the enterprise should be examined to make sure that managerial authority and responsibilities are clearly assigned. The chart of accounts should then be designed to conform to the established responsibility structure. It is the organization structure, not accounting convenience, which is the ruling consideration in the design of the chart of accounts.

The inventory section of the chart of accounts may be designed for the use of the *four-wall* concept of *inventory* accounting. Under this concept, inventories are accounted for only in terms of their material, direct labor, and overhead content, not by stage of production. Responsibility for the control of inventories is properly lodged in the production-planning and -control function.

Individual control accounts are included in the income and expense section of the chart for sales, specific sales deductions, cost of sales, programmed expenses, manufacturing expenses, and commercial expenses. The detail coding underlying these controls provide for classification of each of these elements by responsibility and type of expense. Separate controls are used for variances which may be beyond the control of any one manager.

The detailed descriptive expense accounts to be set up are determined by the control requirements of management and by the classification of expenses required for external reporting. Detailed accounts are not segregated into "product cost" or "period expense" categories.

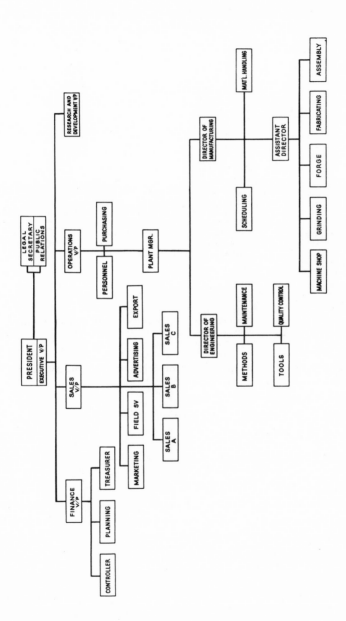

Exhibit 4–1. ABC Manufacturing Company organization chart.

Account Number	Account Title
100	Cash
101	General bank accounts
102	Payroll and dividend deposit account
103	Sales office working funds
104	Petty cash fund
110	Marketable securities
111	U.S. Government securities
112	Other marketable securities
120	Notes and accounts receivable
121	Notes receivable - customer
123	Accounts receivable - customers
125	Claims receivable
127	Intercompany accounts receivable
129	Allowance for doubtful notes and accounts
140	Inventories
141	Beginning inventory - productive materials
142	Beginning inventory - direct labor
143	Beginning inventory - variable manufacturing overhead
144	Purchases of productive materials
145	Direct labor incurred
146	Variable manufacturing overhead
149	Special charges
151	Cost of sales - materials
152	Cost of sales - direct labor
153	Cost of sales - variable manufacturing overhead
155	Standby manufacturing overhead
158	Allowance for inventory losses and obsolescence

Exhibit 4–2 (page 1 of 10). Chart of accounts for ABC Manufacturing Company.

Account Number	Account Title
160	Prepaid expense and deferred costs
161	Prepaid insurance
162	Prepaid taxes
163	Employee travel advances
164	Prepaid group insurance
165	Deferred payroll tax expense
166	Prepaid interest
167	Prepaid rent
200	Investments and other assets
201	Investment in subsidiary
211	Deposits with mutual insurance companies
221	Deferred commission and expense on long-term debt
222	Refunds due from federal and state governments
223	Due from officers and employees
224	Deposits - air travel credit cards
225	Deposits - performance bonds
300	Property, plant and equipment
400	Allowance for depreciation

Under 300 and 400 are following detail plant ledger accounts

-05	Land
-10	Buildings
-15	Machinery and machine tools
-20	Patterns
-25	Autos and trucks
-30	Furniture and fixtures
-35	Additions and improvements in progress
500	Intangible assets
501	Trademarks
505	Patents
506	Allowance for amortization
590	Clearing accounts
598	Freight clearing account
599	Distribution clearing account

Exhibit 4–2 (page 2 of 10). Chart of accounts (*continued*).

Account Number	Account Title
600	Payables
601	Notes payable to banks
602	Accounts payable - trade
604	Dividends payable
605	Advance payments received on future contracts
606	Inter-company account payable
611	Officers and employees accounts payable
613	Withholding taxes
615	Long-term debt - current maturity
621	Union dues
622	Community chest
623	Credit union
624	Red Cross
700	Accrued liabilities
701	Accrued salaries and wages
702	Accrued commissions
703	Accrued royalties
704	Accrued holiday pay
705	Accrued vacation pay
706	Accrued social security tax
707	Accrued real estate and personal property tax
708	Accrued interest
709	Provision for pension trust
710	Provision for federal income tax
800	Long-term debt
801	Mortgage note payable
900	Stockholders' investment
901	Preferred stock, authorized
902	Preferred stock, unissued
903	Preferred stock, in treasury
911	Common stock, authorized
912	Common stock, unissued
913	Common stock, in treasury
931	Additional paid-in capital
941	Retained earnings
942	Dividends paid
943	Current earnings

Exhibit 4–2 (page 3 of 10).　Chart of accounts (*continued*).

SALES

100,000   Gross sales less perfect goods returned at list or
      established prices

SALES PRICE VARIANCES

200,000   Sales price variances

SPECIFIC SALES DEDUCTIONS

210,000   Trade discounts
220,000   Commissions
230,000   Freight out
240,000   Allowances
250,000   Royalties
260,000   Cash discounts allowed

COST OF SALES

310,000   Productive materials
320,000   Direct labor
330,000   Variable manufacturing overhead

DETAIL CODING FOR THE FOREGOING CONTROLS

Third digit: Sales division

--1--- Sales division A
--2--- Sales division B
--3--- Sales division C
--4---

Fourth digit: Customer classification

---1-- Retail
---2-- Franchise
---3-- Jobber
---4-- Manufacturer

Fifth and sixth digits: Detail product

----01
----02
----03
----04
----05

Exhibit 4–2 (page 4 of 10). Income and expense controls.

OTHER EXPENSE CONTROLS

400,000   Programmed expenses

DETAIL CODING

Second and third digits: Department responsibility

420--- Director of manufacturing
445--- Controller
463--- Advertising

Fourth, fifth, and sixth digits: Project number

4--001
4--002
4--003
4--004

500,000   Manufacturing expenses

Second and third digits: Department responsibility

-01--- Manufacturing - vice-president
-02--- Industrial relations
-03--- Purchasing
-10--- Director of engineering
-11--- Methods
-12--- Maintenance
-13--- Tools
-14--- Quality control
-20--- Director of manufacturing
-21--- Scheduling
-22--- Material handling
-25--- Machine shop
-26--- Grinding
-27--- Forge
-28--- Fabricating
-29--- Assembly

Fourth, fifth, and sixth digits: Descriptive expense accounts

Exhibit 4–2 (page 5 of 10).   Income and expense controls (*continued*).

OTHER EXPENSE CONTROLS – Continued

590,000   Variable manufacturing expense absorbed
           (control for all ---998 and ---999 accounts in expense detail)

600,000   Purchase price and yield variations

           610,000 Raw steel purchase price variation
           620,000 Other material purchase price variation
           630,000 Green lumber yield variance

700,000   Commercial expenses

           Second and third digits: Department responsibility

                     -40--- Finance
                     -45--- Controller
                     -50--- Planning
                     -55--- Treasurer

                     -60--- Sales
                     -61--- Marketing
                     -62--- Field service
                     -63--- Advertising
                     -64--- Export
                     -65--- Sales Division A
                     -66--- Sales Division B
                     -67--- Sales Division C

                     -80--- Research and Development

                     -90--- General corporate

           Fourth, fifth, and sixth digits: Descriptive expense accounts

Exhibit 4–2 (page 6 of 10).   Income and expense controls (*continued*).

DIRECT LABOR (memorandum only)

---001	Rated - Productive
---002	Standard day work - Productive
---003	Non-standard day work - Productive
---004	Service labor

LABOR ALLOWANCES AND VARIANCES

---100	Approved absence from duty
---102	Sub-standard material
---104	Hard castings
---106	No power
---108	Machine trouble
---110	Routing not followed
---112	Day work time variance
---114	Day work rate variance
---116	Holiday pay
---118	Sick pay
---120	Night shift premium
---122	Overtime premium
---124	Vacation pay
---126	Make-up guarantees
---128	Miscellaneous allowances

SALARIES AND WAGES

---202	Executive
---204	Supervisory
---205	Staff
---206	Foremen
---208	Engineers
---210	Tool crib
---212	Servicemen
---216	Traffic
---218	Credit and collection
---220	Servicemen
---222	Order and billing
---228	Watchmen
---230	Janitors
---232	Crane operators
---234	Receiving and truck drivers
---236	Storeroom

Exhibit 4–2 (page 7 of 10).   Detail expense accounts.

SALARIES AND WAGES - Continued

---238	Draftsmen
---240	Clerical and stenographic
---242	General accounting
---244	Cost accounting
---246	Restaurant
---248	Nursing
---250	Office services
---258	Miscellaneous non-productive

REPAIRS AND MAINTENANCE - OWN LABOR

---260	To building
---262	To machinery and machine tools
---264	To patterns
---266	To autos and trucks
---268	To furniture and fixtures
---270	To productive materials
---272	To manufactured products
---274	Re-arranging machinery and equipment

REPAIRS AND MAINTENANCE - MATERIALS AND OUTSIDE EXPENSES

---360	To buildings
---362	To machinery and machine tools
---364	To patterns
---366	To autos and trucks
---368	To furniture and fixtures
---370	To productive materials
---372	To manufactured products
---374	Re-arranging machinery and equipment

MATERIALS AND SUPPLIES

---405	Power and light
---410	Water
---415	Gasoline
---420	Fuel oil
---425	Office supplies
---430	Small tools
---435	Welding expenses and supplies
---440	Janitor supplies

Exhibit 4–2 (page 8 of 10). Detail expense accounts (*continued*).

MATERIALS AND SUPPLIES - Continued

---445	Printing and stationery
---450	Drafting supplies
---455	Food purchases
---460	First-aid supplies
---465	Painting materials and supplies
---470	Packing materials not on bill of materials
---475	Experimental materials

SCRAP LOSS

---505	Scrap loss - engineering errors
---510	Scrap loss - defective workmanship
---515	Scrap loss - defective material
---520	Scrap loss - obsolete material
---550	Scrap salvage

MISCELLANEOUS EXPENSES

---602	Postage
---604	Dues and subscriptions
---606	Donations
---608	Legal and other professional
---610	Bad debts
---612	Telegrams
---614	Telephone
---616	Travel expense
---618	Sundry in and out freight
---620	Medical fees and expense
---622	Employer relations
---624	Convention displays and exhibits
---626	Publication space
---628	Sales literature
---630	Instruction manuals
---632	Miscellaneous rent
---634	Personnel tests
---636	Life insurance expense
---638	Directors' fees
---640	Credit and collection expense
---642	Loss on disposition of capital assets
---644	Cost variation due to outside work
---646	Interest expense
---670	Restaurant income (credit)
---698	Sundry expense

Exhibit 4–2 (page 9 of 10). Detail expense accounts (*continued*).

DEPRECIATION, INSURANCE, TAXES

---700	Depreciation
---705	Amortization of patents
---710	Insurance - property
---715	Insurance - workmen's compensation
---720	Insurance - group
---725	Insurance - liability
---730	Insurance - sundry
---750	Taxes - real estate and personal property
---755	Taxes - payroll
---760	Taxes - sundry
---765	Taxes - on income

VARIABLE OVERHEAD TRANSFERS

---895	Departmental expense transferred (credit)

VARIABLE OVERHEAD ABSORBED

---998	Overhead absorbed in properties
---999	Overhead absorbed in production

Exhibit 4–2 (page 10 of 10). Detail expense accounts (continued).

Chapter 5

Standard Cost Data on
Materials and Labor

THE CONCEPT of standard cost had its origin in the latter part of the last century in the scientific management movement headed by Frederick W. Taylor. The factory system, one of the major developments resulting from the Industrial Revolution, had made possible tremendous increases in productivity, but management had not yet learned how to harness its huge potential. Taylor and other pioneers in the scientific management movement developed a program of setting specifications for jobs in terms of the time required to do them and then comparing these predetermined standards with the actual results. This was the first major step on the part of management toward instituting control of factory operations. Others were to follow in the field which came to be known as industrial engineering.

In the early period, cost accounting, when used at all, was based on actual historical data. Its objective was to assign costs to products so that the product costs could be used in pricing inventories and setting selling prices.

Gradually the interchange of ideas and people from production, industrial engineering, and accounting resulted in the recognition of the standard cost concept in cost accounting as well as in plant operations. Subsequent developments and refinements of standard cost techniques were introduced by both industrial engineers and accountants, until standard costs evolved to their present form.

THE CONCEPT OF STANDARD COST

A standard cost is a predetermined cost, an explicit statement of what cost should be under the most efficient methods of operation which can be attained and sustained. It is actually the product of two factors determined separately—quantity and price. For example, the quantity of material required for a product is first determined by drawing up a bill of materials in physical units, such as pounds of steel or board feet of lumber. Then the physical quantities are costed, using predetermined prices, to arrive at standard cost. Similarly, the hours of each type of labor required to produce the product are determined by engineering estimates or time and motion studies and then priced at the corresponding labor rates.

The term *standard cost* refers to two kinds (or areas) of cost: product cost and operation cost. In the typical cost-accounting usage of the term, standard product cost includes standard material, standard direct labor, and standard manufacturing overhead, whereas operation standard costs usually refer only to standard material and standard direct labor. While the former are used for product line accounting and profit planning, the latter are used for measuring actual performance against plan by responsibility.

One of the major problems in administering a standard cost system is that of ensuring consistency between the operating standards and the product standards. This is complicated by the desire to reflect the most current standards for measuring operating performance while holding the product cost standards constant during the period of an annual profit plan. This is discussed later in this chapter in the section on "changing standards."

It is unfortunate that the increasing use and importance of standard costs have not yet been accompanied by a single, uniformly understood, and generally agreed upon concept of what a standard cost should be. With the more or less independent development of standards in so many different companies, however, it is not surprising that several versions of standard costs have evolved:

"Basic" standards are historic standards, never adjusted after an original determination unless the product specifications or production facilities change materially. After a time the standards fail to reflect current, efficient methods, and no longer provide accurate product cost information or effective cost control.

"Ideal" standards include only those elements of cost incurred under optimum conditions. While they provide an ultimate goal that managers may strive for, they do not indicate what a manager can actually expect to achieve on a continuing basis, nor do they provide meaningful cost information.

Standard Costs in Profitability Accounting

Standard costs are an integral part of Profitability Accounting. In fact, the standard concept is broadened considerably to include the planned element of every cost item, including variable manufacturing and commercial overhead, standby costs, and programmed costs as well as direct material and direct labor. Exhibit 5–1 is a simplified diagram of the flow and collection of the various elements of cost in a Profitability Accounting system. It clearly illustrates how the concept of standard cost is applied to each of the building blocks of cost. In each case, provision is made for the separation of planned costs and variances. Variances are recorded by type and reported according to the responsibility structure of the organization as incorporated in the chart of accounts.

The exhibit illustrates that the concept of standard cost in a Profitability Accounting system is not limited to direct material and direct labor. Following traditional usage of the term, however, the discussion of standard costs in this chapter will be focused on these last two elements of cost. Standard costs are used in performing three of the key functions in the operation of a management information system based on Profitability Accounting. These are as follows:

1. Providing measures of performance by responsibility for controlling costs in every segment of the enterprise
2. Developing meaningful cost information for various kinds of management decisions
3. Developing sound inventory costs and useful interim financial statements

The kind of standard desired in Profitability Accounting is a realistic standard, one which is comprehensive and attainable. It should contain provisions for all expected elements of cost, including normal unavoidable waste, spoilage, and scrap, also expected average losses in labor cost because of defective materials and equipment, excessive set-up time, use of non-preferred equipment, idle time, overtime premiums, and failure of workers on incentive to make guaranteed earnings. It should not be based on a theoretically perfect operation but should represent what can reasonably be expected to occur under the probable operating conditions. This is the only kind of a standard which provides meaningful information for controlling cost, for evaluating product profitability, and for making decisions based on cost.

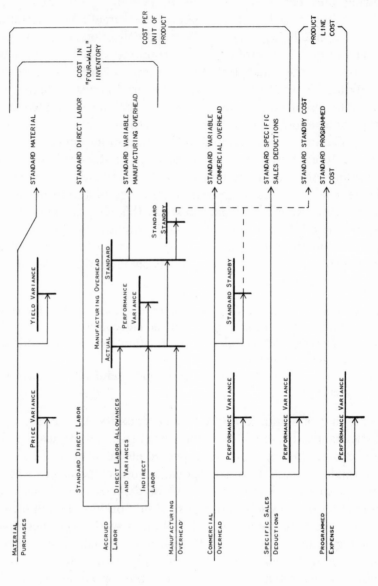

Exhibit 5-1. Flow of costs in Profitability Accounting.

Establishing Control of Costs

In Profitability Accounting, control of costs is based upon a comparison of the actual and planned results of every cost item for each responsibility unit in the organization. The differences between planned and actual achievements are a measure of the performance of managers and employees. In any given situation, however, this measure may be influenced by either or both of two factors:

1. The planning may be basically in error.
2. Actual conditions beyond the control of the responsible manager may differ from the conditions which were anticipated.

Since the objective of the control system is to isolate each element of the difference between planned costs and actual costs which is the result of individual performance, the effect of extraneous influences must also be isolated.

In most situations, basic errors in planning can be avoided or reduced to a minimum by following proper procedures and by creating a favorable attitude toward planning in the organization. Top management must exercise accuracy in planning; all managers must devote sufficient time and attention to the process of making and reviewing plans; and responsible managers must agree that their planned results can be achieved. The fulfillment of these conditions will create an atmosphere in which a manager will feel more responsible for performing according to plan because the planning was done carefully and with his participation.

The effect of changed conditions, beyond the control of responsible managers, can be dealt with in several ways:

1. Planned performance may be automatically adjusted to prevailing conditions. This is the approach to the application of flexible budgets for controlling many cost items where usage should vary with some measure of volume. Allowable amounts of expense are keyed to a measure of activity, and planned performance is automatically adjusted to take into account any change in activity. This approach is also inherent when determining the standard costs of direct labor and materials in the products which are actually produced rather than those which were planned.

2. Certain variances from planned performance may be isolated as soon as they are incurred so that they will not distort the reporting of cost control performance at subsequent points in the operation. For example, the difference between the planned price and the actual price of purchased materials is labeled "purchase price variance," and is usually segregated at the time materials are purchased. In all subsequent operations, materials are priced at the planned (standard) purchase price.

3. Plans may be revised when it becomes obvious that conditions have changed materially.

If none of these suggested methods deal satisfactorily with the situation, the specific changes in conditions may be cited as a partial explanation of the difference between planned and actual results, otherwise attributable to managerial performance.

Standards and Budgets for Control of Costs

In Profitability Accounting, both standards and budgets are used for first-line control of costs. This sometimes leads to confusion about the role that each of these tools plays.

Standards for control of material and direct labor costs are based upon material specifications of a unit of product and the specific operations necessary to manufacture it. These standards are generally set forth on a bill of materials and a process-routing sheet. The total standard materials and direct labor will vary directly and proportionately with the number of units manufactured.

However, the same technique cannot be used for first-line control of overhead costs. Overhead within a responsibility unit is composed of a variety of cost items with different behavior characteristics. It includes average expected losses in labor cost and may include normal unavoidable waste, spoilage, and scrap. Some of the overhead items are of a standby nature and should not vary at all with change in the volume, for example, the salary of the plant manager, property taxes, and building depreciation. Other overhead cost items will vary in direct proportion to some measure of activity of the responsibility unit, such as direct labor hours or invoices. Still others may vary with activity, but not proportionately.

The point is that allowable amounts of overhead costs within a responsibility unit cannot always be set by reference to the specified material and operations necessary to manufacture a particular product. Allowable amounts of cost are best determined by constructing schedules which take into account the standby element and the variability of each overhead cost item in relation to some measure of the responsibility unit's activity. Such schedules are called "variable budgets" or "flexible budgets." This type of budget is the tool used for control of overhead costs by responsibility, and various methods of developing such budgets are described at length in Chapter 6.

Standard Costs for Management Information

The same planned costs that are used for control by responsibility are also used to develop standard product cost for management information purposes such as determining interim earnings and product line profitability, and making pricing and profit-planning decisions. This is one aspect of the integration and flexibility provided with Profitability Accounting. The building blocks of standard cost data provide information which is appropriate for a variety of purposes, yet entirely consistent from one application to another.

The major problem is to convert budgeted overhead costs from a responsibility basis to standards for a unit of product. For control purposes, overhead costs are classified by individual responsibility unit. A cost center, on the other hand, refers to a function or group of functions, the costs of which are related to a common measure of volume. It is a means of compiling the overhead costs of a function in order to assign a fair share of these costs to each of the products passing through.

The cost center idea had its origin in traditional cost accounting. It was developed and is used in an effort to make a more accurate distribution of overhead costs, particularly in situations where a variety of products are manufactured in a single plant. Not all products affect all of the functions in the plant, or, if they do, they affect them in varying proportions. Also, the overhead costs of different functions vary widely when related to any common measure of volume.

Profitability Accounting uses the cost center method of assigning planned variable overhead costs to products. Planned standby and program costs, of course, are assigned and allocated only to product lines or profit centers. The specific techniques for accomplishing these assignments and allocations, and the distribution of service department costs, are discussed in detail in Chapters 6 and 7.

The classification of costs for control purposes need not, and often will not, coincide with the classification of costs by cost center for product and product line costing, but this need not cause concern. Costs are originally recorded on a responsibility basis because this facilitates reporting, and quick reporting is absolutely essential for good cost control. Product costs, while no less important, do not have to be reported as urgently. The standard product and product line costs used most frequently are developed in the initial planning and are readily available.

To recapitulate, planned costs are originally developed for control in these two forms:

- *Standard Costs for Materials and Direct Labor.* These costs are associated directly with a unit of product.
- *Budgeted Overhead Costs.* These costs are associated directly with the responsibility unit.

The rest of this chapter is concerned with the first of these forms.

BASIC DATA ON MATERIALS

Material cost standards should be based upon the type and quality of material required in the product, the quantity to be used, and the price to be paid. Each of these elements must reflect the conditions predicted for the ensuing period. The development of standard material costs is best handled in two steps:

1. Development of the physical standards, i.e., type and quantity of materials required by the product
2. Development of the material price standards, i.e., the current or contemplated prices of materials during the period in which the standard will be effective

By summarizing the standard physical quantities of each type of material required for a product before extending this by the standard price of the material, the cost standard can be more easily adjusted for price changes. With the existence of standard material prices, the difference between actual and standard price, the purchase price variance, can be isolated when the material is purchased, and the subsequent inventory transactions, including the calculation of material usage variances, can be costed at standard material prices.

Physical Standards for Materials

The specifications for the type and quantity of material required are commonly expressed in the bill of material, in a parts list, or in some similar document. This document is usually prepared by the engineering department or an equivalent function from engineering drawings, blueprints, or formula records. It is a permanent record which will change only when the specifications of the product change or when the manufacturing process changes in such a way that the specifications of the required materials are affected.

A separate sheet is usually prepared for each component part or intermediate product where the manufacturing process involves the making and assembly of parts, or where an intermediate material is used in several end products. A "where used" file of common parts or intermediate materials is an invaluable aid for production and inventory control and product engineering and can reduce considerably the effort required to establish and maintain current product standards.

Nominal Cost Materials

In most manufacturing companies, there are some direct materials in which the cost per unit of product is insignificant, even though large quantities may be used. Paint, certain finishing materials, and packing or crating supplies are items of this nature.

If it is feasible to determine the usage of such materials per unit of product, these items should be included in the material standard and should be charged to the inventory accounts as purchased. If it is not practicable to establish usage per unit of product, the items should be considered indirect materials and charged to an overhead account. The basis for their treatment must be thoroughly understood and consistently applied. Charging to inventory materials which are not included in the material standards used for relieving inventory can lead to inventory shortages when a physical inventory is taken.

Material Price Standards

Having developed standard physical quantities, the second step in the development of standard material costs is the determination of the price standards for purchased materials. Standard prices permit management to view material prices on an exception basis. Those material prices which are not at the planned level will be brought to management's attention.

The purchasing department is best qualified to set standard prices for purchased materials, but its prices should be reviewed by someone else in the organization who is quite familiar with the basic price movements of at least the more important purchased materials. In a smaller company this may be the president, while in a larger organization, it may be someone in the planning department or the economic analysis section.

The objective is to set as the standard price the net delivered price expected to prevail over the ensuing period. If the market price fluctuates rather widely, as might be the case with a basic commodity such as copper or wool, a "normal" price, reflecting an average of past experience, might be used as a standard in the absence of other evidence. If a part or material is to be purchased for the first time, the commitment is frequently on the basis of "price to be negotiated." In these situations, an estimated standard can be used. If the price finally arrived at is significantly different from the estimate, the standard price should be adjusted and the purchase price variance resulting from the use of the estimate should be isolated.

In some cases, as a matter of policy, the company may wish to utilize several sources of supply for a particular material even though prices differ. A weighted average, using the proportion to be purchased at each price, will provide a satisfactory standard. However, if the objective is to emphasize the cost of the multiple source policy, the lowest price should be used as the standard. The same solution would apply where a part of the required material is manufactured within the company and the remainder is purchased from an outside source.

The availability of quantity discounts on the purchase of certain materials should also be taken into consideration. Obviously, a company should not always order in quantities which simply yield the lowest purchase cost per unit. The standard unit price should be based on a standard quantity which minimizes the total cost per unit, including the inventory carrying cost as well as the purchase cost and the cost of ordering.

Purchase Price Variances

The *purchase price variance* is the difference between the amount actually paid for materials during a period and the amount which would have been paid at standard prices. It is reflected directly as one of the deviations from planned profits. It may be the basis for such management decisions as a change of selling prices, a change in make or buy policy, or a change to a substitute material. In some cases, a single purchase price variance account will provide all the information management needs. In most situations, however, where a wide variety of materials is purchased, where price fluctuations tend to be irregular, or where purchased materials represent a large share of total costs, the purchase price variance should be classified in greater detail. It may be classified by purchasing agent in order to assign individual responsibility within the purchasing department, by commodity groupings, or by product or product line where materials are peculiar to either.

The purpose of classifying purchase price variances by purchasing responsibility is to report the information to the proper person in the organization and to facilitate analysis of the variances. The purchase price variance cannot be used as a measure of the purchasing department's efficiency except in a very limited fashion. Market conditions are likely to have a far more pronounced influence on prices than any actions of the purchasing department. In fact, the objective of purchasing is not necessarily to obtain the lowest possible price. Such factors as quality, technical assistance provided, and the ability of the vendor to meet delivery schedules must also be considered, and any one of these might outweigh a small difference in the purchase price per unit.

The purchase price variance should be separated at the time of purchase. The simplest, most economical procedure for determining and recording the variance requires the purchasing department to record the standard unit cost, as well as the price to be paid to the vendor, on the accounts payable copy of the purchase order. When the invoice is received in the accounts payable department, the actual unit price is compared to the standard unit price and the purchase price variance is computed. The variance and the remainder of the cost distribution are marked on the face of the invoice, and a single handling of the vendor's invoice enables the recording of price variance as an integral part of the accounting distribution.

Some companies, especially those with centralized accounts payable and decentralized or divisionalized cost departments, prefer to compute the purchase price variance in the cost department. This procedure usually necessitates duplicate invoices and extra clerical effort. Typically, the original invoice is paid and recorded at actual cost in accounts payable while the duplicate invoice is sent to the cost department, where the price variance is calculated and recorded on the duplicate. The price variances are summarized periodically, and the summary is used to adjust the actual amounts previously charged to the inventory via the distribution of the original invoices. Attempting to route the original invoice through the cost department first may result in losing cash discounts because of delayed payment.

Inbound Transportation Charges

Since the standard purchase price includes a provision for inbound transportation, the actual transportation costs must be considered along with the invoice cost of materials in determining the purchase price variance. Except where unusual circumstances prevail, the simplest procedure is the periodic addition to inventory of an amount for standard freight cost. To determine the standard freight cost, a standard percentage, relating freight charges to standard purchase price, is applied to the standard cost of materials purchased during the period. Then the standard freight cost is compared to actual freight charges for the period and the difference is reported as a freight variance.

Another somewhat more complicated method is to charge the total standard cost of the material on each purchase invoice and the standard freight provision to the *four-wall inventory*. The difference between this total and the actual invoice cost is credited to the purchase price variance account, which is later charged with the actual cost of the freight bill.

A third, even more refined, method is to collect the inbound freight charges in a clearing account until they can be matched with material invoices. At that time an entry to the purchase price variance account may be made.

Material Quantity Variances

The *four-wall inventory* method used in Profitability Accounting takes full advantage of standard costs and adopts the exception approach to inventory accounting. It aims at reducing the amount of clerical effort in inventory accounting on the principle that although such accounting is necessary it cannot control inventories. As mentioned in the previous chapter, the materials section of a *four-wall inventory* usually consists of a single combined inventory amount. This includes in summary form the standard cost of all productive materials and the material content of all work in process, finished parts, assemblies, and finished products. All purchased materials are charged at standard prices. Certain raw materials, such as foundry metal, lumber, and formula ingredients, may be carried in separate accounts to facilitate the calculation of yield variances. Once this is accomplished, however, only the standard specified quantities at standard costs are carried to the combined inventory accounts.

The use of the *four-wall inventory* is based on the assumption that materials and parts once received in the plant leave in one of two ways: Either they become incorporated in the final product and leave the company when the product is sold or they are lost or spoiled in the course of production. The relief of inventory for items sold can be easily accomplished by accumulating the total standard cost of all products sold. Attention, therefore, can be focused on materials lost in production.

The ways in which materials may be lost and the methods used to determine and report the losses depend to a great extent upon the particular manufacturing processes being employed. Generally such losses occur in four primary areas and are treated as is described in the following paragraphs.

1. *Yield.* Material standards should include a provision for waste and shrinkage which are an unavoidable result of the manufacturing process.

- For example, if circular pieces are to be stamped out of sheet steel, the "lost corners" of steel are unavoidable waste. The material standard should include the cost of the total amount of sheet steel required per piece.
- Similarly, in the manufacture of paint or certain chemicals, a portion of the volatile ingredients will necessarily be lost through evaporation, and the material standard should include provision for expected shrinkage.

The relationship of expected usable material to the material put into the process is the yield, and it is generally expressed as a percentage. The adequacy of the allowance for the normally expected shrinkage or waste should be tested by comparing it to actual yield and developing a yield variance, and adjusting the inventory accordingly.

Yield may be measured at any point in a process where the unit of measure changes or where the material undergoes a change of form or state. Frequently, the first production operation results in conversion of the purchased unit of measure to the final product unit or measure and is the point at which yield and yield variance are measured. The yield concept generally does not apply to assembly of fabricated materials.

2. *Scrap.* Production scrap and spoilage are clearly different from waste shrinkage. They are material which has been lost because of some failure in the operation. Such loss is avoidable in the sense that no scrap or spoilage would occur if operations were perfect. As a practical matter, perfect operations are seldom achieved. The prudent manager attempts to provide for the normal expected scrap in his cost planning and at the same time institutes such procedures as may be necessary to keep scrap and spoilage within this limit. The cost of scrap is the accumulated standard cost through the last production operation on which the scrap occurred. It includes the standard cost of materials, direct labor, and variable manufacturing overhead. The provision for scrap should not be hidden in the material cost standard of the product. Since scrap reflects the performance of people, the pro-

vision for it should appear in expense budgets by responsibility. The standard cost of actual scrap is then relieved from inventory and charged to the responsible department to develop a performance variance against budget.

Where standard quantities of material are issued for a specific job or run, special requisitions may be required for the issuance of excess stock to replace spoiled materials. The special requisition is, in effect, a scrap report and must contain the necessary cost data to relieve inventory and charge scrap loss with the proper amount. In other cases, where spoiled materials are not replaced, a scrap report is prepared at the time an item is scrapped.

3. *Substitution of Material.* The standard material cost of the end product is based on specific usages of specified materials. To the extent that a more or less expensive material is substituted, there is a gain or loss of value which must be reported and recorded as a material substitution.

4. *Non-productive Use of Materials.* The product development function, the model shop, and, on occasion, the maintenance department may have need for productive materials. These materials should be issued on special requisitions which will be costed and which provide for the relief of inventory and a charge to the appropriate expense account.

BASIC DATA ON LABOR

The two steps of determining standard quantity and standard price apply to the development of standard direct labor costs as well as to standard material costs. Quantity in this case is the direct labor time required to perform all of the operations necessary to manufacture the product, while price is the wage rate paid for this time. Direct labor cost standards are an expression in money terms of attainable levels of worker performance under the planned manufacturing methods.

Direct vs. Indirect Labor

Normally, *direct labor* is that labor which is applied directly to products and which varies directly with volume. Actually there is no fine line of distinction between direct and indirect labor. In a given situation, the identification usually depends upon how closely the cost can be associated with a unit of product.

Certain labor directly benefits the manufacturing operations but does not necessarily vary directly with the quantities produced. The set-up of machine tools is an example. This kind of direct service labor can easily be identified with a specific product, but it may be difficult to decide upon the volume of product over which to spread the cost. If direct service labor is relatively insignificant in amount or if it is performed by workers other than the direct workers, such as a special crew of set-up men, it is best treated as an item of overhead cost. In other cases, it is desirable to consider direct service labor as direct labor because this permits greater accuracy in developing product costs and gives better control over time spent.

When direct service labor is included in the direct labor standards, it is often treated as direct labor for control purposes, even to the extent of being performed on the basis of routings. Any difference between the actual time taken to perform the service labor and the standard time will result in a variance. For product cost purposes, the standard cost of service labor is spread over a standard volume of production. Any difference between the actual size of a production run and the standard size will result in a labor cost variance, usually called a scheduling variance.

Other types of labor may vary more or less with volume, but either they cannot be specifically identified with a unit of product or it is impractical to do so. Such labor is classified as indirect and treated as manufacturing overhead.

Time Standards for Direct Labor

The time standards for direct labor are based upon the specifications of the product. The production or engineering department determines the specific operations required to manufacture the product with the available facilities and skills. Then these operations are usually listed on a document called a process routing sheet. This document is a permanent record which will be revised only when the specifications of the product change or when the availability of improved facilities or skills dictates a change in the standard method of manufacture. Generally, the routing sheet contains the sequence of operations, a brief description of each operation to be performed, the machines and special tools to be used, make-up of the crew or group if more than one worker is required for an operation, the department in which the work is to be done, and the standard time per unit for each operation. Exhibit 5–2 shows a typical process routing sheet with provision for standard time data.

It is possible to establish standards for direct labor by one or more of the following methods:

1. An estimate, made by a foreman or someone with shop knowledge of the machine to be used, the crew required, and the production per hour
2. The selection of representative actual labor time data from historical cost or output records
3. A time study analysis of operations as they are performed

Estimates and past experience may be adequate in particular situations for limited uses. Generally, however, if labor standards are to be fully effective for controlling labor costs and for developing accurate product cost information, they should be based on time studies and standardized job conditions.

One of the most important prerequisites of good time standards is the standardization of job conditions and methods. There are wide variations in the methods workers can use to perform the same task with identical tools and equipment, and there are usually several combinations of tools and equipment which can be used to perform a given task.

Assuming that the task is undertaken with equal determination, effort, and speed of movement, the required time will be influenced by the efficiency of the method. Therefore, standard times must be based on use of the proper tools and equipment and a worker must be trained in the proper method. In many cases, the development of standard times is the occasion for a methods study to determine the most efficient ways of doing jobs. The methods study, especially if it is broad in scope and includes consideration of plant layout and work flow, is a most effective means of discovering cost reduction opportunities.

In considering the importance of standardized job considerations, it is interesting to note that Frederick W. Taylor, the father of industrial engineering and the originator of labor standards,

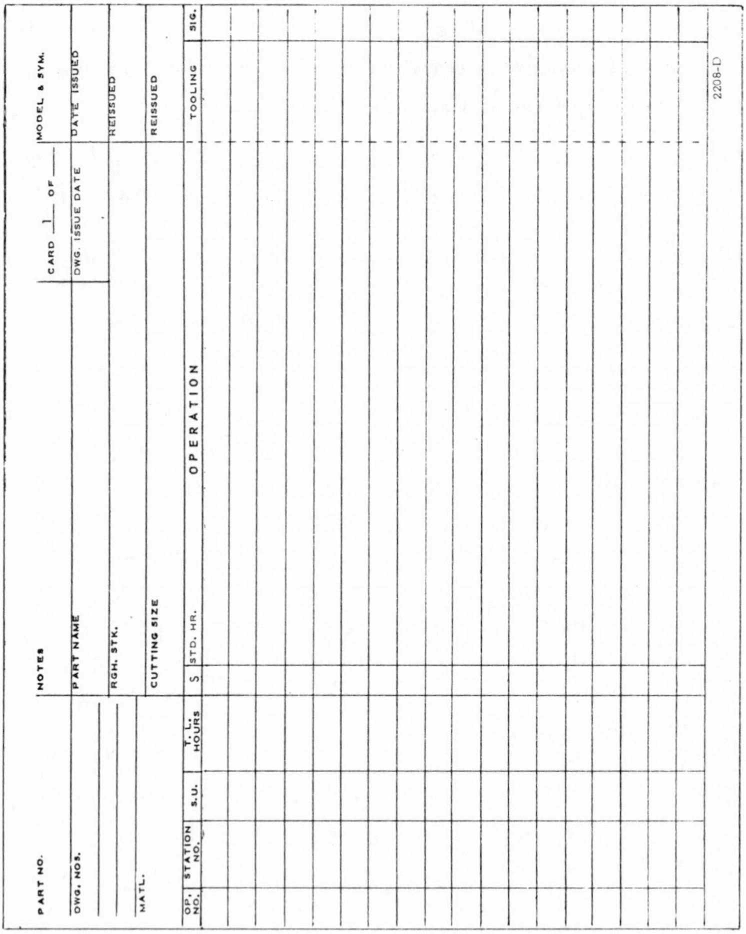

Exhibit 5–2. Process routing sheet.

quickly recognized that, without reliable tooling, manufacturing labor standards were ineffective. His own research in the field of metallurgy resulted in the development of the tool steels necessary for reliable, standardized tooling, and it was with these developments that he made his fortune.

Obviously, occasions will arise in which the worker will encounter non-standard conditions. The most common of these results from the use of non-standard materials.

- During a steel shortage, for example, one manufacturer was unable to obtain steel sheets in the proper size for forming a component of his product. He improvised by welding together smaller sheets to create the sheet size required. The workers in the forming operation had to exercise greater care, and consequently use more time, with the welded sheets than with sheets mill rolled to the desired size. Obviously the standards for performance in terms of both quantity and quality of output had to take into consideration the type of sheets being used.

In other cases, machine failures or peak production volumes and attendant scheduling problems may make it necessary to manufacture an item on sub-standard equipment, i.e., equipment with a lower capacity or slower speed than that normally used. Or, if tooling is in poor repair, an extraordinary amount of set-up and running time may be required.

If a non-standard condition is encountered and is expected to persist for some time, as in the case of the welded steel sheets, a new standard can be developed and used until conditions return to normal. If, on the other hand, the non-standard condition is encountered only occasionally, as in the case of the occasional "hard casting" in a machining operation, a special allowance may be granted to the operator by the industrial-engineering or standards function on an exception basis. In both cases, the non-standard conditions are recognized and adjustments are made for them so that they will not adversely affect the operator's performance measure.

Direct Labor Allowances

Direct labor time standards, whether established by time study, estimate, or past experience, should be at a level which can be attained by an average worker at a normal pace under standard conditions. The standard will provide reasonable allowances for personal needs, unavoidable delays, and make-ready time. These allowances are similar in nature to waste and shrinkage allowances for material. While they actually represent nonproductive labor, they are unavoidable for all practical purposes and can usually be predetermined. Therefore, they should be included in the labor time standard.

There is another element of direct labor cost which is analogous to scrap or spoilage of material. The extra time required to machine an abnormally hard casting, the time lost because of machine breakdown or power failure, and the re-work required because of a machining error—these are examples of this type of labor cost. Labor cost in excess of standard is incurred because of imperfect performance on the part of men, materials, and machinery.

Again, a prudent management will attempt to avoid this cost by programs such as preventive maintenance of machinery, tooling maintenance, and inspection of purchased materials, but only to the point where each dollar spent on a program produces savings of more than a dollar. The objective is least cost production, not operationally perfect production. The costs occasioned by any remaining imperfections should be planned for and included in overhead cost.

The incurrence of direct labor allowance costs of this nature should be controlled on an exception basis. That is, an allowance ticket should be issued by the departmental supervisor or industrial engineer for each occurrence to cover the additional time required because of the non-standard condition. By setting up the appropriate detailed expense accounts in the labor allowance section of the chart of accounts, the labor allowance can be classified and reported by cause as well as by departmental responsibility.

"If Necessary" Operations

It frequently happens that some productive work must be done on an irregular basis—that is, sometimes an operation may be necessary and sometimes not.

- For example, when a trimming die is new or recently repaired, it may cut sheet metal so cleanly that grinding to remove burrs is unnecessary. As this trimming die wears, however, the edges may become dull and all or part of the parts produced may require a grinding or filing operation to remove burrs.

- Similarly, re-striking, polishing, welding, or other operations may be necessary on a certain percentage of output, although the percentage may vary with such factors as quality of material, temperature, humidity, condition of dies, tools and equipment, and other unpredictable circumstances.

From the viewpoint of measuring performance of individual workers or groups, it is important that standards be established for "if necessary" operations. This causes no great trouble, because the number of pieces processed through the operations is known and actual time can be compared with standard for those pieces. A problem arises, however, in determining the standard cost of the finished product. The "if necessary" operations have been performed and charged to inventory on only a portion of the finished product. If the standard cost for relief of inventory includes the cost of these operations as though they had been performed on all of the finished product, an inventory difference will occur. Two possible methods of solving the problem are as follows:

1. The "if necessary" operations may be treated as a cost variance and not included in the standard cost. While not theoretically correct, this method is the simplest and has many practical advantages.

2. A weighted standard cost of finished product may be established, based upon performing the operations on an estimated percentage of the total production. The standard cost of the "if necessary" operations is charged to inventory as performed. If the estimated percentage is approximately correct, relief of inventory at the weighted standard cost should produce a negligible inventory difference.

Rate Standards for Direct Labor

The price factor for direct labor is the rate paid per labor hour. The standard rate per direct labor hour is used to price the standard time in order to develop standard labor cost.

The standard rate per hour should be the rate normally paid for the type of skill required to perform a particular operation. The method of determining the standard rate will depend upon conditions in a given company.

In some cases a worker is paid a fixed hourly rate, but varying rates may be paid for the same operation. The variation may be due to skill or length of service. Standard wage rates are usually established by occupational groups or codes. The standard rate may be simply the arithmetical average of the actual hourly rates of all present employees in each occupational group, or it may be some other figure representative of the actual rates to be paid during the coming period. Where differences between occupational wage rates are insignificant, departmental or plant-wide average rates may be used as the standard.

If an operation requires a crew of two or more workers, a standard crew size should be determined and the standard rate should be the weighted average of the standard labor rates for the occupations represented in the crew.

If employees are paid on a piece rate basis, the quantity and price factors of labor cost are merged into a single figure. The rate per piece is actually the standard labor cost. This is the simplest type of incentive pay plan to administer, but compared with an earned hour plan it has disadvantages:

1. The standard times and standard rates originally used to set standard piece rates are often lost sight of through direct adjustments of the piece rate. Subsequently, over-all adjustments of the piece rate must be made to compensate for changes in the standard time of the operation or the wage level.
2. Labor hours rather than labor dollars are the common shop language. A piece rate is an unwieldy statistic and must be converted to labor time before the standard data can be used for production scheduling.
3. The extra cost resulting from using a high-priced man on a low-priced job is buried in an over-all efficiency variance.

It has become increasingly common for employees to be paid on some type of earned hour plan in which the separate identity of the time and rate elements of cost is constantly maintained. Administration and accounting under the plan should not be much more complex than under a piece rate system, and the benefits in terms of good wage administration and control information more than offset any extra effort. An earned hour plan results in a constant direct labor cost per unit of product, and the standard rate is established in the same way as it is under an hourly rate plan. Some other incentive plans result in varying labor costs per unit of production by paying a different rate per piece as labor performance exceeds a standard level.

Direct Labor Variances

Once the labor standards for both time and rate have been determined, the problem is to establish a recording and analyzing procedure to segregate the standard labor cost from the direct labor variances and allowances. Standard direct labor cost will be charged to inventory. Direct labor variances and allowances are classified by type and responsibility, and thus they provide a starting point for an analysis by responsible managers to determine and correct the basic cause of the excess cost.

Direct labor allowances present no particular problem. An allowance is classified by type and by responsibility at the time the allowance ticket is issued. Allowance tickets are summarized by type and by responsibility and charged to the proper allowance account, a departmental overhead account. Labor allowances are controlled at this point by a comparison of the actual cost with the budgeted cost. Any excess of actual expense over the planned amount is reported as a performance variance.

Note that this is a control over labor allowances at the secondary level. Original control was exercised when the allowance ticket was issued. At that point, a determination was made that non-standard conditions existed, beyond the control of the individual worker, and that these conditions would hinder him in attaining his expected level of performance. The labor allowance ticket removed the effect of the non-standard condition from his performance measurement and made possible effective reporting and control of his performance on direct labor operations. At the secondary level, the objective is to control the occurrence of non-standard conditions. If actual allowances exceed planned or budgeted allowances, it may be because of improper inspection of purchased materials, inadequate maintenance, or failure in any of several support functions. The secondary control of labor allowances is designed to indicate to the responsible manager the existence of a problem so that he can isolate it and take corrective action to maintain the least cost of production.

Direct labor cost variances can be segregated into two types— a rate variance and a time (or performance, or efficiency) variance. The efficiency variance is the difference between the standard direct labor cost and the actual direct labor cost arising because the actual time required to perform an operation differed from the standard time. It is calculated according to the formula

$$(\text{Standard Time} - \text{Actual Time}) \times \text{Standard Rate} = \text{Efficiency Variance}$$

The rate variance is the difference between actual and standard direct labor cost arising because the actual wage rate paid differed from the standard wage rate. The rate variance is calculated according to the formula:

$$(\text{Standard Rate} - \text{Actual Rate}) \times \text{Actual Time} = \text{Rate Variance}$$

Together, these two variances account for the difference between actual direct labor cost and standard direct labor cost.

The original data for calculation of direct labor variances are obtained from the job time ticket, an example of which is shown in Exhibit 5–3. The job ticket contains much of the standard data that appear on the routing, such as part number and name, operation number, description of operation, department number, and standard time per unit or per one hundred units. It may also contain standard rate per hour, if standard rates vary within a department. In addition, the timekeeper, supervisor, or worker will enter on the job ticket certain variable information such as employee's name and clock number, the date, the time started and time finished or the elapsed hours, and the number of units completed. If workers are paid a straight hourly rate, the formulas above must be used to determine the efficiency variance and the rate variance.

If a piecework plan is in use, no variance will occur unless the earnings of the operator fall below a guaranteed rate per hour and an allowance must be made to bring the piecework earnings up to the guarantee. Such allowances should be classed as labor variances, and they are usually classed as efficiency variances even though they may include a rate variance. The rate and efficiency

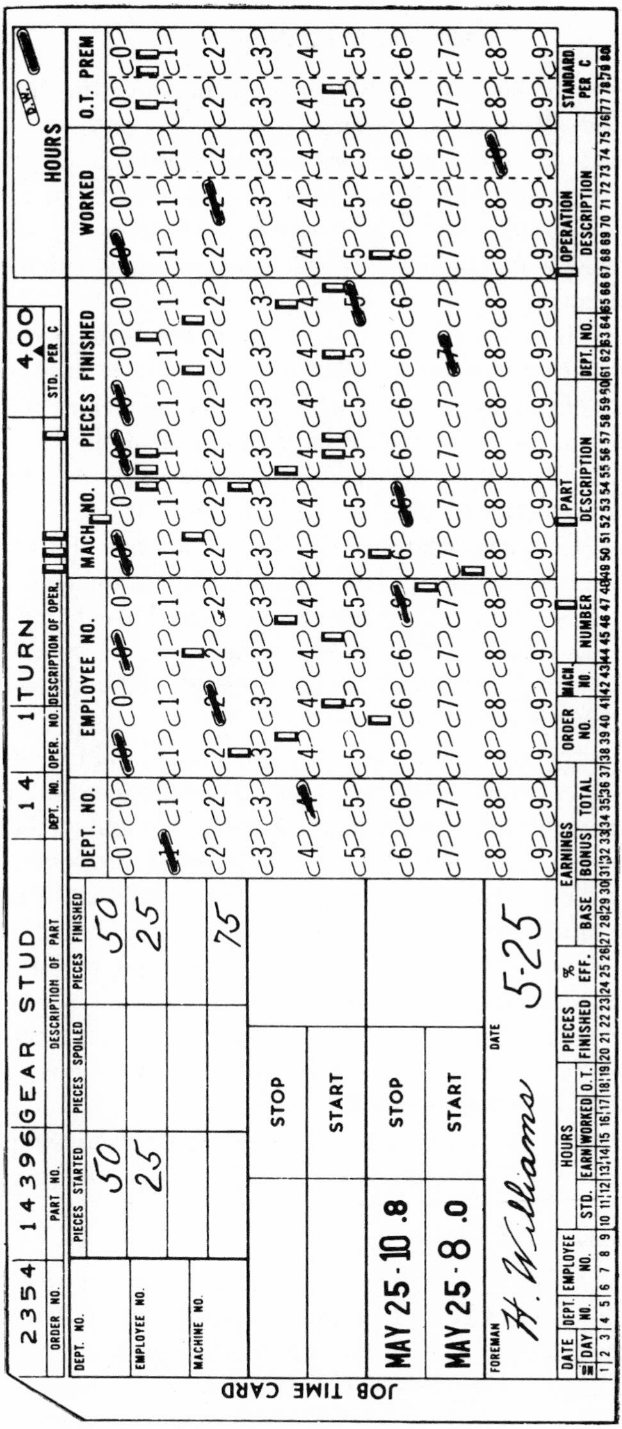
JOB TIME CARD

2354 | 14396 | GEAR STUD | 14 | 1 | TURN | 400
ORDER NO. | PART NO. | DESCRIPTION OF PART | DEPT. NO. | OPER. NO. | DESCRIPTION OF OPER. | STD. PER C

	PIECES STARTED	PIECES SPOILED	PIECES FINISHED
DEPT. NO.	50		50
EMPLOYEE NO.	25		25
MACHINE NO.			
			75

STOP
START
MAY 25-10.8 STOP
MAY 25-8.0 START

FOREMAN H. Williams DATE 5-25

DEPT. NO. | EMPLOYEE NO. | MACH. NO. | PIECES FINISHED | HOURS WORKED | O.T. PREM

DATE MO. DAY | DEPT. NO. | EMPLOYEE NO. | HOURS STD. EARN WORKED O.T. | PIECES FINISHED | % EFF. | EARNINGS BASE BONUS TOTAL | ORDER NO. | MACH. NO. | PART NUMBER DESCRIPTION | OPERATION DEPT. NO. DESCRIPTION | STANDARD PER C

Exhibit 5–3. Job time ticket.

variances cannot be separated without recourse to the time and rate data underlying the piece rate.

In the earned hour plan, where the operator is paid a uniform rate per unit at all levels of efficiency as long as the guaranteed hourly rate is earned, the allowance to bring earnings up to guaranteed rates will also be the only efficiency variance which shows up in the accounts.

However, if the incentive plan is one in which the operator is paid a varying rate per unit as efficiency rises, it is necessary to calculate an efficiency variance whenever the efficiency achieved by the operator differs from that on which the standard is based, in addition to computing the make-up allowance for any employees who fail to earn the guaranteed wage.

Because efficiency variance is usually a more meaningful measure of the control over direct labor than the rate variance, it is not uncommon to calculate the former and "force" the latter. This "forced" rate variance is the difference between the actual labor cost and the sum of the standard labor cost, the labor allowances, and the labor efficiency variance.

In most situations, a daily labor report is essential for effective control of direct labor efficiency. Variances are brought to the attention of responsible managers promptly enough so that corrective action can be taken before significant losses occur. Furthermore, a daily labor accrual and balancing minimizes the peak clerical workload at the end of a pay period. The daily report is usually in terms of hours only. Dollar extensions and the rate variance are determined only at the end of the pay period. A daily departmental labor report usually shows for each worker the attendance hours, labor allowance hours, actual productive hours, earned or standard hours of productive work, and make-up or day work guarantee hours. Often an efficiency percentage is reported which is the ratio of earned hours to actual productive hours.

Accounting Flow of Labor Costs

The flow of labor costs in the accounts is illustrated in Exhibit 5–4. Standard direct labor is originally charged to departmental direct labor accounts. These are only memo accounts, however, as was explained in Chapter 4. The objective is to obtain standard direct labor by department as a basis for charging overhead into

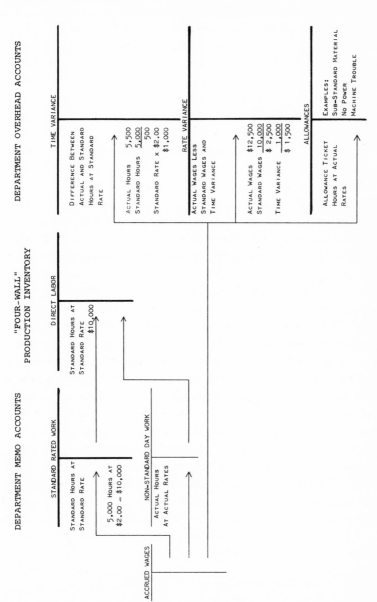

Exhibit 5–4. Flow chart of labor costs.

inventory in those situations where overhead is absorbed on standard direct labor hours or dollars. From the memo accounts, standard direct labor is charged directly to inventory.

The labor section of the *four-wall inventory* used in Profitability Accounting consists of a single account which includes the standard direct labor cost of all work in process, finished parts, assemblies, and finished products. This considerably reduces the clerical effort required to account for inventory and lessens the opportunities for clerical errors.

Labor allowance costs are charged to the proper labor allowance accounts, which are a part of departmental overhead. The charge is made on the basis of hours shown on labor allowance tickets at the actual rate paid. The planned variable amounts are applied to product and enter the inventory as standard variable manufacturing overhead, as was illustrated in Exhibit 5–1.

Labor variances are charged directly to departmental variance accounts. They represent amounts by which actual earnings will differ from planned earnings.

In most companies, there will be occasions when productive direct labor is performed for which no standards are available. When this occurs, the labor cost should be charged to a separate departmental non-standard labor account. The common practice is to charge the cost to inventory and ultimately to cost of sales on a job order basis. This procedure is illustrated in Exhibit 5–4.

As in the case of materials under a *four-wall inventory*, once standard direct labor enters the inventory it can leave in only two ways: Either it is relieved from inventory as part of the cost of products sold or it is lost in subsequent operations. A separate procedure is not required to account for losses in subsequent operations, however. In every case direct labor is associated with some kind of material. The procedures used to determine and report material losses in production should also provide for reporting the direct labor costs incurred in the operations up to the point of loss.

Overtime and Shift Premiums

A question arises as to whether overtime premiums should be treated as direct labor, a direct labor variance, or an overhead item. The company policy with respect to the number of regularly scheduled working hours per week should be considered in arriving at the answer. If the normal working hours are such that overtime premium is usually not paid, the premiums that are paid should be treated as a labor variance or an overhead item. When overtime is scheduled regularly as a planned operation, the premium should be included in standard labor cost by a labor rate adjustment.

If overtime is scheduled only upon the specific requests of customers and they are expected to pay for the excess cost, the premiums may be collected on a factory work order and charged to a specific product or customer. In general, however, overtime is attributable more to over-all operations than to particular products.

When a plant operates more than one shift, it is a frequent practice to pay a premium of perhaps $.05 or $.10 an hour for employees on the second and third shifts. This shift premium is usually included in the standard wage rate. The amount included should be based on a careful estimate of future activities and should be weighted according to the expected mix of hours worked during the various shifts.

Production Counts

The importance of accurate production counts to accurate determination of cost variances and inventory balances is obvious. Furthermore, when an incentive pay plan is being used, erroneous production counts will affect the amounts paid to workers. Some of the procedures and devices that aid in obtaining accurate production counts are

1. Proper selection of points at which production is to be counted (In some cases the production counts are taken at the end of every operation. In assembly line operations, counts may be taken only at the end of a series of operations through which each product must move.)
2. Scale or hand counting of production at the selected points
3. Use of mechanical or electrical counters on presses, machines, or conveyors wherever this is practical
4. Maintaining lots of predetermined size which move from operation to operation as a unit, or attaching a traveler to each lot to

carry forward the count of good pieces completed at the previous operation
5. Checking reported production against a master control record in the production control department

CHANGING STANDARDS

Any of several factors may change permanently after standard costs are established, making it desirable to change the standard. These changes include

1. Changes in standard labor time as a result of different tooling, machinery and equipment, or processing methods
2. Changes in material specifications
3. Changes in the price level of material or labor

The problems which arise in changing standards are

1. The clerical effort involved in changing the standards themselves
2. The difficulty of determining the effect of the adjustments on inventories

Price standards for both material and labor are generally set at a level which takes into consideration anticipated changes over a given future period. It is a frequent and desirable practice to revise the price standards annually, and the revision can often be timed to coincide with the annual physical inventory and the signing of a new labor contract. Where these are not coincident, favorable variances may be programmed for the early part of a year and unfavorable variances may be programmed for the period following the price rise. The effect of any unanticipated price level changes which may occur between annual revisions can be reflected in purchase price variances or labor rate variances without causing a particular problem in most cases. These variances are not performance variances in the strict sense of the term. If the variance is of particular concern to management, it can be set apart in a separate variance account.

Changes in material specifications and manufacturing methods should be reflected currently in the operating or performance standards, if these are to remain useful as a measure of performance. It is usually not desirable, however, to change the product cost standards for inventory during the year, because this complicates the task of reconciling planned and actual profit and because it increases the possibility for serious inventory difference to arise at the time of taking a physical inventory. More than one company has found that it could only avoid these inventory differences by resorting to a system of dual standards. Under this system, one set of standards is kept very current for performance measurement, and another set, not changed during the year, is used for charging inventory. The accumulated difference is compiled and gives a valuable indication of cost trends.

SUMMARY

Under Profitability Accounting, all costs are treated as planned or standard costs. The term has been used here, however, in the more common cost-accounting sense, to refer to direct labor and direct material. The standard costs of these items, as specified in bills of material and routing sheets, can be identified directly with a unit of product.

These standard costs are first used to determine performance variances by responsibility in terms of material yield and scrap variances and labor efficiency variances. Material price and labor rate variances are also developed before charging the direct material and labor content of production to the "four-wall inventory" at standard quantities and standard prices.

The operation standard costs used for segregating performance variances from the cost input to inventory must be consistent (or reconcilable) with the product cost standards used for relieving inventory for cost of goods sold, although this may be complicated by the desire to keep operating standards as current as possible while holding product cost standards constant during the period of the annual profit plan.

Chapter **6**

Variable Overhead
Budgets Based on
Work Measurement

In the past, managers have had more difficulty controlling overhead costs than they have had with those costs incurred for direct material and direct labor. Overhead costs are incurred in every area of the firm's operations and include a variety of cost items with different behavior characteristics. Some are of a standby nature and remain stable with changes in the workload volume, while others fluctuate in various manners. They are seldom specifically identifiable with a unit of product.

Another difficulty in the control of overhead costs arises from the complex interrelationship of the various cost-incurring departments or functional groups. Some functions precede actual production or sales by weeks or months, others occur simultaneously, and still others may lag by varying periods. The related costs will lead, coincide with, or lag behind the production or sales program. A common base, such as direct labor hours or dollars, as an index of the allowable costs for all operating groups may have very little relationship to the workload volume of a department at any particular time.

Trouble often occurs when volume is low for long periods and costs are sustained at high levels in anticipation of greater production. An expensive time lag may intervene between the reduction of volume and the reduction of overhead costs, or a hasty cost-cutting effort based on inadequate or unreliable information may produce unbalanced operations. The application of work measurement techniques has often produced overhead cost savings, but these may prove only temporary unless they are incorporated in a continuing budgetary control system.

In recent years, variable (or flexible) budgets have been widely recognized as the best available tool for the control of overhead costs. The bulk of this chapter details the most comprehensive variable budget program used in Profitability Accounting, one which recognizes both long-range and short-range cost behavior and which may be applied to all the operating areas of a complex enterprise. It recognizes the idiosyncracies of cost relationships within operating units, resulting from operational requirements, management decisions, and changing volume. Budgets are based on the scope, completeness, and quality of the tasks to be accomplished, as explicitly determined by the use of work measurement techniques. This chapter describes, too, how the allowable costs provided by these variable budgets are also used to develop variable overhead rates for purposes of product costing, thus illustrating the building block principle.

The first part of this chapter, however, describes the evolution of successively more refined types of variable budgets, leading up to the most sophisticated type detailed here. Companies usually have to acquire some experience with one of these simpler types before they can make intelligent use of the most sophisticated and complex budgets. The next chapter shows how a company that is not yet ready for the most sophisticated budgetary procedures can still develop variable overhead rates and determine product line profitability. Subsequent chapters illustrate how the same costs are also used for return on investment calculations, planning, and aiding pricing decisions.

Although the examples presented in this chapter apply to departments and functions closely associated with the manufacturing operation, these variable budget techniques are equally effective in the control of commercial costs.

THE EVOLUTION OF VARIABLE BUDGETS

Variable budgets for overhead costs have appeared in several forms and have met with varying degrees of success, depending partly on how they were designed and partly on how they were used. The three major steps in the evolution of variable budgets are illustrated in Exhibit 6–1.

The earliest type of variable budget was based on plotting a crude "scatter graph" of historical cost behavior (the level of actual cost at various actual levels of volume) and drawing the straight line which best fitted the plotted points. The slope of the line was the rate at which cost was assumed to vary with volume, and it was used both for determining the budget allowance and for absorbing variable overhead into product cost. Projection of the line back to zero volume determined the assumed level of fixed costs. The use of this crude but simple method was an improvement over the use of fixed budgets (pre-set lump sum amounts which may not reflect actual operating conditions), and it was a useful device for approximating the variable overhead portion of both operation and product costs. It had little value as a cost control budget, however, because it was not based on how costs should behave, but on how they were behaving, and because the straight line was usually an over-simplified representation of cost behavior.

The second type of variable budget, illustrated in the middle graph of Exhibit 6–1, is the most widely used by companies in their initial adoption of Profitability Accounting. It is a useful compromise between the over-simplification of the "scatter-graph" budget and the complexity of the more sophisticated system described below. In the middle graph, the dotted, stair-step line labeled short-range budget indicates how costs should behave in a department. It is actually the *summary* of how a number of individual overhead expense accounts within that department should behave. Some of these, such as indirect labor, should increase in steps as people are added at various volume levels. Others, such as supplies, may increase linearly with volume; while still others, such as depreciation, may be completely unaffected by volume. Many accounts will have both a standby and a variable component.

The determination of how each of these costs should behave may be based on discussion with knowledgeable supervisors, or it may be based on more sophisticated work measurement techniques. In any event, the short-range budget summarizes the allowable department expenses, which are determined account

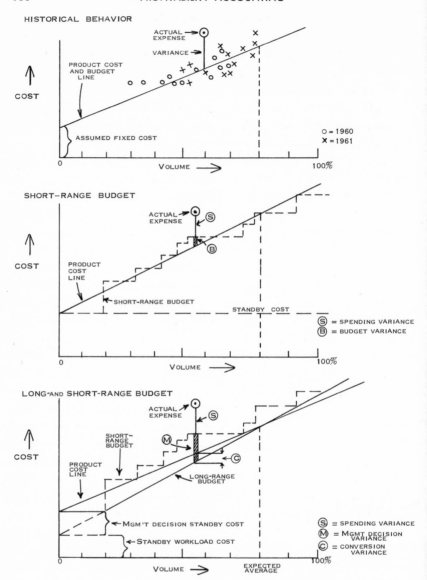

Exhibit 6–1. The evolution of variable budgets.

by account for cost control purposes. The straight line starting at standby cost and zero volume is drawn so as to best fit the budgeted costs over the normal range of operating volumes. The slope of the line determines the variable overhead rate for product cost purposes and input to inventory. The standby cost allowed in the budget is the same amount charged to standby cost in inventory or, where the monthly adjustment for this is not made, charged directly against monthly income.

At any particular, actual volume, the difference between the departmental budget allowance and the total of the actual expenses is the spending variance, an over-all measure of departmental cost control. The difference between the budget allowance and the amount of variable overhead absorbed into product cost (based on the straight-line rate) is usually called the "budget variance." It is the reconciling item between the variable overhead in the budget allowance and that in standard product cost. Although this variance often tends to average out to zero over the course of the year, it may accumulate into a significant amount, depending upon the relation of the budget line to the product cost line and the volumes encountered during the year. Therefore, the budget variance is computed monthly to avoid deferring unpleasant surprises to the end of the year.

Although it is a simple matter to determine the monthly amount of budget variance for the whole company and only a little more difficult to determine it by department, it is extremely difficult to isolate the reasons for this variance. Not only does the budget vary with volume in a non-linear manner, but it is likely to be based on one measure of volume, such as machine hours or invoices processed, that is converted into another volume measure, such as direct labor dollars, for product costing purposes. This arithmetic conversion has to be based on assumptions as to average mix and volume, and these assumptions may not be borne out by actual events.

Companies that have worked for a while with the simpler budgets and encountered significant, unexplainable budget variances are the most receptive to the more sophisticated budgeting system illustrated in the bottom graph of Exhibit 6–1. Since this system is discussed in detail in this chapter, only a few points need be mentioned here. Under this method, there is a short-range budget, similar to that described above, one which is always based on the use of work measurement for determining indirect labor and clerical workloads. There is also a so-called long-range budget, the straight line on the graph that never goes above the short-range budget and only touches it at a few points. The slope of this line reflects the lowest obtainable overhead rate. The difference between this line and the short-range budget allowance is reported as a "management decision variance," the cost of operating at any volume other than the one that results in the lowest cost rate.

The variable product cost (overhead absorption) line is drawn from standby cost at zero volume to the long-range budgeted cost at the forecast volume. A comparison of product cost overhead rates under this method and under the one described immediately above is given in the next chapter in connection with Exhibit 7–1. The "conversion variance," the reconciling item between the long-range budget and the product cost line, is not likely to get as large as the budget variance in the previous method, and it can be analyzed more readily.

ANALYSIS OF OVERHEAD DEPARTMENT WORKLOADS

In most well-organized enterprises, the responsibility for incurring a cost rests with the manager who directs the activities creating that cost. He is the man best qualified to control the cost. He is familiar with the tasks to be performed, knows what skills are required, and is aware of the equipment needed.

Thus the cost of service functions, such as inspection and maintenance, should be charged first to the supervisor of the service department. The managers of the departments requisitioning the service are charged secondarily, at a predetermined standard rate, for services rendered, and the service department receives credit through overhead transfer accounts. This procedure is described in greater detail in Chapter 4.

However, there are situations in which the secondary charges would serve no useful purpose. For example, it would be pointless to allocate the total cost of electric current to departments on the basis of machine hours, horsepower ratings, or any similar measurement, for such allocations cannot be positively identified with the individual departments and the individual manager's efforts will not thus be reflected.

Basic Elements of Overhead Costs

In order to provide management with the information needed to gain positive control over overhead costs, the variable budget program must take into account the basic elements that generate and influence these costs. These elements are as follows:

1. The *function*, or task which has to be performed
2. The *workload*, or size of the task in terms of some kind of completed units
3. The *method* of carrying out a function which influences the workload
4. The *productivity*, or efficiency with which the task is performed

In order to express workload in quantitative terms, to relate it to cost and to evaluate productivity, the measure of Control Factor Units (CFU) is used. A Control Factor Unit is a common measure of the quantity of workload resulting from the various functions performed within a department or responsibility group.

The operation of a department is analyzed to determine the workloads created by each function, when it is performed according to the prescribed method. Control Factor Units and the appropriate cost are analyzed, and the relationship between them is determined at an acceptable level of performance or efficiency. A schedule is then developed showing the allowable cost in relation to a varying amount of workload as expressed in Control Factor Units.

Thus functions, methods, workloads, and control factors are all explicitly considered and integrated in the variable budget program to provide the means for practical control of overhead costs at the departmental level.

Workload and Cost Behavior Characteristics

The design, construction, and use of a practical variable budget requires an understanding of the relationship between workloads and costs. It also requires a thorough knowledge of the behavior of both workloads and costs in response to the different factors which influence them. As mentioned in Chapter 2, overhead costs are classified into two groups—variable costs and standby costs.

Standby costs include costs resulting from the retention of facilities, such as depreciation, rent, insurance, and real estate and personal property taxes, and from the retention of certain key people, even at zero volume. The size of the basic organization to be maintained and the related standby costs are determined by two factors:

1. The amount of the functional workloads which exist at zero volume (Certain functions are a "must" even though there are no production or sales. For example, a financial statement must still be prepared, various tax forms and reports must be filed, and buildings must be heated and protected against fire, theft, and vandalism.)

2. The decisions as to whether it would cost more to hire and train employees for jobs requiring certain abilities and skills than would be saved if they were laid off when the workload did not justify their employment

When an enterprise suffers a temporary shutdown, the ready recognition of which standby costs exist because of standby workloads and which are the result of management decisions becomes extremely important.

For those cost items in which the entire amount of the standby cost is the result of a standby workload, or in cases where there is no standby cost, any additional workload will be accompanied by an increase in costs. The first of these conditions is illustrated in the top graph of Exhibit 6–2. This condition is readily understood and usually handled correctly.

However, it is important to take note of any cost item in which part or all of the standby cost is the result not of standby workload but of a management decision. Such an item can absorb a certain amount of variable workload without an increase in cost. This is illustrated graphically by the "long-range budget" line in the bottom half of Exhibit 6–2. Frequently this point is overlooked and the variable budget is developed by connecting a straight line from the standby cost to the expected cost at expected average volume. This "absorption line," shown in the graph, may be useful for inventory costing, but it is not valid for budgetary control.

STANDBY COST EQUALS COST OF STANDBY WORKLOAD

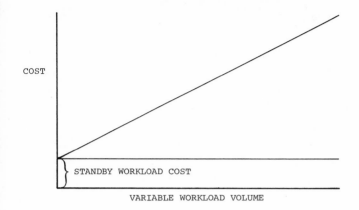

STANDBY COST EXCEEDS COST OF STANDBY WORKLOAD

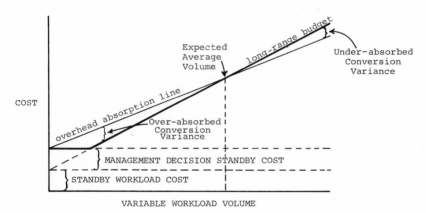

Exhibit 6–2.

When used as a budget, it over-provides for costs at the lower volumes and under-provides at the higher volumes. It only provides the correct allowance when actual volume is at the expected average volume. (See Chapter 7, for more on this subject.)

Analysis of Departmental Functions

Because functions are such a basic determinant of costs, they should be carefully analyzed. The analysis of functions is intended to accomplish a number of purposes.

1. Challenge the need for each function
2. Challenge its place in the organization
3. Reveal any peculiarities in the function which will affect cost occurrence

Sometimes the need for a function disappears when the organization, facilities, or products change, but the function itself may remain because no one questions it. Organizational changes may result in duplication of functions, in whole or in part, in different parts of the company.

The functions of each department should be reviewed from the standpoint of placement within the organization. A number of unrelated functions may be grouped in a department for no real reason. As a result, some functions may be poorly supervised or, in effect, uncontrolled.

Any peculiarities inherent in a function should be thoroughly noted, as well as any limitations of equipment or facilities.

Exhibit 6–3 illustrates the typical data collected for an analysis of departmental functions. It lists the functions of the payroll department and provides other pertinent data.

Development of the necessary data as well as much of the analysis itself can best be achieved by working closely with the supervisors of the various departments. If there is an organizational manual discussing the functions of each department, information collected from the supervisors can be checked and possible discrepancies resolved. Very often the actual organization of the company differs considerably from that depicted in the manual; thus it is necessary to check the operation with what is described.

Analysis of Current Work Force

The activities of the current work force in each department should be analyzed to learn what functions its members are supposed to perform and what they are actually doing. This analysis will frequently reveal minor functions which result from major functions. For example, supervision is not considered a departmental function, because it does not produce an output in the form of a tangible item or service, yet it is essential if the major functions are to be accomplished.

Very frequently, the existence of minor functions is revealed only when the analysis is directed at the specific assignments of

DEPARTMENTAL
FUNCTIONAL ANALYSIS

DEPT. NO. 11   Dept. Name - Payroll   Date   6/16

FUNCTIONS PERFORMED

This department is responsible for the following functions:
1. Process daily time cards.

2. Process payroll change notices, including rate changes, new hires and terminations.

3. Issue new insurance policies.
4. Maintain insurance records.

REMARKS

Time cards are sent to the tabulating department where the payroll is prepared mechanically.

Signed —————   A. J. Spencer ————
                                Supervisor

Exhibit 6–3.

everyone in the department, whether the functions themselves are proper or improper. The analysis may also reveal workload flows within and between departments, and it will also be of later assistance in the identification and classification of workload control factors. Exhibit 6–4 is an illustration of the typical data developed for an analysis of the current working force.

The analysis of departmental functions and the analysis of the current working force together are a catalogue of the functions being performed in each department and in the entire company.

ANALYSIS OF CURRENT WORKING FORCE

DEPT. NO. 11   Dept. Name -   Payroll   Date   6/16

No. of Employees		Employee Classification		Functions Performed	Ref.
Sal.	Hrly.	No.	Description		No.
1		1632	Supervisor	Responsible for supervision	
				of payroll department.	
1		2017	Secretary	Performs secretarial duties.	
				Assists with insurance	
				records and reports.	
1		1994	Supervisory Clerk	Assists with supervision of	
				payroll activities, keeps	
				insurance records and prepares	
				insurance reports.	
	14	2415	Payroll Clerks	Processes daily time cards,	
				change notices, new hires &	
				terminations.	
3	14		Total		

Signed ___A. J. Spencer___
                        Supervisor

Exhibit 6–4.

They serve as a basis for a systematic and continuing evaluation, organization, and control of all functions.

Selection of Workload Control Factors

The Control Factor Unit is a common measure of the workload within a department. It is also the means of converting workload into allowable costs. In addition to their role in the control of costs, control factors can also be used to measure and control the synchronization of the company's operations. When their relationship to the production or sales program has been established, they can be used in forecasting functional workloads and personnel requirements in accordance with the predicted production or sales schedule.

A control factor may be an actual unit of a tangible item or service produced by a department, or it may be units which are in some way related to the output of the department. The analyses of functions and the current work force can be of great assistance in selecting the proper control factors.

Exhibit 6–5 is an illustration of the analysis and selection of control factors for the clerical employees in a payroll department. Wage expense is incurred as a result of time spent by employees in carrying out the functions of the department listed in the functional analysis. The control factors are units of output requiring the time of employees. In this case, several control factors were selected, each with a different unit value. For example, it takes considerably more time to process an employee change notice than it does to perform the necessary operations on a time card, and it requires even more time to process a labor price change notice.

When several such control factors are used in a department, all are converted to a common Control Factor Unit by a weighted process. In this case, each control factor was weighted by the number of minutes required to complete one unit of that control factor. The total workload of the department is then the sum of the products obtained by multiplying the raw units of each control factor (change notices, operation pricing, etc.) produced in a period by the relative weight assigned to that control factor.

Determination of the weighting of each control factor requires some form of work measurement. It may be as simple as an estimate by the department supervisor or as scientific as a time study.

Expressing the workload in Control Factor Units of time, such as minutes, may create confusion and misunderstanding. When this is done, people tend to relate the wage rate to the Control Factor Unit and attempt to compute their budget allowance directly. This will not give the proper allowance if there is any standby cost involved in the function. In order to reduce the opportunity for this kind of misunderstanding, it may be advis-

CONTROL FACTOR ANALYSIS

DEPT. NO. 11 DEPT. NAME - PAYROLL
ACCT. NO. 249 ACCT. NAME - CLERICAL WAGES DATE 6/19

POSSIBLE CONTROL FACTORS	REMARKS
NO.1 EMPLOYEES ON ROLL	(Creates workload but is not the workload. (Does not reflect important workload variances.
2 OPERATIONS ON TIME CARDS	(Piecework price posted on time cards by the (payroll clerks. Extensions are made and (total pay accumulated by the Tabulating Dept.
3 LABOR PRICE CHANGE NOTICES	(Workload caused by changes in piecework (price, operations, and cancellation or (addition of operations.
4 EMPLOYEE CHANGE NOTICE	Workload created by change in employee status.
5 NEW HIRES, TRANS. & TERM.	Workload resulting from employee turnover.
6 NEW INSURANCE POLICIES	(Variable portion of workload resulting (from employees' group insurance plan
7 MONTHLY INSURANCE REPORTS) 8 MAINTAINING INSURANCE FILES)	(Fixed workload resulting from administration (of employees' group insurance plan. Standard (monthly reports required by insurance (companies & management. Necessary to keep (employees record files up to date at all (times. (Address changes, etc.)
9 MISCELLANEOUS STANDARD REPORTS	(Fixed workload created by standard monthly (reports for management & government.

CONTROL FACTORS SELECTED	MINUTES PER UNIT INCL. PERSONAL TIME ALLOWANCE	(MINUTES ÷ 5) WEIGHTED VALUE
NO.2 OPERATIONS ON TIME CARDS	1.1	.22
3 LABOR PRICE CHANGE NOTICES	16.0	3.20
4 EMPLOYEE CHANGE NOTICES	6.4	1.28
5 NEW HIRES, TRANS. & TERMINATIONS	8.5	1.70
6 NEW INSURANCE POLICIES	4.3	.86
7 MONTHLY INSURANCE REPORTS) 8 MAINTAIN INSURANCE FILES)	151.5 HOURS PER MO.	STANDBY WORKLOAD 1818
9 MISCELLANEOUS STANDARD REPORTS	+77.3 HOURS PER MO.	STANDBY WORKLOAD + 928

SOURCE OF DATA AND COMMENTS
NO.2 COUNT SHOWN ON TABULATING REPORT RESULTING FROM PAYROLL CALCULATIONS.
3 ISSUED IN NUMERICAL SEQUENCE. FIRST & LAST NUMBER INDICATES USAGE.
4 INFORMATION AVAILABLE FROM WORKING FORCE REPORT SUMMARY.
5 INFORMATION SHOWN ON EMPLOYMENT ACTIVITY REPORT.
6 INFORMATION SHOWN ON INSURANCE REPORT.
7-8-9 FIXED WORKLOAD. NO MONTHLY COUNT NECESSARY. ALL ITEMS CAN BE AUDITED FOR ACCURACY.

SIGNED _____ A.J.SPENCER
SUPERVISOR

Exhibit 6–5.

able to use a Control Factor Unit which is a multiple or fraction of minutes.

Whenever possible, the entire workload output should be related to a major control factor in order to reduce the amount of detail work in the preparation of current budget reports.

It is usually desirable to begin by selecting the control factors for indirect labor costs in the case of a productive department, or those for salaries and wages in the case of a service or commercial department. Typically, these costs give rise to the greatest number and variety of control factors, because (1) salaries and wages are probably the largest item of overhead expense in any department, and (2) people are so flexible that even a relatively unskilled worker can perform a variety of tasks. Because people or their activities are directly or indirectly responsible for most costs, some or all of the same control factors will usually be used for the other cost items.

- For example, the control factors for salaries in a metallurgical testing laboratory might include the different types of tests performed, with each raw unit of control factor weighted in relation to the time required for that type of test. The control factors selected for supplies expense might also be the different kinds of tests performed. The only difference might be that the raw units of control factor could be weighted in accordance with the value of supplies required for that type of test rather than in terms of time required. Some types of tests might not require any supplies, in which case they could be excluded as a control factor, or assigned a weight of zero.

At all points in the development of a variable budget program, and especially in the selection of control factors, the materiality of the cost to be controlled and the probability and magnitude of potential savings or losses should be kept in mind.

BUDGETING INDIRECT LABOR COSTS

The salaries and wages paid to employees, except payments for direct labor, will be referred to as *indirect labor costs*. It was pointed out earlier that indirect labor is usually the largest single item of cost in a department or in a company and that it is extremely flexible. Also, it is perishable in the sense that it has to be properly used from day to day, for the cost of an idle day is irretrievably lost.

In Profitability Accounting, after the control factors have been selected and weighted, the development of the variable budget program for indirect labor involves three further tasks in each department:

1. Evaluation of the productivity of the current work force
2. Preparation of a schedule of personal requirements, or, as it is sometimes called, a manning table
3. Construction of the variable budget itself

Current Work Force Productivity Evaluation

First to be prepared is the evaluation of the productivity of the current work force. It compares the capabilities of the work force with the actual output for the most recent period. It also measures over-staffing.

Exhibit 6–6 is a productivity evaluation of the clerical work force in a payroll department. During the period studied, the variable workload output totaled 24,238 Units. However, the actual organization had capabilities totaling 27,494 Units, after allowance for a standby workload of 2,746 Units. On the basis of the workload output, the organization was over-staffed by 1.7 persons.

The productivity evaluation serves several purposes:

1. It provides a rough check on the functional analysis and the selection and weighting of control factors.
2. It gives the department supervisor an opportunity to review the basic data and deal with disagreements or questions.
3. It informs the department supervisor of the efficiency of his organization.
4. It represents a base volume of output, measured in Control Factor Units, which can be used to establish the volume scale on the schedule of personal requirements and in the variable budget.

The Personnel Requirements Schedule and the Variable Budget

The schedule of personnel requirements and the variable budget are usually prepared at the same time. The schedule of

CURRENT WORKING FORCE PRODUCTIVITY EVALUATION

DEPT. NO. 11   DEPT. NAME - PAYROLL
ACCT. NO. 249   ACCT. NAME - CLERICAL WAGES   DATE 6/19

VARIABLE CONTROL FACTOR UNITS EARNED FROM 5/16 TO 6/15

CONTROL FACTORS	ACTUAL RAW UNITS	WEIGHTS APPLIED	WEIGHTED UNITS	ORGANIZATION WORKLOAD CAPABILITIES	STANDBY WORKLOAD UNIT VALUE	VARIABLE WORKLOAD CAPABILITIES OF CURRENT ORGANIZATION	NUMBER OF PEOPLE OVER STAFFED DURING PERIOD
OPERATIONS ON TIME CARDS	104,123	.22	22,907.0	157.5 HRS.X	TAKEN	USE AS BASE	27,494 -
LABOR PRICE CHANGE NOTICES	202	3.20	646.4	60 MIN = 9450	FROM	VARIABLE	24,238 =
EMPLOYEE CHANGE NOTICES	172	1.28	220.2	9450 ÷ 5 =	CONTROL	WORKLOAD	3256 C.F.U.
NEW HIRES, TRANSFERS &	214	1.70	363.8	1890 CONTROL	FACTOR	VOLUME	3256 ÷ 1890 =
TERMINATIONS				FACTOR UNITS	ANALYSIS	FOR THE	NO. OF
NEW INSURANCE POLICIES	117	.86	100.6	PER EMPL.	REPORT	CURRENT	PEOPLE OVER
				PER MONTH.		ORGAN-	-STAFFED OVER
				1890 UNITS X		IZATION	WHICH IS
				16 EMPL.			
TOTAL WEIGHTED CONTROL FACTOR UNITS			24,238	30,240 =	- 2,746 =	27,494	1.7

Signed _____ A. J. SPENCER
                 SUPERVISOR

Exhibit 6-6.

personnel requirements specifies the number of employees of each classification needed to handle various volumes of workload in a department or group. It also shows the average pay rate of each classification and the total cost of salaries and wages at each of the various volumes. This schedule, which is coordinated with other control tools, is a valuable aid for the supervisor in estimating and controlling personnel requirements and costs.

Exhibit 6–7 is the schedule of clerical personnel requirements for the payroll department. For this department, which does not have the problem of minimum staffing limitations discussed in the subsequent example of the inspection department, the data at standby and base volume would first be entered in the personnel requirements schedule. The remaining data would be entered after the variable budget graph is completed.

The original and permanent record of the variable budget itself is primarily a graphic representation of the planned relationship of costs and workload volumes at all levels. The horizontal axis of the graph represents workload volumes, and the vertical axis represents costs. The same workload volume scale is used for both the schedule and the budget. It is so designed that the range from 0% to 150% or 160% of base volume encompasses all workload volumes which can reasonably be expected. The usual procedure is to use as the base volume, or 100%, the amount of variable workload capability of the work force during the period covered by the productivity evaluation.

However, if the work force during the evaluation period was much larger or smaller than usual, the workload capabilities of an average work force should be used as the base volume. Calculations are simpler if the base, or 100% on the workload volume scale, represents the workload capabilities of a whole number rather than a fractional number of employees. The particular volume scale selected has no further significance in balancing operations within or between departments.

In determining personnel requirements and costs in a department or group, there are two basically different situations which may be encountered:

1. Where personnel requirements depend only on the volume of workload, except for management decisions about standby crews
2. Where personnel requirements are affected by minimum staffing

PERSONNEL REQUIREMENTS SCHEDULE

DEPT. NO. 11
ACCT. NO. 249

DEPT. NAME – PAYROLL
ACCT. NAME – CLERICAL

DATE 6/19

AVE. RATE	CONTROL FACTORS	% OF BASE	0	10	20	30	40	50	60	70	80	90	BASE	110	120	130	140	150
		No. OF UNITS*	0	2.8	5.5	8.3	11.0	13.8	16.5	19.3	22.0	24.8	27.5	30.3	33.0	35.8	38.5	41.3
400	SECRETARIES		1	1	1	1	1	1	1	1	1	1	1	1	1	1	1	1
400	SUPERVISORY CLERKS		1	1	1	1	1	1	1	1	1	1	1	1	1	1	1	1
336	PAYROLL CLERKS		0	1	3	4	6	7	9	10	12	13	14	16	17	19	20	22
	TOTAL PERSONNEL		2	3	5	6	8	9	11	12	14	15	16	18	19	21	22	24
	TOTAL PAYROLL *		$.8	$1.1	$1.8	$2.1	$2.8	$3.2	$3.8	$4.2	$4.8	$5.2	$5.5	$6.2	$6.5	$7.2	$7.5	$8.2

* IN THOUSANDS

Signed _____ A. J. SPENCER
SUPERVISOR

Exhibit 6–7.

limitations as well as the volume of workload (The term *minimum staffing limitations,* as used here, does not mean merely that each additional employee hired is a "whole person," but rather that workloads are not evenly balanced among all work stations and that one employee is limited to working at one work station.)

The first of the two situations described above is the one most frequently encountered. The payroll department illustrated in Exhibits 6–3 through 6–8 is such a case.

Budgeting for Workload Requirements

The variable budget in Exhibit 6–8 was established solely on the basis of workload as follows:

The workload potential of the current clerical force of 16 employees in the payroll department was determined as 27,494 units of control factor, and this was established as the base volume, or 100%. It was determined that the cost of these sixteen employees totaled $5,504 a month, and a point (A) was plotted on the variable budget graph to represent this cost at the base volume.

Next, it was determined that two employees would be retained at the standby level at a cost of $800 a month. A point (B) representing this standby cost was plotted on the variable budget at zero volume. The two employees are to be retained at zero volume, because of their particular skills, to handle the standby workload of 2,746 Control Factor Units. However, these two employees have a total workload potential of 3,780 Units (two employees @ 1,890 Units apiece). This means that, in addition to the standby workload of 2,746 Units, they are also capable of completing 1,034 Units of variable workload without incurring any additional wage or salary cost. To reflect this information on the variable budget graph, another point (C) was plotted at $800 on the cost scale and 1,034 Units on the variable workload volume scale.

The cost-volume relationship line was placed on the variable budget graph by drawing a straight horizontal line from the point at $800 cost and zero volume (B) to point C and then drawing a straight upward-sloping line through point A. The sloping portion of the cost-volume relationship line represents the planned cost to be incurred at various volumes when the workload is being

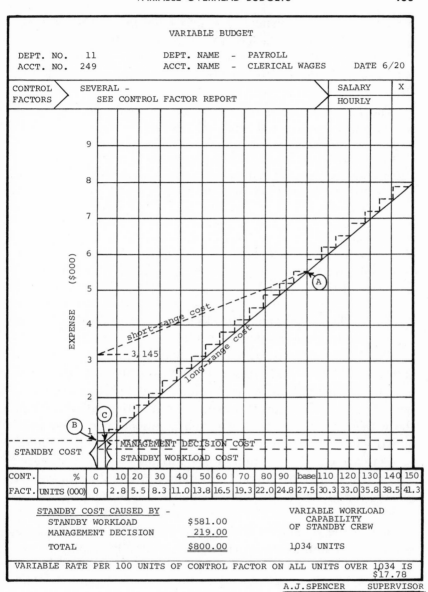

Exhibit 6-8.

performed at full efficiency. The horizontal line at the $800 cost level, covering volume levels from zero to 1,034 Units, indicates that the cost will remain at $800 even if the variable workload volume should drop to any level from zero to 1,034 Control Factor Units.

The information recorded below the variable budget graph was developed by the following calculations:

- Standby cost of $800 was apportioned between the cost of standby workload and management decision cost, based on the relation of the 2,746 Units of standby workload to the 1,034 Units of additional capability of the standby crew. This resulted in costs of $581 for one and $219 for the other.
- The monthly cost per variable employee, $336, was divided by the workload capability of the employee, 1,890 Units, to determine the variable rate of $17.78 per 100 Units of control factor on all Units over 1,034.

The staffing requirements for the variable workload of the department were then developed as follows:

Starting with the standby cost of $800 and adding cost in increments of $336 (and workload in increments of 1,890 Units) a point was plotted on the cost-volume line. This process is repeated for each addition of a man. The resulting points indicate the workload volumes at which each additional person could be added while maximum utilization and efficiency is still retained.

For example, the addition of one variable employee produced a total cost of $1,136. A point was plotted where the cost-volume line crossed $1,136 on the cost scale and 2,924 Units on the volume scale.

This is the volume level at which the services of one variable employee, as well as the services of two standby employees, can be fully and efficiently utilized. The dotted "stair-step" line in Exhibit 6–7 never goes below the straight cost-volume line which is the variable budget. This means that there is only one workload volume at which any particular number of employees will show full efficiency.

A staffing problem will occur when the workload volume requires something less than the full time of an additional employee. If a person is added at that point, the group will operate at less than full efficiency. If the operating budget provides only for full utilization and efficiency, as does the cost-volume relationship line, an unfavorable cost performance or spending variance will result. The amount of the variance will be the difference between the actual cost incurred and the cost provided by the cost-volume line at the actual volume of workload.

In some variable budget systems, the planned cost line is drawn as a series of steps to provide for the addition of a full person at various volumes even though he cannot be fully utilized at those volumes. However, this procedure over-simplifies the true cost-volume relationship and limits the usefulness of the budget.

It implies that there are no alternative approaches to meeting the workload requirements. Actually, if the amount of extra help required is less than one person, the use of overtime is usually a more economical solution. In some cases, a temporary need can be filled by supplementary help from another department where an employee does not have a full workload. Or the workload may be re-scheduled to take advantage of periodic volume fluctuations.

In some cases, supervisors, technicians, skilled employees, and even some clerical employees are not laid off or hired when volume fluctuations last for only a short period. This may be because certain skills are difficult to find and perhaps require long training. Employees in the "critical" classes are hired or laid off only when there are basic changes in the long-range average volume. When this situation exists, the costs during short-range volume fluctuations will not follow the long-range cost-volume relationship line shown in Exhibit 6–8. Instead, they will follow a different cost trend line peculiar to the expected average volume of the department at that particular point in its history. The short-range cost line will shift its position from year to year, and may change its slope in response to increases or decreases in the expected average volume. The straight dotted line in Exhibit 6–8 represents a short-range cost line which might prevail in the department and which indicates that $3,145 of cost will be incurred at zero volume.

The short-range cost line for indirect labor in a given department at a given time is subjective to a certain extent. However, if the variable budgets are built in detail according to practical staffing requirements, the short-range budget can be reasonably determined. The difference between the actual cost incurred and the short-range budgeted cost at the actual volume is the spending variance.

The long-range cost-volume line represents the lowest cost level that is considered possible under reasonable operating practices with existing facilities. It is the base from which each succeeding short-range cost trend takes its departure, following a change in the average expected volume. The difference between the short-range budget and the long-range budget at the actual volume is called the management decision variance. It is the result of staffing for a particular volume plateau which differs from current volume. It puts a cost value on the staffing policies followed by managers, or, viewed in another way, it puts a cost value on the effect of volume changes.

With sudden changes in expected average volume, the long-range cost-volume relationship line is an extremely valuable tool for helping managers adjust quickly to new conditions without incurring excess costs. A short-range cost budget and the management decision variance may also be used to advantage in the situation where the function, product, or facilities impose certain minimum staffing limitations. This will be described in the next section.

Budgeting with Minimum Staffing Limitations

Some personnel requirements are determined by a combination of minimum staffing limitations and workload requirements. Certain skill requirements or the separate location of work stations may generate minimum staffing limitations because workloads are not balanced at all locations. An example of work station staffing limitations could be that of inspectors stationed at various points along an assembly line. The points at which they are stationed are often determined by the accessibility of the parts to be inspected as the unit moves along the assembly line, or by the need for performing the inspection between particular successive operations.

The re-location or consolidation of inspection points with changes in volume is not always possible. Thus the result may be an organization in which flexibility and efficiency are limited by product design and assembly requirements. When workloads are not balanced at all stations, the minimum staffing restrictions may limit the possibilities for full utilization and efficiency to only a few widely separated volume levels.

The budget should recognize these staffing limitations, but this does not mean that it should be built so as to show only the number of personnel needed at various volumes. Since the objective is to provide the kind of information that will help reduce the costs, the excess costs resulting from the incompatibility of staffing needs and workloads at certain volume levels should be reported to managers. These costs should not be accepted as inevitable.

Any cost greater than the lowest attainable under reasonable operating practices with existing facilities should be considered an excess cost, regardless of its cause. This "hard-line" approach, which provides highly useful information for managers, will ultimately result in the most economical operation.

In a situation where personnel requirements are determined by a combination of minimum staffing limitations and workload requirements, the variable budgeting begins with an analysis of workload, the work force, and its workload capabilities. This is intended to produce much the same kind of information as that developed for the payroll department through the selection and weighting of control factors as shown in Exhibit 6–5.

Because of the wide variety of possible situations, the analysis of the assembly inspection group, as shown in Exhibit 6–9, is merely illustrative. No single type of analysis is applicable to all such cases.

The inspection department consists of five inspection stations at separate physical locations on an assembly line. The time required for the inspection operation is constant per Unit at any one station; however, it varies between stations. Because of the product design and the sequence of assembly operations, it is not possible to combine the inspections at the various stations. Although no stations can be eliminated, except at zero volume, inspectors could be added, should this be justified by the volume.

The unit of product was selected as the Control Factor Unit for this function, since workload requirements at any one inspection station are directly proportionate to the units produced. The proportion, and therefore the workload capability, varies from one station to the next. This makes it difficult to get maximum effi-

ANALYSIS OF ASSEMBLY INSPECTION
WORKFORCE AND WORKLOAD CAPABILITIES   DATE 6/9

	INSPECTION POINTS WHERE INSPECTORS CAN BE ELIMINATED, NEW WORK FORCE AND WORKLOAD CAPABILITIES						CURRENT INSPECT. WORK FORCE / WORKLOAD OUTPUT			INSPECTION POINTS WHERE INSPECTORS CAN BE ADDED, NEW WORK FORCE AND WORKLOAD CAPABILITIES					
INSPECTION POINT (WORK FLOW)	No. Empl.	W.L. Cap.	No. Empl.	W.L. Cap.	No. Empl.	W.L. Cap.	NO. EMPL.	CUR-RENT	CAP.	No. Empl.	W.L. Cap.	No. Empl.	W.L. Cap.	No. Empl.	W.L. Cap.
1	1	8640	1	8640	1	8640	1	5040	8640	1	8640	1	8640	1	8640
2	1	2880	2	5760	2	5760	2	5040	5760	3	8640	3	8640	3	8640
3	1	3744	1	3744	1	3744	2	5040	7488	2	7488	2	7488	3	11232
4	1	5760	1	5760	1	5760	1	5040	5760	2	11520	2	11520	2	11520
5	1	3600	1	3600	2	7200	2	5040	7200	2	7200	3	10800	3	10800
	5	2880	6	3600	7	3744	8	5040	5760	10	7200	11	7488	12	8640

S. E. LUTHER
————————————
SUPERVISOR

Exhibit 6-9.

ciency at all stations simultaneously, but the fact that Control Factor Units have different values at different stations is not a problem, since each station must be treated differently anyway.

The analysis of the work force and the workload at each inspection station revealed that the workload capacity was considerably greater than the current volume produced—5,040 Units. These data are recorded in the center section of Exhibit 6–9. Because the work flows from station to station, the station with the lowest workload capacity limits the capacity of the entire line. In this case, the lowest workload capacity is at Stations 2 and 4. Each has a capacity of 5,760 Units.

This capacity was set as the base volume, or 100%, on the volume scale of the variable budget graph. The manning of the current organization supplied the personnel requirements and cost data at base volume. It was also determined that no standby workload would exist and that no personnel would be retained or costs incurred in the inspection operation under standby conditions.

In the determination of personnel requirements at volumes greater than base volume, the lowest possible cost was assured by successively adding one person to the organization at the inspection station or stations which had the lowest capacity. This is illustrated in the columns of data on the right in Exhibit 6–9. For example, to increase the capacity of the organization above 5,760 Units per month, personnel must be added at Stations 2 and 4, both of which are bottleneck points at base volume. Adding one person at Station 2 increases its capacity to 8,640 Units per month. Adding one person at Station 4 increases its capacity to 11,520 Units per month. After these changes, the capacity of the entire organization is 7,200 Units per month. This is the capacity of Station 5, which has become the bottleneck point.

To assure the lowest possible cost at volumes less than base volume the reverse procedure was followed. The organization was reduced by successively dropping one person from that station which had the highest capacity and was also staffed by more than one employee. This procedure is illustrated in the columns of data on the left in Exhibit 6–9.

The productivity evaluation (analogous to Exhibit 6–6 for payroll) for the assembly inspection department at current volume is not included in this chapter, but it would have shown no over-staffing, even though the organization operated at a utilization rate of only 87.5%. The reduction of the work force by one person at any inspection station would have reduced the capacity of the organization to, at most, 3,744 Units, considerably less than the actual volume experienced.

The personnel requirements data, not included here, are similar to those of Exhibit 6–7 for payroll, except that the various personnel levels are not necessarily spaced at equal volume intervals of 10% above and below base volume as they were in Exhibit 6–7. Data were only entered for volume levels of 50%, 62.5%, 65%, 100%, 125%, 130%, and 150%. These (as seen in Exhibit 6–10) are the only levels at which the size of the work force must change because of capacity limitations at one or another of the inspection stations. They are the points of greatest efficiency and utilization for those particular staff levels.

The personnel requirements at any volume level between these volumes or below 50% of base volume are governed by minimum work station staffing requirements. For example, in order to operate at 110% of base volume, 6,300 Units per month, two inspectors must be added to the base volume staff, one each at Stations 2 and 4. This raises the capacity of the organization to 7,200 Units per month, or 125% of base volume, even though it will only be utilized at the rate of 6,300 Units a month. The personnel requirements are identical at the two levels and at any other volume level between base volume and 125% of base volume. The dotted line in Exhibit 6–10 indicates how the work force must react to volume changes because of minimum staffing limitations, and it, consequently, represents the short-range cost for the department.

The long-range cost-volume line in Exhibit 6–10 was drawn through the point of zero volume and zero cost because no standby cost was planned for this operation. Note that once again it was drawn as a straight line passing through the plotted points which represented the lowest cost per unit produced. In this case, the points at base volume, 125% and 150%, are the only volumes at which personnel are most fully and efficiently utilized. All other points in the short-range cost line lie above the straight line.

An examination of the variable budget graph reveals that poor utilization of personnel is inherent in this operation as it is now

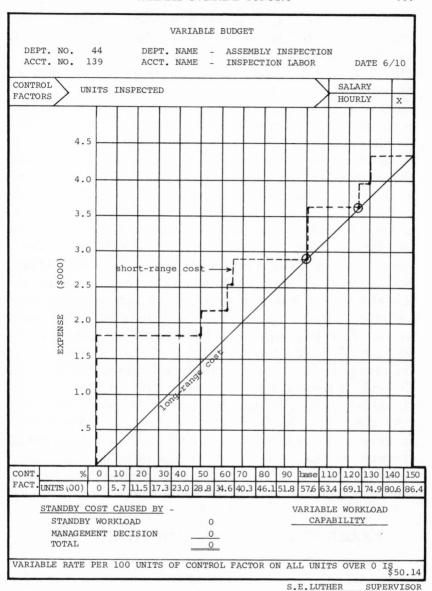

VARIABLE BUDGET

DEPT. NO.   44   DEPT. NAME - ASSEMBLY INSPECTION
ACCT. NO. 139   ACCT. NAME - INSPECTION LABOR   DATE 6/10

CONTROL FACTORS	UNITS INSPECTED	SALARY	
		HOURLY	X

EXPENSE ($000)

short-range cost →

long-range cost

CONT. FACT.	%	0	10	20	30	40	50	60	70	80	90	base	110	120	130	140	150
	UNITS (00)	0	5.7	11.5	17.3	23.0	28.8	34.6	40.3	46.1	51.8	57.6	63.4	69.1	74.9	80.6	86.4

STANDBY COST CAUSED BY -   VARIABLE WORKLOAD
    STANDBY WORKLOAD   0   CAPABILITY
    MANAGEMENT DECISION   0
    TOTAL   0

VARIABLE RATE PER 100 UNITS OF CONTROL FACTOR ON ALL UNITS OVER 0 IS
                                                              $50.14

                              S.E.LUTHER   SUPERVISOR

Exhibit 6–10.

constituted. The cost per unit of $.5014, as represented by the cost-volume relationship line, can be achieved at only three volume levels. Even at these volumes, only 85% of the total workload capabilities of the personnel is actually being utilized, although the utilization rate is 100% at one or two inspection stations. At other volumes, notably in the range from 50% to 80% of base volume, the cost per unit may rise by 40% or more.

Management should be kept informed of conditions such as these. A change may not be possible or practicable, but, unless the condition is revealed, the responsible managers may not be aware of a cost reduction opportunity.

In the variable budget program in Profitability Accounting, the manager in charge of the inspection function is directly responsible for costs which vary from the amounts provided by the short-range cost lines. The amount represented by the vertical distance between the short-range cost line and the cost-volume relationship line at the actual volume is reported as a management decision variance. It is an excess cost incurred through operating in some manner other than that which would generate the lowest possible cost, even though this may not be the result of a conscious decision but merely the effect of producing the volume which satisfies the demand. It points out, however, an area in which the managers should be alert for cost reduction opportunities, since alternatives may be available. Mathematical techniques performed on a computer have been used successfully to balance the workloads among the work stations on an assembly line and thereby reduce costs. A budget program directed toward isolating the various kinds of costs may well lead to action which will reduce them.

BUDGETING COSTS OTHER THAN INDIRECT LABOR

If indirect labor costs are budgeted first in a department or responsibility group, much of the data required to budget other overhead costs will be readily available. In the service and commercial functions, many of the other costs are closely related to salaries and wages. In direct manufacturing departments, many of the other costs are related to direct labor, to indirect labor, or to both. The analysis of control factors for indirect labor costs frequently assists in determining the relationship of other costs to other control factors.

A list of the expenses actually incurred by or charged to a department in one or more prior periods can be a starting point for determining the overhead costs for which budgets should be established. This is only a starting point, however. The installation of a variable budget program is frequently accompanied by changes in the organization and control within the enterprise. Procedures used in the past may differ substantially from those planned for the future. Consequently, all cost items should be reviewed to determine that each is properly classified in relation to the responsibility structure of the organization. Listings of costs incurred in prior periods may also be used to make sure that no cost item previously incurred has been overlooked in the realignment of costs and in the budgeting process. There still remains the need to look ahead and to incorporate in the plans and budgets those cost items which were not incurred in the past but which will be incurred in the future.

The kinds of overhead cost items incurred may differ substantially from one company to another, or from one department to another within the same company. This is to be expected. However, consistent classification of costs to appropriate accounts is essential if budgetary and other cost-oriented reports are to provide a medium of communication among managers, and if cost information is to be properly utilized for decision making. The variable budgeting process, particularly when it is centrally coordinated, can do much to establish and encourage consistent classification.

The original and permanent record of the variable budget for other overhead expenses is a graphic presentation quite similar to that used for indirect labor costs. The horizontal axis of the graph represents workload volumes, and the vertical axis represents costs. The cost-volume relationship line indicates the planned cost at any volume of workload from zero up to the maximum that can be expected to occur during a period.

Any factual data used to develop a particular variable budget should be preserved on a Budget Data Sheet for use later in revising or refining the budget, or clearing up any questions which may arise. The reverse side of the variable budget graph is frequently used for this purpose.

Exhibit 6–11 is a graphic presentation of the historical behavior of the utilities cost in a machine shop, with a cost-volume relationship line fitted to the historical data. This type of graphic approach is sometimes used to establish a variable budget. While it may provide a useful *test* of the budget, it is not a very reliable basis for establishing the budget itself, because of the tendency to build the costs of past mistakes into the allowances. Furthermore, it tends to limit the view of the future to nothing more than an extrapolation of the past. It does not encourage the anticipation of changes or new ideas.

Wherever it is practical to do so, and especially for the major items of expenditure, the budget should be established on the basis of specified costs rather than historical costs. That is, actual requirements should be determined objectively by studies and measurements. Further, the data should first be expressed in physical units and related to volume, then priced to obtain the budget in dollars. For example, the original relationships for the machine shop should be established in numbers of kilowatt hours, quantities of cutting tools, or the gallons of cutting oil to be used at different volumes. This technique has a number of important advantages:

1. It permits the budgeting of quantities, which are frequently more meaningful than dollars to operating managers.
2. It facilitates the analysis of cost variances into the elements of usage and price by special studies when these are helpful in analyzing a variance.
3. It simplifies the task of budget revision. The cost effects of different factors are readily apparent, and adjustments are easily made.

Some of the costs related to facilities, such as depreciation, rent, taxes, and insurance, are entirely of a standby nature and will not vary at all with volume within the range for which provision has been made. Current accounting schedules of charges can be used to establish budgets for these items. However, the costs of any new and planned facilities which are not reflected in the accounting schedules should be given proper consideration.

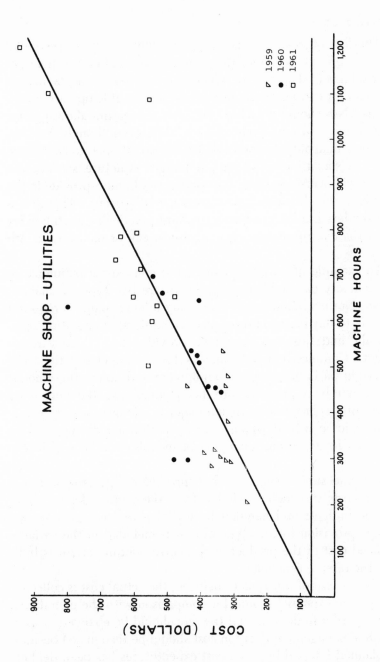

MACHINE SHOP - UTILITIES

COST (DOLLARS)

MACHINE HOURS

△ 1959
● 1960
□ 1961

Exhibit 6–11. Historical behavior of an expense account.

Reserve Budget

The first objective of the variable budget program presented here is to provide a tool for the positive control of cost at the cost-incurred level. The budget which does this should not include a provision for extra costs resulting from undesirable operating conditions. Nor should it include an average monthly allowance for costs which will occur only once a year, even though they are expected, unavoidable costs related to normal operations. These costs are sometimes built into a budget structure so that the budget will over-provide in most periods and under-provide in the periods in which the irregular costs actually occur. This procedure renders the budget insensitive and practically worthless for use in the control of cost on a week-to-week or month-to-month basis.

An example of an infrequent cost is cumulative maintenance of machinery or machine tools. There are two types of maintenance. Normal maintenance, including minor repairs, is required on a day-to-day basis to keep a piece of equipment operating satisfactorily, and this cost should be provided for in the variable budget. Cumulative maintenance is the result of cumulative wear on certain parts of a piece of equipment. Although the amount of wear will be in proportion to the machine's use, the worn parts are usually replaced only when a major breakdown occurs or during a major overhaul which may be performed during a plant shutdown for vacations, changing of models, or taking of inventory.

This and similar necessary but infrequent and irregularly occurring costs should be excluded from the normal departmental variable budgets and handled by use of a reserve account. An average provision for this type of cost is included in the variable overhead cost of the product, and a corresponding credit is built up in the reserve account.

When a cost of this type is incurred, the actual cost is collected in a specific expense account for comparison with the cumulative credit in order to determine if the rate should be changed or, perhaps, if a management decision cost should be recognized because the planned interval between cost expenditures has been deliberately changed.

• For example, the management of a mill which intended to re-line furnaces every three years may re-line one after two years because the market is slow this year and expected to improve next year. The unamortized cost resulting from the earlier overhaul should be treated as a programmed cost.

The reserve variable budget is included in the variable overhead rate for product cost purposes so that it is entirely consistent with the planned costs used for control purposes.

A reserve budget can be established at the department, cost center, or plant level in the manufacturing area and at the department, division, or corporate level in the commercial organization. However, it is quite difficult to identify with an individual department the continuing need and specific amount of a reserve budget. Consequently, the reserve budget is usually established at the plant, division, or corporate level.

The particular cost items and amounts to be included in the reserve variable budget are obtained from several sources. Some items may be discovered and set aside for the reserve budget during the process of establishing departmental budgets. Others may be identified by analyzing extraordinarily high costs which appeared in past cost statements of individual departments. They should be reviewed with responsible managers and an amount established in accordance with expected requirements. Cumulative maintenance costs to be included in the reserve budget can often be predicted very accurately by the plant engineer and maintenance manager on the basis of machines scheduled for major overhaul and major breakdowns anticipated. Only the costs of these items resulting from normal operating requirements should be included. The costs associated with specific management decisions such as the accelerated furnace re-lining should be included in neither the departmental control budget nor the reserve budget but should be treated as a programmed cost.

Budgeting Programmed Costs

Programmed costs were described in Chapter 2 as project-type costs incurred by management decision. Like the costs included in the reserve budget, they may be high during one period and low or non-existent during another period, without any relationship to the volume of activity. Unlike the reserve costs, however, they are not merely an inherent cost of normal operations, where there is only a problem of predicting the timing of the cost. They are actually incurred or avoided on the basis of specific management decisions. They may be incurred in any area of the company. Examples of programmed costs are major research and development programs, engineering programs, and advertising media.

The budgeted amount of a programmed cost as determined by a management decision is treated as an appropriation or fixed budget. It is not considered a part of normal variable overhead, and it is not included in the variable overhead rate or variable product cost. Whenever it is practical to do so, a detailed programmed expense budget should be established, showing planned expenses by specific item in the program, and by the period in which they will be incurred. Budget reports for individual periods will compare actual costs incurred during the period with costs planned for that period. The detailed programmed expense budget is necessary to properly evaluate a reported cost variance. The variance may be the result of a different timing of expenditures than that planned, or it may represent a real difference between planned costs and actual costs of specific items. Programmed expenditures by period are also used in profit planning and cash planning.

A Budget Data Sheet should be prepared for each program. It should contain a description of the program, the reasons it is being undertaken, and the objectives or anticipated results. In addition it is always desirable to record any specific, interim check points which may be established to measure the progress of the program in relation to a time schedule and a cost schedule. These data may be used to produce cost status reports on individual programs at significant points during the life of the program.

USING THE VARIABLE BUDGET DATA

Up to this point, the development of variable budgets has been viewed almost entirely from the standpoint of cost control. Consequently, workloads and cost have been considered only at the level of the department or functional group. In Profitability

Accounting, however, the same planned costs used for cost control are also used for other purposes.

After all of the detailed budgets have been prepared, it is necessary to determine the relationship of the variable workload in a department to a common measure of volume, such as sales dollars or standard direct labor dollars, which is forecast in the beginning of the profit-planning process. When this relationship is known, the production and sales forecasts can be used to forecast the variable workloads and variable costs in each manufacturing and commercial department to develop variable overhead rates for use in product costing, profit planning, and income determination. The forecasted workloads provide information for advance planning and coordination of the various functional operations which support the production or sales programs.

Workload Relationships to Production and Sales

The workload of each department or group which supports the production or sales effort is affected by changes in the production or sales schedules. However, because of the variety of functions involved, the workloads of all departments are not affected to the same extent by any given change; nor are the workloads all affected at the same time. The normal relationship of the variable workload in a department to the production or sales program can be determined by graphic analyses of historical data.

The variable workload in a department is measured in variable Control Factor Units. The production or sales schedule is expressed in a common measure of volume such as sales dollars or standard direct labor dollars. By plotting the workload quantities and the volumes on a time scale for a succession of periods, it is possible to determine lead or lag relationships between production or sales schedules and the workload levels. Then, after adjusting the data for the lead or lag, it is possible to determine the normal volume relationship of the workload and the production or sales schedule.

The illustrations used here, and in the remainder of this chapter, include only departments which support the production effort. The same techniques are used in commercial departments. It is assumed, for purposes of illustration, that standard direct labor cost is a common measure of volume and a satisfactory base for

		CONTROL FACTOR SUMMARY					
DEPT. NO. 16		DEPT. NAME - PURCHASING					
	STD.	C O N T R O L	F A C T O R S				
MONTH	DIRECT LABOR COST (000)	PURCHASE ORDERS WT.FACTOR 5.0		LINE ITEMS ON P.O. WT.FACTOR 1.0		P.O. CHANGE NOTICES WT.FACTOR 1.5		TOTAL WTD. UNITS
		RAW UNITS	WTD. UNITS	RAW UNITS	WTD. UNITS	RAW UNITS	WTD. UNITS	
NOV. 1960	$306.8	600	3000	915	915	45	68	3983
DEC.	255.6	625	3125	955	955	35	53	4133
JAN. 1961	289.7	700	3500	999	999	26	39	4538
FEB.	316.5	700	3500	1025	1025	48	72	4597
MAR.	353.0	750	3750	1170	1170	40	60	4980
APR.	379.8	725	3625	1115	1115	24	36	4776
MAY	430.9	680	3400	1000	1000	52	78	4478
JUN.	374.9	675	3375	940	940	30	45	4360
JUL.	362.8	625	3125	900	900	25	38	4063
AUG.	340.8	625	3125	822	822	60	90	4037
SEPT.	325.8	560	2800	800	800	33	50	3650
OCT.	316.5	520	2600	745	745	28	42	3387
NOV.	292.2	590	2950	1025	1025	32	48	4023
DEC.	267.8	615	3075	1037	1037	30	45	4157

Exhibit 6–12.

the absorption of variable overhead. In many cases, standard direct labor cost is not suitable for these purposes. The selection and development of appropriate measures of volume and overhead bases is discussed in Chapter 7.

Exhibits 6–12 through 6–14 demonstrate how the normal relationships between the variable workload in a purchasing department and the production program would be obtained by graphic analysis. Exhibit 6–12 lists the actual Control Factor Units produced in the purchasing department and shows the total standard direct labor for each of 14 consecutive periods. Both of these variables are plotted in relation to time in Exhibit 6–13. An examination of this chart reveals that the purchasing workload factor in control units tends to lead production, as expressed in standard direct labor, by about two months. This apparent lead or lag relationship should be verified by reference to operating policies and work flows whenever possible.

Exhibit 6–14 illustrates the apparent relation between production volume and the functional workload in the purchasing department. It was prepared from the data presented in Exhibit 6–12,

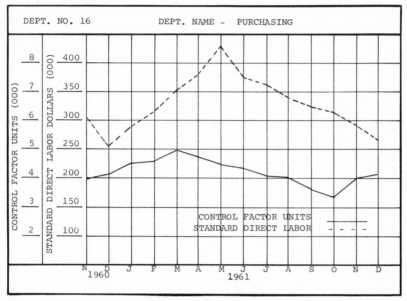

LEAD OR LAG - 2 MONTHS LEAD

Exhibit 6–13. Control factor lead and lag chart.

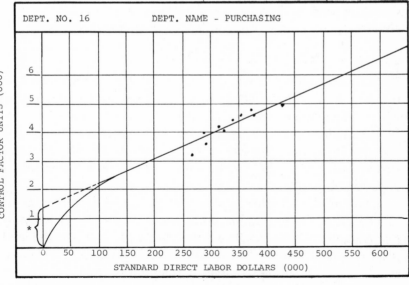

Variable rate per $100 standard direct labor -   .8564 C.F.U.
*Volume adjustment factor -   1350. C.F.U.

Exhibit 6–14. Production volume effect on variable control factors.

after adjusting for the two months' lead time. For example, January, 1961, standard direct labor was matched with the Control Factor Units for November, 1960, in order to plot a point at 3,983 units of control factor and $289,700 of direct labor. The result of doing this for each month was the 12 points shown in the exhibit. The line fitted to these points indicates the rate for variable workload, a change of .8564 units of control factor for each $100 change in standard direct labor over a wide range of operating volumes. The change in workload should occur two months in advance of the scheduled volume. The exhibit also shows that the relation of workload to direct labor becomes non-linear at very low volumes because there is no standby workload for this department. The difference between zero workload and the projection of the straight line back to zero volume, 1,350 Control Factor Units, is a volume adjustment factor to be added to the amount of variable workload computed by use of the rate.

In analysis of the historical data to determine the relationship of workload volume to production or sales programs, some significant variations from the general pattern may appear because of abnormal operating or economic conditions. The variations should be reviewed and adjusted to eliminate the effect of these abnormal conditions when establishing the budgetary relationship.

Developing Variable Overhead Rates

Overhead rates are intended to transfer overhead costs from the department level where they are incurred to the product where they may be used to price inventory and determine income. In Profitability Accounting, only variable costs are included in unit product cost. Consequently, the overhead rates are constructed using only the variable elements of overhead cost at the department level.

The variable overhead rates are developed by dividing the planned amount of variable overhead costs for the year by the planned annual volume. The rate per unit of volume is the overhead rate, and it is applied to each unit of product according to the units of volume represented by that unit of product.

Planned volumes are obtained from forecasts of sales and production. The forecast volumes by product are extended by the direct labor per unit for each production department to convert forecast unit production into forecast standard direct labor cost. Forecast standard direct labor cost, as is often the case, is the measure of planned manufacturing volume used here. This type of calculation is illustrated in Chapter 7.

Planned Workloads

Planned variable overhead costs are the costs developed for control purposes at the department level. They vary with work-load as measured in Control Factor Units. Therefore, it is necessary to forecast the workload in units of control factor for each department before it is possible to forecast the amount of variable overhead costs which should result from the planned production and sales programs. The previously determined relationships of workloads to production or sales can be applied to the forecast of the latter to obtain forecast units of control factor.

Exhibit 6–15 illustrates how this relationship is used to forecast Control Factor Units by department for a 12-month period. The lead or lag relationships listed in Column 1 were determined by graphic analyses such as that shown in Exhibit 6–13, but they do not affect the forecast shown here. It was assumed that the total variable workload over the entire 12 months could be determined

TWELVE-MONTH FORECAST

VARIABLE CONTROL FACTOR UNITS

DEPARTMENT NAME	LEAD OR LAG	VOLUME ADJUST-MENT (Thousands)	VARIABLE RATE	VARIABLE UNITS* (Thousands)	TOTAL UNITS (Thousands)
GENERAL FACTORY	None	18.0	6.9510	330.0	348.0
PURCHASING	2 Mo.Lead	16.2	.8564	40.6	56.8
PAYROLL	None	120.0	5.2924	251.3	371.3
COLUMN	1	2	3	4	5

* Forecast standard direct labor $4,747,500

Exhibit 6–15.

by applying the variable rate directly to the annual direct labor without adjusting for lead or lag in workload requirements.

The volume adjustment factor in Column 2 of Exhibit 6–15 is the annual amount of Control Factor Units which represent nonvariable workload. In other words, the figure of 16,200 Units shown for the purchasing department is 12 times the monthly adjustment factor shown in Exhibit 6–14.

The variable rates in Column 3 represent the variable relationship of Control Factor Units to direct labor, and this is equal to the slope of the trend line on a graphic analysis such as Exhibit 6–14. Application of these rates to total standard direct labor gives the quantities of variable workload in Control Factor Units which are shown in Column 4. The last column merely totals the variable workload and the volume adjustment to give the total forecast Control Factor Units for each department.

Planned Overhead Costs and Rates

The planned overhead costs for the year, by department and by account, are then determined from the variable budgets. The variable budgets specify the long-range standby cost per month and the rate for relating long-range variable costs to variable Control Factor Units, as was shown in Exhibits 6–8 and 6–10. Monthly standby costs are converted to annual costs, and the variable budget rates for each account in each department are multiplied by the forecast variable workload for the department. Exhibit 6–16 shows the data used and the forecast amounts of overhead cost for the payroll department. Note the line of "clerical" data in the exhibit. The long-range standby cost of $9,600 is 12 times the monthly standby shown in the graph of Exhibit 6–8, and the long-range variable cost rate of $17.78 per 100 CFU's is the slope of the line in that budget graph.

This rate was multiplied by the total forecast units of control factor for the department, after deducting the workload capabilities of the standby crew (1,034 Units per month in Exhibit 6–8, or 12,408 Units for the year). The resulting 358,849 CFU's extended by the variable rate produce $63,803 of long-range variable cost as shown in Column 3 of Exhibit 6–16. Dividing this cost by the total forecast direct labor gives the rate of $1.344 per $100 shown in Column 6.

TWELVE-MONTH FORECAST
MANUFACTURING OVERHEAD EXPENSE

DEPT. NO. 11   DEPT. NAME - PAYROLL

		THOUSANDS				VARIABLE RATES		
	FORE-CAST UNITS OF CONTROL FACTOR	LONG RANGE		SHORT RANGE		LONG RANGE BASED ON -		SHORT (3) RANGE BASED ON DEPT. CONTROL FACTOR
		STANDBY COST	VARIABLE COST	NON-VARIABLE COST	VARIABLE COST	TOTAL STANDARD DIRECT LABOR (1)	DEPT. CONTROL FACTOR	
SUPERVISION		$10,500		$10,500				
CLERICAL		*9,600	63,803	$37,740	$35,663	1.344	*17.780 (2)	9.606
OTHER PAYROLL EXP.		2,700	9,581	6,931	5,350	.202	2.670 (2)	1.441
OTHER EXPENSES		1,800	7,428	1,800	7,428	.156	2.001 (3)	2.001
TOTAL	371,257	$24,600	$80,812	$56,971	$48,441	1.702		13.048
COLUMNS	1	2	3	4	5	6	7	8

Totals to Exhibit 6-17

(1) PER $100.00 OF DIRECT LABOR

(2) PER 100 UNITS OF CONTROL FACTOR IN EXCESS OF WORKLOAD CAPABILITIES OF STANDBY ORGANIZATION (371,257 - 12,408 = 358,849)

(3) PER 100 UNITS OF CONTROL FACTOR (TOTAL UNITS)

* From Exhibit 6-8

Exhibit 6-16.

The short-range variable rates (Column 8) and non-variable amounts (Column 4) reflect the expected relationship of costs and workload volumes for relatively short time periods. When the short-range relationship differs from the long-range relationship, the difference is usually caused by management's decision to retain certain employees in excess of workload requirements when volume falls below the expected average level. The short-range non-variable amount of $37,740 in Column 4 is the annual equivalent of the $3,145 shown in Exhibit 6–8. The short-range variable cost of $35,663 is merely the difference between total long-range costs (Column 2 plus Column 3) and short-range non-variable costs.

The short-range variable rates are obtained by dividing the short-range variable costs by the forecast units of control factor.

Both the short- and the long-range rates in Columns 7 and 8 are used to calculate budget allowances, spending variances, and management decision variances for periodic budget reports, to be illustrated shortly.

Planned Variable Overhead Rates

The planned variable overhead rates are obtained by dividing the forecast long-range variable cost for the year by a measure of planned volume, which in this case is standard direct labor. This was illustrated by the calculation for Column 3 in Exhibit 6–16.

The totals of Exhibit 6–16 can be traced to the payroll line in Exhibit 6–17, which is a summary of the forecasts of control factors, overhead costs, and variable overhead rates for departments related to production. Note that a reserve budget is included in the forecast. The reserve amount is intended to cover the expenses, such as cumulative maintenance, which occur at infrequent and irregular intervals. Although these expenses are related to production volume, they are not included in departmental budgets. If these amounts were included at the departmental level, the budget allowances would be over-stated in most periods and under-stated in the periods in which the costs were actually incurred. This would considerably reduce the usefulness and effectiveness of the variable budgets for day-to-day and month-to-month cost control.

TWELVE-MONTH FORECAST
ALL MANUFACTURING DEPARTMENTS
SUMMARY OF CONTROL FACTOR UNITS, OVERHEAD COSTS
AND VARIABLE OVERHEAD RATES

THOUSANDS

	FORECAST UNITS OF CONTROL FACTORS		LONG RANGE		SHORT RANGE		VARIABLE OVERHEAD RATE PER $100 STANDARD DIRECT LABOR
	TOTAL	OVER STANDBY ORG. CAPA-BILITIES	STANDBY COST	VARIABLE COST	NON-VARIABLE COST	VARIABLE COST	
GENERAL FACTORY	348.0	278.4	$480.0	$ 991.8	$ 648.0	$ 823.8	$20.891
PURCHASING	56.8	40.6	32.9	60.1	76.8	16.2	1.266
PAYROLL (From Exhibit 6-16)	371.3	358.8	24.6	80.8	57.0	48.4	1.702
STORES - MATERIAL HANDLING	310.2	310.2	14.4	377.3	21.4	370.3	7.947
INSPECTION - MACHINE SHOP	3,287.5	3,287.5	7.2	311.3	21.6	296.9	6.557
INSPECTION ASSEMBLY							
PRODUCT A	50.0	50.0	7.5	46.0	7.5	46.0	.969
PRODUCT B	35.0	35.0	7.2	42.7	7.2	42.7	.899
PRODUCT C	12.5	12.5	7.5	44.0	7.5	44.0	.927
MACHINE SHOP	3,287.5 *	3,287.5	82.2	2,382.1	97.2	2,367.1	50.176
ASSEMBLY - PRODUCT A	780.0 *	780.0	19.8	255.0	34.8	240.0	5.371
PRODUCT B	455.0 *	455.0	13.8	123.0	21.3	115.5	2.591
PRODUCT C	225.0 *	225.0	15.0	92.0	22.5	84.5	1.938
TOTAL-ALL DEPARTMENTS			$712.1	$4,806.1	$1,022.8	$4,495.4	$101.234
RESERVES	4,747.5 *	4,747.5		142.4		142.4	2.999
GRAND TOTAL			$712.1	$4,948.5	$1,022.8	$4,637.8	$104.233

TO Exhibit 6-18

Exhibit 6-17.

* Standard direct labor

COMPUTATION OF STANDARD VARIABLE OVERHEAD ABSORPTION
BY PRODUCTIVE DEPARTMENTS
(BASED ON 12-MONTH FORECAST OF OVERHEAD AND DIRECT LABOR)

	Total Plant	Machine Shop	Assembly Departments Product (A)	Product (B)	Product (C)
Variable Expenses					
Direct Departments	$2,852.1	$2,382.1	$255.0	$123.0	$ 92.0
General Factory	991.8	686.8	156.7	80.4	67.9
Purchasing	60.1	41.5	9.5	4.9	4.2
Payroll	80.8	55.9	12.8	6.6	5.5
Stores - Material Handling	377.3	261.3	59.6	30.6	25.8
Inspection	444.0	311.3	46.0	42.7	44.0
Reserves	142.4	98.6	22.5	11.6	9.7
Total Expense	$4,948.5	$3,837.5	$562.1	$299.8	$249.1
Standard Direct Labor	4,747.5	3,287.5	780.0	455.0	225.0
Standard Variable Overhead Rates by Productive Departments			116.73	72.06 65.89	110.71

COMPUTATION OF STANDARD VARIABLE OVERHEAD ABSORBED IN JUNE

	Standard Direct Labor	Overhead Absorption Rate	Variable Overhead Absorbed
Machine shop	$241,120	116.73	$281,459
Assembly - A	54,600	72.06	39,345
Assembly - B	32,368	65.89	21,327
Assembly - C	18,050	110.71	19,983
	$346,138		$362,114

Exhibit 6–18.

The long-range variable costs which appear in Exhibit 6–17 are also used for computing the variable overhead absorption rates for the direct production departments, rates which are used in determining standard variable product cost. In this case, the standard direct labor in the four direct departments is used as the basis for charging all standard variable manufacturing overhead to inventory because these same rates are used in relieving inventory for the cost of goods sold. The top portion of Exhibit 6–18 shows how the annual forecast of variable overhead of the indirect departments is distributed to the direct departments in order to develop the absorption rates for these departments. The lower portion of the exhibit shows the application of these rates to the standard direct labor for the month of June. The resultant total of standard variable overhead absorbed into inventory for the month is used to develop a variance which helps to reconcile budgeted overhead with that used for standard product cost and inventory purposes.

Calculating Budget Allowances and Variances

Exhibit 6–19 is an example of the actual expenses, budget allowances, and variances for the payroll department for a particular month. The calculation of the budget amounts and variances in this exhibit is illustrated in Exhibit 6–20 by reference to the clerical wages of the payroll department.

The long-range budget allowances for any account include both the standby and the variable portions of the cost. The standby portion is a constant amount for each period as specified in the variable budget. The variable portion of the budget allowance is the product of the variable rate and the number of units of control factor produced during the period, less the variable workload capacity of the standby organization ($26,400 - 1,034 = 25,366$). This is illustrated in the first portion of Exhibit 6–20, where the long-range budget allowance for payroll clerical wages is calculated as $5,311 for the month.

The short-range budget allowance is computed in essentially the same manner, except that monthly short-range non-variable amounts, short-range variable rates from Exhibit 6–16, and the total earned units of control factor for the month ($26,400$) are used. This results in a short-range budget allowance of $5,680.

The standard overhead absorbed, on total standard direct labor in this case, is computed by multiplying the total plant standard direct labor for the month by the long-range variable rate to direct labor as shown in Exhibit 6–16. Remember that this rate was obtained by dividing total forecast overhead for the overhead account by total forecast direct labor for the plant. The relation of this "absorption cost" to the long-range budget is similar to that illustrated in Exhibit 6–2. The two coincide only at the forecast level of volume.

The special allowances granted are the amounts transferred from the reserve budget because of infrequent or irregular costs.

The variances calculated in the lower portion of Exhibit 6–20

DEPARTMENTAL BUDGET REPORT

MONTH OF JUNE

DEPT. NO. 11   DEPT. NAME - PAYROLL   () Indicates unfavorable variance

| | | BUDGET ALLOWANCE BASED ON DEPARTMENT CONTROL FACTORS | | | | VARIANCES | | | |
EXPENSE	ACTUAL EXPENSES	SPECIAL ALLOW. GRANTED	SHORT-RANGE BUDGET (1)	LONG-RANGE BUDGET	TOTAL STANDARD DIRECT LABOR	SPENDING	MANAGEMENT DECISION	CONVERSION	TOTAL
SUPERVISION	$ 875		$ 875	$ 875	$ 875				
CLERICAL WAGES	5,714		5,680	5,311(2)	5,451	$(34)	$(369)	$ 140	$(263)
OTHER PAYROLL EXPENSES	962		957	902(2)	924	(5)	(55)	22	(38)
OTHER EXPENSES	1,044	$ 340	678	678(1)	690	(26)		12	(14)
TOTAL	$8,595	$ 340	$8,190	$7,766	$7,940	$(65)	(424)	174	(315)
Column	2	3	4	5	6	7	8	9	10

(1) Based on earned variable control factor units for the month

(2) Based on earned variable control factor units for the month in excess of the capacity of the standby organization   26,400 - 1,034 = 25,366

Exhibit 6-19.

BUDGET COMPUTATIONS

Long-Range Budget Allowance:

Variable workload produced in excess of the variable capacity of the standby crew (Exhibit 6-19)	25,366	C.F.U.	
Variable rate (Exhibit 6-8 or 6-16)	x $17.78/100	C.F.U.	
			$4,511
Standby cost (Exhibit 6-8 or 1/12 of Exhibit 6-16)			800
Long-range budget allowance			$5,311

Short-Range Budget Allowance:

Variable workload produced (Exhibit 6-19)	26,400	C.F.U.	
Variable rate (Exhibit 6-16)	x 9.606/100	C.F.U.	
			$2,535
Short-range standby (Exhibit 6-8 or 1/12 of Exhibit 6-16)			3,145
Short-range budget allowance			$5,680

Standard Overhead Absorbed Direct Labor:

Standard direct labor (Exhibit 6-18)	$346,138	
Variable overhead rate to direct labor (Exhibit 6-16)	x 1.344/$100	
		$4,652
Standby cost (as above)		800
Standard overhead absorbed on direct labor		$5,452

Actual Payroll Clerical Salaries Expense (Exhibit 6-19)	$5,714

VARIANCE COMPUTATIONS

Actual expense	$5,714
Short-range budget allowance	5,680
Spending variance (unfavorable)	$ (34)
Short-range budget allowance	$5,680
Long-range budget allowance	5,311
Management decision variance (unfavorable)	$ (369)
Long-range budget allowance	$5,311
Standard overhead absorbed on total standard direct labor	5,452
Conversion variance - favorable	$ 140

Exhibit 6–20. Budget and variance computations of clerical salaries of payroll department for month of June.

illustrate how actual overhead is reconciled with planned amounts. Spending, management decision, and conversion variances are determined by accounts by departments. Each type of variance has a significance which should be thoroughly understood.

Spending Variance

The spending variance is the difference between the actual expenses incurred and the short-range budget allowance. For clerical costs in the payroll department, the variance is "unfavorable," since actual expense is $34 higher than the short-range budget. An "unfavorable" variance may be caused by poor utilization of personnel, materials, or services, or by operating problems. All variances of a significant amount, whether "favorable" or "unfavorable," should be investigated to determine their cause.

Management Decision Variance

The management decision variance is the difference between the short-range budget allowance and the long-range budget allowance. An "unfavorable" variance, such as the $369 calculated in Exhibit 6–20, occurs whenever the short-range allowance exceeds the long-range allowance. It results from management's retention of personnel in excess of the requirements of the current workload. This course of action and the resulting variance may be justified by the fact that it is less costly to retain certain skilled employees beyond the workload requirements for a short period of time than it would be to hire and train new personnel when needed. The management decision variance, however, focuses attention on the cost of this excess capability. Because, as was described in connection with Exhibit 6–8, the short-range budget for any given volume is never set any lower than the long-range budget, this management decision variance is never "favorable."

Conversion Variance

The conversion variance is the difference between the long-range budget allowance and the standard overhead absorbed on a common measure of volume, in this case standard direct labor for the plant. The typical relationship between these two is illustrated in Exhibit 6–2, where the budget line exceeds the absorption line, an "unfavorable" conversion variance, until volume reaches the forecast level used for setting the absorption rate. At higher volumes, a "favorable" variance results.

The overhead absorbed is essentially the standard variable overhead charged to inventory plus the standard standby cost of overhead. It would be exactly that, if the variable overhead of each department were related directly to product cost. For example, the proportion of variable payroll expense to total standard labor might be added directly to the standard labor in each product. It is not precisely that, however, because product costs were developed by distributing the overhead in the indirect departments to the direct production departments (Exhibit 6–18) in order to include all overhead in the direct department rates. This calculation was based on the forecast mix of direct labor among the production departments. When the actual mix is different, the overhead absorbed on a departmental basis will differ from the overhead absorbed on a product cost basis, and the latter is what will be relieved from inventory when the product is sold.

Exhibit 6–21 summarizes the budget reports for the month of June, including the overhead allowance based on total standard direct labor. The amount shown, $420,128, includes standard variable overhead absorbed at departmental variable rates, standard standby, and the provision for reserves. After deduction of the standby costs, the variable overhead absorbed at individual department rates is $360,788. Comparison of this with the variable overhead absorbed at direct department rates (bottom portion of Exhibit 6–18) produces the so-called production mix variance shown in Exhibit 6–21, in this case a "favorable" variance of $1,326.

This is actually a plant-wide adjustment to the sum of the individual departmental conversion variances, and it eliminates the possibility of developing variance in inventory because of inconsistencies between input and relief of inventory.

The conversion variance includes

1. The adjustment for workload that leads or lags the over-all volume base of sales or production, as was illustrated earlier for the purchasing department
2. The adjustment for differences between the departmental long-range budget and the departmental absorption rate, as was illustrated by the calculation for the payroll department
3. The adjustment for changes in actual volume or mix from the forecast volume and mix on which the direct departmental variable overhead rates and product cost standards are based, as illustrated above

The conversion variance is the device which makes it possible to reconcile the costs for product costing, income determination, and profit planning with those used for cost control. Ordinarily

SUMMARY OF
DEPARTMENTAL BUDGET REPORTS
MANUFACTURING DEPARTMENTS
MONTH OF JUNE

() Indicates unfavorable variance

DEPARTMENT	EARNED UNITS OF CONTROL FACTOR	ACTUAL EXPENSES	BUDGET ALLOWANCE BASED ON DEPARTMENT CONTROL FACTORS			TOTAL STANDARD DIRECT LABOR	VARIANCES			
			SPECIAL ALLOW. GRANTED	SHORT-RANGE BUDGET	LONG-RANGE BUDGET		SPENDING	MANAGE-MENT DECISION	CONVER-SION	TOTAL
GENERAL FACTORY	25,230	$116,998		$113,725	$111,677	$112,312	$(3,273)	$(2,048)	$ 635	$(4,686)
PURCHASING	4,540	7,543		7,692	7,464	7,122	149	(228)	(342)	(421)
PAYROLL (From Ex. 6-19)	26,400	8,595	340	8,190	7,766	7,940	(65)	(424)	174	(315)
STORES - MATERIAL HANDLING	23,569	32,865	847	29,918	29,867	28,708	(2,100)	(51)	(1,159)	(3,310)
INSPECTION - MACHINE SHOP	241,120	23,219		23,576	23,432	23,296	357	144	(136)	77
INSPECTION - ASSEMBLY										
PRODUCT A	3,500	3,998		3,845	3,845	3,979	(153)		134	(19)
PRODUCT B	2,490	3,867		3,638	3,638	3,712	(229)		74	(155)
PRODUCT C	1,003	4,012		4,156	4,156	3,834	144		(322)	(178)
MACHINE SHOP	241,120 *	200,711	15,800	181,714	181,563	180,527	(3,197)	(151)	(1,036)	(4,384)
ASSEMBLY - PRODUCT A	54,600 *	16,727		19,700	19,500	20,241	2,973	(200)	741	3,514
PRODUCT B	32,368 *	9,043		9,992	9,900	10,118	949	(92)	218	1,075
PRODUCT C	18,050 *	8,855		8,654	8,630	7,958	(201)	(24)	672	(897)
TOTAL ALL DEPARTMENTS	346,138 *	$436,433	$16,987	$414,800	$411,438	$409,747	$(4,646)	$(3,362)	$(1,691)	$(9,699)
RESERVES			16,987	10,381	10,381	10,381	(6,606)			(6,606)
GRAND TOTAL		$436,433	-	$425,181	$421,819	$420,128	$(11,252)	$(3,362)	$(1,691)	$(16,305)

Less standby expense ($712,080 for year ÷ 12)	59,340			
Standard variable overhead at individual department rates	360,788			
Variable overhead absorbed at direct department rates (Ex. 6-18)	362,114			
Production mix variance	1,326		1,326	
Composition of overhead variance	(11,252)	(3,362)	(365)	(14,979)

*Direct Labor

Exhibit 6-21.

the conversion variances will tend to balance out to zero over the course of a year, although this will not necessarily happen if forecast volume and mix are drastically different from actual volume and mix for the year.

SUMMARY

Variable budgets based on work measurement provide the same performance measures by responsibility for overhead that standard costs provide for direct material and labor. These budgets should be based on analyses of departmental functions, workloads, and productivity and on the selection of control factors which best reflect departmental activity. The behavior of costs is related to activity, or volume of workload, expressed in units of the appropriate control factor, with particular attention to indirect labor. In this area, the short-range budget reflects minimum staffing limitations, if such exist, as well as workload requirements.

Irregularly occurring, but necessary, costs may be handled by the use of reserve (accrual) budgets, and project-type costs may be controlled by use of programmed expense budgets.

Occasionally, the first installation of a Profitability Accounting system may incorporate rather crude budgets, based partly on "fitting" straight lines to "scatter graphs" of points plotted to show historical relationships of cost to volume. Obviously, such budgets do not provide the control over performance that results from detailed analyses of workloads and the use of work measurement techniques, such as work sampling and Methods-Time-Measurement, which underlie the budgetary structure discussed in this chapter.

Because variable overhead costs are not specifically and directly variable with units of product, variable overhead absorption rates are necessary for determining standard product costs for purposes of profit planning, product line decisions, and inventory accounting. The conversion variance enables a reconciliation of the overhead cost used for these purposes with that used for budgetary control. The use of both short-range and long-range budgets permits the determination of an actual spending variance from the short-range budget while also focusing managerial attention on any variance which is associated with a decision to follow the short-range rather than the long-range budget, during volume fluctuations of short duration.

However, the state of system development in some companies may not be sufficiently advanced so that the practical problems of incorporating these sophisticated budgetary procedures into a smoothly working system can be solved in the initial installation. In such cases, although some control may be sacrificed, most of the advantages of Profitability Accounting may still be obtained by using only the short-range budgets based on some type of work measurement.

In general, the use of the simpler budgets will result in higher variable overhead rates, higher conversion variances (or as they are sometimes called, "budget variances"), less knowledge about costs, and less accounting effort than will the use of the more sophisticated budgets. An illustrative comparison of these differences is given early in the following chapter, in connection with the development of variable overhead rates for purposes of product line accounting.

Chapter 7

Product Line Profitability and the Profit Plan

	Page
THE PROBLEM OF OVERHEAD COSTS	188
Cost Centers and Product Lines	190
Developing Variable Overhead Rates	191
ASSIGNING MANUFACTURING OVERHEAD COSTS TO PRODUCT LINES	195
Summary of Overhead Costs by Cost Center	196
Assigning Overhead Costs to Direct Cost Centers	197
Assigning Overhead Costs to Product Lines	199
ASSIGNING COMMERCIAL OVERHEAD COSTS TO PRODUCT LINES	203
ASSIGNING PROGRAMMED COSTS TO PRODUCT LINES	205
CONSTRUCTING A PROFIT PLAN	205
PROBLEMS IN MECHANICS	208
Product Cost Centers	208
Distribution of Indirect Department Overhead Costs	213
Organizational Complexities	217
SUMMARY	218

THE LAST three chapters have emphasized the control of costs by responsibility, through the use of standard costs for direct labor and material, variable budgets for overhead, and a chart of accounts designed to conform to the responsibility structure of the organization. Planned costs and other statistics are compared with the actual data for each responsibility center. This procedure facilitates prompt reporting, essential for continuous control, to the manager responsible for each function.

Several other managerial objectives, however, must also be served by essentially the same data, converted into various other forms. In order to develop a successful profit-planning strategy, managers with product responsibility need to know the margin between the cost and the selling price of a product or group of related products. They must be kept informed of current selling prices, volumes, and profits in order to be ready to take any necessary corrective action.

Cost, volume, profit, and turnover data by product and product line are extremely useful in make or buy decisions; in determining cost of sales; in establishing a pricing policy and setting individual selling prices; in long-range planning for investment in facilities, research, and development; as well as in measuring the performance of managers.

Moreover, the financial manager must know the cost of each product in order to price inventories correctly. In the past, this use has frequently but wrongly been considered to be the primary, if not the only, objective of internal accounting. Of course, accurate inventory costs are an essential for determination of net income, but that is only one of several significant benefits to be obtained from imaginative, well-conceived internal accounting.

In Profitability Accounting, only a minimum of effort is required to convert the same planned costs used for control of performance into product and product line costs. Product line costs are matched with product line revenues in order to determine product line profitability, at the level of profit contribution and at the level of net profit.

THE PROBLEM OF OVERHEAD COSTS

Many of the data required for a profit plan are recorded in the accounts only by responsibility and must be converted to a product or product line basis. Sales and direct costs, which include standard materials, standard direct labor, and specific sales deductions, are originally planned and recorded in the accounts by product or product line and, therefore, require no conversion. Planned manufacturing and commercial overhead costs, however, are summarized by product cost center.

Only the variable elements of planned overhead costs are assigned to units of product. This means that some commercial costs are included and some manufacturing costs are excluded from unit cost. The costs included are applied to products by use of a variable rate to sales or direct labor. Collecting only the variable costs permits the determination of profit contribution, which is the difference between selling price and variable cost per unit of product. The rate of profit contribution to sales can be used to calculate the effect on profits of changing volumes when considering decisions on product pricing, make or buy, and selective selling.

It is also important, however, to know the non-variable costs which are incurred because of a particular product line, and to consider all other costs in determining a figure which corresponds to the net profit by product line. Therefore, both the standby and programmed groupings of costs are classified as either "specific," those which can be specifically identified with product line, or "general," those which can only be allocated to product lines. In these four groupings, the costs are assigned to product lines in separate lump sum amounts, and not merged with the variable costs. In this way, managers are provided with the information necessary for a variety of decisions without the need for a special study.

This chapter is intended to illustrate in detail the mechanical problems involved and the techniques used to develop a profit plan by product line, against which actual results will be reported. Much of this chapter is devoted to examples of allocations which may be familiar to many cost accountants. For simplicity, most of the examples in this chapter are based on the functions of a small company with several product lines. However, the basic approach would be essentially the same in a large, multi-division company.

It should be noted, however, that these are systematic memorandum allocations developed only once each year in the determination of various product line costs and cost rates which are used in constructing the profit plan. The steps in the development of the profit plan do not reflect the day-to-day accounting routines. The accounting records are maintained on a responsibility basis only, and the formal accounting routines need not be complicated by the memorandum product line allocations. The identification of overhead costs with products and the detailed segregation of standby and variable costs are not accomplished in the accounts themselves. It is necessary, however, that the determination of variances and standard costs which appear in the interim earnings statements be formally integrated with the accounting records.

Before proceeding to illustrate the assigning of overhead cost to product lines and the mechanics of constructing a profit plan, it is well to define a few terms which are used extensively in this chapter and to demonstrate alternative methods of developing overhead rates depending upon the type of variable budgets adopted by a company.

Cost Centers and Product Lines

The four terms mentioned below are used frequently in this chapter. While most readers may be generally familiar with these terms, a specific mention of the sense in which they are used here may help to avoid misunderstanding.

A *product line* is a grouping of products which are related for purposes of at least some management decisions. They may be similar in design and in manufacturing requirements. They may be sold through a common distribution channel and be under a single sales responsibility. They may face similar competitive pressures and be priced as a group. A single product may be treated as a "product line" if it is sufficiently different from other products in the above characteristics, and if such treatment will provide better information for management decisions.

A *profit center* is an organizational sub-division of a company, which can be held responsible for the profit of a specific segment of the business because it is responsible for both sales and production of a group of products. Most often a profit center is a semi-autonomous division in a decentralized company, but occasionally product line managers will have such responsibility within a centralized company.

A *cost control center* is the basic organizational unit having first-line responsibility for the control of a specific segment of costs. It can be a direct or indirect manufacturing department under a foreman, a commercial department under a department head, a sales division under a sales manager, or even a group of administrative costs over which the president of the company exercises first-line control. In many situations cost control centers will also serve directly as product cost centers, but this does not always hold true.

A *product cost center* is a grouping of overhead costs which tend to vary with a common measure of volume, such as sales dollars or direct labor hours or dollars, and where the incidence of overhead cost per unit of volume is essentially the same for all products.

Developing Variable Overhead Rates

The problem of identifying overhead costs with products is usually complex. Typically, a variety of different products or components are worked on in each of a number of direct productive departments, and other, so-called indirect, departments provide services to one or more productive departments, or to some or all of the different products. In these circumstances the identification of each specific bit of overhead cost with a specific unit of product is usually impossible. However, the planned overhead costs which tend to vary with volume can usually be related to some common measure of product volume, such as direct labor, material content, or sales. The amount of *variable overhead* cost per unit of this volume measure is the *overhead absorption rate* used here and in Chapter 6. It does not include the standby and programmed costs which are usually included in the typical full overhead absorption rate. The term *absorption* is used to identify the rate with product costing in contrast to the budgetary overhead rates discussed in Chapter 6. While this variable overhead (absorption) rate does not identify every specific bit of overhead cost with a specific unit of product, it does provide a reasonable method for assigning variable overhead costs to each unit of product.

At this point, it is desirable to identify and compare two different approaches to developing variable overhead (absorption) rates for product costing. One was detailed in Chapter 6, where the long-range expense budget allowance for the forecast average units of control factor in the payroll cost center (Exhibit 6–8) was related to the forecast average volume of total direct labor in the plant (Exhibits 6–15 and 6–16). This was used to determine a

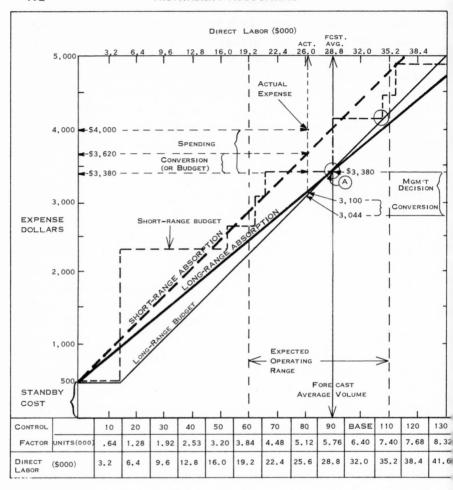

Exhibit 7–1. Comparison of overhead absorption based on short-range budget with absorption based on long-range budget.

straight overhead absorption cost line which went from standby cost at zero volume to long-range budgeted cost at forecast average volume.

Much the same thing is illustrated in Exhibit 7–1, but for a cost center where the short-range budget is similar to that for the assembly inspection labor in Exhibit 6–10 except for the addition of standby cost. The long-range absorption line is drawn through point A, budgeted cost at expected volume. The slope of the line is the variable overhead rate for product cost purposes. (For pur-

poses of simplicity, this example ignores any distribution of indirect department overhead to direct departments, as was shown
in Exhibit 6–18, thus the volume base can be shown in both direct
labor dollars and units of workload.)

As was brought out in Chapter 6, the long-range budget based
on work measurement reflects the best attainable efficiency, and
the difference between it and the short-range budget is reported
as a management decision variance. The difference between it
and the absorption cost is shown as a conversion variance.

The management of a company may prefer not to use the long-
range absorption line for one of two reasons:

1. Their state of systems development may not be sufficiently ad-
    vanced for them to incorporate variable budgets based on dual
    budgeting into a smoothly working system.
2. If the difference between short-range and long-range budgets is
    considerable and cannot be reduced by management decision,
    they may be unwilling to use a variable overhead rate which
    excludes a considerable portion of costs.

In either case, they need not lose the other benefits which can
be obtained by the use of Profitability Accounting.

An alternative method of determining variable overhead (absorption) rates is shown by the dotted lines in Exhibit 7–1. It is
still necessary to obtain some idea of how overhead varies with
short-range volume fluctuations. For comparative purposes, it is
assumed that the short-range budget in Exhibit 7–1 is available
for either method of developing overhead rates, although this will
be known less precisely if work measurement is not used.

Once the short-range behavior of overhead has been plotted
with respect to the common measure of volume in the cost center,
direct labor in this case, a straight line can be drawn which starts
from standby cost at zero volume. It is drawn so as to best fit the
cost behavior over the expected operating range, 60% to 110% in
Exhibit 7–1. Although this line might be computed by using the
statistical "method of least squares," it is usually satisfactory to fit
it by eye. (The rather poor fit of the short-range absorption line
in Exhibit 7–1, and its unnecessary parallelism with the long-range
budget line, resulted from a deliberate effort to produce simple,
whole-number, variable rates for the calculations in Exhibit 7–2.)

	Short-Range Absorption	Long-Range Absorption
Actual Expense	$4,000	4,000
Less: Short-range budget allowance	3,380	3,380
Spending Variance (unfavorable)	($620)	($620)
Workload in control factor units		5,200
Less: Capabilities of standby crew		960
Variable Workload		4,240
Long-range overhead budget rate		x $.600
Variable portion of long-range budget		$2,544
Add: Standby cost		500
Long-range budget allowance		$3,044
Short-range budget allowance		$3,380
Less: Long-range budget allowance		3,044
Management Decision Variance (unfavorable)		($ 336)
Actual amount of standard direct labor	$26,000	$26,000
Overhead absorption rate	x .120	x .100
Standard variable overhead absorbed	$ 3,120	$ 2,600
Add: Standby cost	500	500
Standard overhead absorbed	$ 3,620	$ 3,100
Short-range budget allowance	$3,380	
Long-range budget allowance		$3,044
Less: Standard overhead absorbed	3,620	3,100
Conversion Variance – favorable	$ 240 *	$ 56

* (or Budget Variance)

Exhibit 7–2. Comparison of variance calculations based on short-range absorption and on long-range absorption.

The comparative variances under the two methods are shown graphically in Exhibit 7–1 and computed in Exhibit 7–2. Under both methods, the spending variance is the difference between actual expense and the short-range budget, and it reflects the cost control in the department or account. In using the method of Chapter 6, the next step is the calculation of the long-range budget allowance and the resulting management decision variance. Then, the calculation of overhead absorbed is used to determine a conversion variance. The alternative method ignores the long-range budget, and compares the short-range budget with short-range absorption to force the conversion (budget) variance.

As a general rule, the use of the short-range absorption method will result in higher variable overhead rates, higher conversion variances, less knowledge about costs, and less accounting effort than will use of the long-range absorption method. It is also possible to use work measurement in developing long-range budget standards which are used to review performance but which are not incorporated in the monthly accounting. The management decision variance might be computed strictly as a memorandum figure which does not enter into the formal accounting reconciliation of planned and actual cost.

ASSIGNING MANUFACTURING OVERHEAD COSTS TO PRODUCT LINES

The common measure of volume in a direct cost center, one engaged in making products, is usually direct labor hours or dollars, machine hours, or product units, any of which are readily identifiable with the product. When variable overhead costs in the cost center can be related to the common measure of volume, it is relatively easy to transfer these costs to products. Similarly the standby costs of a direct department can be allocated among product lines on the basis of the expected long-term volume of the product line in the cost center.

The overhead costs of indirect manufacturing cost centers cannot be as readily identified with products. The best procedure in most cases is to summarize the overhead costs of each indirect cost center, distribute them to the direct cost centers, and redistribute them to products and product lines along with the overhead costs of the direct cost center. The theory is that indirect cost centers are service functions which provide benefits to the direct cost centers served. The direct cost centers should receive, and in turn pass on to products and product lines, the cost of indirect centers in proportion to the benefits received.

This is the procedure which is illustrated in this chapter, although there are cases in which the overhead of indirect departments can be carried directly to product cost with as much accuracy and less computational effort. Material-handling costs might be related directly to product on the basis of the material in each product, and other departments might be related on the basis of product labor. Use of such direct overhead rates may reduce the conversion variance.

The following method of assigning all manufacturing overhead costs to products and product lines is accomplished entirely on a memorandum basis apart from the formal accounting records. It may be visualized as a three-stage process:

1. Summarize standby and variable overhead costs for each direct and indirect cost center.
2. a. Incorporate indirect cost center variable overhead in direct cost center variable overhead rates.
    b. Allocate indirect cost center standby costs to direct cost centers.
3. a. Summarize variable overhead costs by product line.
    b. Allocate standby costs to product lines in lump sum amounts.

The three-stage concept of assigning overhead costs to products and product lines will be illustrated in the following sections.

Summary of Overhead Costs by Cost Center

A hypothetical set of direct cost center standby amounts and variable rates are summarized in Exhibit 7–3. In order to keep the illustration simple, each department is assumed to be a single cost control center and a single product cost center. It is also assumed that departmental direct labor dollars are the common measure of volume which accurately reflects the incidence of variable overhead costs in each direct department.

Direct Departments	Annual Standby Cost	Variable Rate Per $1.00 Own Direct Labor
A	$24,000	$.40
B	12,000	.30
C	6,000	.20
D	8,000	.50
E	10,000	.60
	$60,000	

Exhibit 7–3. Summary of standby costs and variable rates of direct departments.

The annual standby cost in each department is obtained by adding together the monthly budgeted standby for all expense accounts in the department and converting the monthly total to an annual basis. The variable rate in each department is obtained by adding together the variable rates of all budgeted expenses in the department or by a graphic procedure similar to that in Exhibit 7–1.

The indirect department standby amounts and variable rates are summarized in Exhibit 7–4. It is assumed that total direct

Department	Annual Standby Cost	Variable Rate Per $1.00 Total Direct Labor
Tool room	$ 48,000	$.05
Engineering	24,000	.08
Material handling	36,000	.10
Maintenance	12,000	.15
General factory	120,000	.22
	$240,000	$.60

Exhibit 7–4. Summary of standby costs and variable rates of indirect departments.

labor dollars in all direct departments are a common measure of volume which reflects the incidence of variable overhead costs in each indirect department. If the services of an indirect department such as the tool room are requisitioned by other departments, the variable costs of the services are usually transferred to the requisitioning department on the books of account to provide the dual control over cost described in Chapter 4. Only the remaining variable costs would be included in the summary and memorandum distribution to direct cost centers.

Assigning Overhead Costs to Direct Cost Centers

The variable overhead rates of the indirect departments are combined with the variable rates of the direct departments as shown in Exhibit 7–5. Since the indirect department rates are

Direct Department	Own Rate Per $1.00 Own Direct Labor	Indirect Rate Per $1.00 Direct Labor	Combined Rate Per $1.00 Own Direct Labor
A	$.40	$.60	$1.00
B	.30	.60	.90
C	.20	.60	.80
D	.50	.60	1.10
E	.60	.60	1.20

Exhibit 7–5. Combining variable overhead rates of direct and indirect departments.

based on total direct labor dollars and the direct department rates are based on "own department" direct labor dollars, the combination is effected by simply adding the total of the indirect department rates to the variable rate of each direct department.

The next step is to distribute the indirect department standby costs to direct departments. This is also a part of the second stage in the three-stage process of assigning all overhead costs to product lines. If indirect departments provide services to the direct departments, the standby costs should be allocated among direct departments on the basis of the expected amount of services to be provided in the long range. Temporary fluctuations or shifts in activity between departments should not affect the bases of allocation. The problem is to select bases which reflect the relative amount of services provided. One example of the allocation of indirect department standby costs to direct departments is illustrated in Exhibit 7–6.

		Standby allocated on basis of:			
Department	Own Department Standby Cost	Space Occupied	Use of Toolroom Facilities	Direct Labor	Standby Cost After Allocation
Direct:					
A	$24,000	$ 9,000	$30,000	$64,000	$127,000
B	12,000	3,000	5,000	32,000	52,000
C	6,000	2,000	9,000	16,000	33,000
D	8,000	4,000	4,000	16,000	32,000
E	10,000	12,000	2,000	32,000	56,000
Total direct	$60,000				
Indirect:					
Toolroom	48,000	6,000	(54,000)		
Engineering	24,000	2,000		(26,000)	
Material Handling	36,000	6,000	2,000	(44,000)	
Maintenance	12,000	2,000	1,000	(15,000)	
General Factory	120,000	(46,000)	1,000	(75,000)	
	$300,000	$ -o-	$ -o-	$ -o-	$300,000

Exhibit 7–6. Allocation of indirect department standby costs to direct departments.

In Exhibit 7–6, certain general factory department standby costs related to building occupancy, such as real estate taxes, insurance on the building, heat, and plant protection, were deemed allocable on the basis of space occupied. Standby costs of the tool room were allocated on the basis of the expected long-term use of the tool room services by the departments served. All other standby costs of the indirect departments were allocated to direct departments on the basis of the long-term forecast of the relative amounts of direct labor in the direct departments. The long-term forecast of direct labor is illustrated in Exhibit 7–7.

Department	Percentage of Total Direct Labor
A	40%
B	20
C	10
D	10
E	20
	100%

Exhibit 7–7. Long-term forecast of relative direct labor in direct departments.

The example in Exhibit 7–6 is over-simplified in that only three bases of allocation are used. As many may be used as are necessary in order to properly allocate the standby costs to direct departments. Individual standby costs within a cost center may be allocated on a basis different from that used for other costs in the same cost center.

Assigning Overhead Costs to Product Lines

Planned variable manufacturing overhead costs are absorbed into inventory by the routine costing procedure of applying the variable overhead rate to the common measure of volume of the

Department	Standard Direct Labor Hours	Standard Labor Rate	Standard Direct Labor Dollars	Variable Overhead Rate	Variable Overhead Cost
A	20.0	$1.75	$35.00	$1.00	$35.00
B	5.0	2.00	10.00	.90	9.00
C	2.0	1.75	3.50	.80	2.80
D	–	–	–	–	–
E	6.6	2.50	16.50	1.20	19.80
			$65.00		$66.60

Exhibit 7–8. Product standard direct labor and variable overhead cost: Product X-1037.

direct departments. Since the common measure of volume can be traced to specific units of product, the variable overhead costs are effectively assigned to products at this point.

To illustrate this procedure, assume that during a particular period a plant produced 500 units of Product X-1037. The standard direct labor and standard variable overhead cost per unit are summarized in Exhibit 7–8. Variable overhead is absorbed into inventory on the basis of direct labor dollars in direct departments, as illustrated in Exhibit 7–9. The total variable overhead absorbed is $33,300. It is represented in inventory by 500 units of Product X-1037 at $66.60 per unit, or $33,300.

Department	Standard Direct Labor Dollars	Variable Overhead Rate	Variable Overhead Absorbed
A	$17,500	$1.00	$17,500
B	5,000	.90	4,500
C	1,750	.80	1,400
D	-	-	-
E	8,250	1.20	9,900
			$33,300

Exhibit 7–9. Variable manufacturing overhead absorbed.

In developing the profit plan by product line, the sales forecast for the current year in units of product is extended by the product direct labor standards to obtain a current forecast of direct labor by product line in each department, such as that shown in Exhibit 7–10.

The current forecast of departmental standard direct labor by product line is extended by the variable overhead rates to produce a current forecast of variable manufacturing overhead cost by

Department	Product Lines			
	X	Y	Z	Total
A	$ 70,000	$38,000	$ 20,000	$128,000
B	20,000	21,000	39,000	80,000
C	7,000		25,000	32,000
D		16,000	16,000	32,000
E	33,000	5,000	10,000	48,000
	$130,000	$80,000	$110,000	$320,000

Exhibit 7–10. Current forecast of standard direct labor.

product line. Continuing the example with the data presented above, this forecast of variable overhead costs is illustrated in Exhibit 7–11.

		Product Lines					
		X		Y		Z	
Department	Variable Overhead Rate	Standard Direct Labor	Forecast Variable Overhead	Standard Direct Labor	Forecast Variable Overhead	Standard Direct Labor	Forecast Variable Overhead
A	$1.00	$ 70,000	$ 70,000	$38,000	$38,000	$ 20,000	$ 20,000
B	.90	20,000	18,000	21,000	18,900	39,000	35,100
C	.80	7,000	5,600			25,000	20,000
D	1.10			16,000	17,600	16,000	17,600
E	1.20	33,000	39,600	5,000	6,000	10,000	12,000
		$130,000	$133,200	$80,000	$80,500	$110,000	$104,700

Exhibit 7–11. Current forecast of variable manufacturing overhead cost by product line.

To complete the third stage in the distribution of overhead costs to product lines, the manufacturing standby cost which has all been assigned to direct departments, as shown in Exhibit 7–6, must be allocated to product lines. The standby costs are allocated to product lines on the basis of the long-term expected usage of the direct departments to produce the items which comprise the product line. The intention is to relate long-term fixed costs to products which are intended to support them in the long run, and thereby provide a proper perspective for the evaluation of product line profitability.

An example of the allocation of manufacturing standby costs to product lines is illustrated in Exhibits 7–12, 7–13, and 7–14. The assumption is that in this situation the standard which best measures the usage of direct departments is direct labor dollars.

	Product Lines			
Department	X	Y	Z	Total
A	$ 80,000	$40,000	$ 40,000	$160,000
B	20,000	20,000	40,000	20,000
C	6,600		33,400	40,000
D		20,000	20,000	40,000
E	26,700	13,300	40,000	80,000
	$133,300	$93,300	$173,400	$400,000

Exhibit 7–12. Long-term forecast of departmental direct labor dollars by product line.

Exhibit 7–12 is a long-term forecast of departmental direct labor by product line. It would be obtained by "exploding" the long-term forecast of product sales into the direct labor requirements of each product line in each direct department.

The standby costs assigned to direct departments in Exhibit 7–6 are then allocated to product lines, using the percentage distribution shown in Exhibit 7–13. The lump sum amounts of man-

Department	Product Lines X	Y	Z	Total
A	50 %	25 %	25 %	100%
B	25 %	25 %	50 %	100%
C	16 2/3%		83 1/3%	100%
D		50 %	50 %	100%
E	33 1/3%	16 2/3%	50 %	100%

Exhibit 7–13. Percentage distribution of direct labor dollars in long-term sales forecast.

ufacturing standby cost distributed to product lines on a memorandum basis are shown in Exhibit 7–14.

The distribution of manufacturing standby costs to product lines on a basis such as this recognizes the long-term readiness to serve which must be maintained in all departments. Furthermore, the amount allocated to a product line will not vary widely from year to year because of temporary shifts in volume between departments or between product lines. A product manager, faced with the problems of setting selling prices and earning a proper return on investment, should not be confronted each year with substantial changes in the amount of standby cost allocated to his product line as a result of temporary volume changes.

Department	Product Lines X	Y	Z	Total
A	$ 63,500	$31,750	$ 31,750	$127,000
B	13,000	13,000	26,000	52,000
C	5,500		27,500	33,000
D		16,000	16,000	32,000
E	18,667	9,333	28,000	56,000
	$100,667	$70,083	$129,250	$300,000

Exhibit 7–14. Summary of standby manufacturing overhead costs by product line.

ASSIGNING COMMERCIAL OVERHEAD COSTS
TO PRODUCT LINES

The distribution of commercial overhead costs to product lines involves many of the same factors and techniques encountered in the distribution of manufacturing overhead costs. However, the distribution may be less complex because the commercial overhead costs are usually associated with product lines more easily. In many cases the direct cost centers are concerned exclusively with one product line. As a consequence the three-stage process of distributing overhead costs to product lines is reduced to two stages because direct cost center is equivalent to product line. Very often the common measure of volume in a cost center will be total sales dollars of one, several, or all product lines so that overhead costs may be associated with a product line without any intervening distribution.

| | | Variable Cost Rate Per $100 | |
Department	Standby Cost	Own Product Sales	All Product Sales
Sales expense - Product X	$ 15,000	$3.00	
Sales expense - Product Y	10,000	2.00	
Sales expense - Product Z	15,000	4.00	
General selling expense	15,000		$ .90
Sales promotion	30,000		1.00
Market research	15,000		.60
Field service	10,000		.20
Personnel	20,000		.20
Data processing	15,000		.50
Treasurer	15,000		.10
Controller	20,000		.15
General administration	30,000		.35
	$210,000		$4.00

Exhibit 7–15. Summary of standby costs and variable rates of commercial departments.

To illustrate the assignment of commercial overhead costs to product lines, the planned standby costs and variable cost rates of the commercial departments in a company are assumed to be those shown in Exhibit 7–15. Again, in order to keep the illustration clear and simple, it is assumed that each department is a single product cost center, and that sales dollars are the common measure of volume. The commercial variable overhead rates by product line would be obtained as shown in Exhibit 7–16. The commercial standby costs might be distributed to product lines as shown in Exhibit 7–17.

	Variable Rate Per $100 Sales of Product Line:		
	X	Y	Z
Own department variable rate	$3.00	$2.00	$4.00
General variable rate	4.00	4.00	4.00
Total variable rate	$7.00	$6.00	$8.00

Exhibit 7–16. Summary of commercial variable rates by product line.

Just as in the distribution of manufacturing standby costs, any number of bases may be used to assign commercial standby costs to product lines. The standby cost of an individual cost center or account should be distributed on the basis which is most appropriate. For example, in Exhibit 7–17, certain costs in the Market Research Department are classified as "specific" and distributed directly to product line X.

These are costs incurred for only the one product line, and they are in addition to the costs of the normal program of market research carried on for all product lines. The remaining standby costs of the department are general to all product lines and were

		Standby distributed on basis of:			
Department	Own Department Standby Cost	Specific to Product Line	Long-term Personnel Requirements	Long-term Sales Forecast	Standby Cost After Allocation
Sales - Product X	$ 15,000	$8,000	$6,000	$71,000	$100,000
Sales - Product Y	10,000		5,600	28,400	44,000
Sales - Product Z	15,000		8,400	42,600	66,000
General selling	15,000			(15,000)	
Sales promotion	30,000			(30,000)	
Market research	15,000	(8,000)		(7,000)	
Field service	10,000			(10,000)	
Personnel	20,000		(20,000)		
Data processing	15,000			(15,000)	
Treasurer	15,000			(15,000)	
Controller	20,000			(20,000)	
General Administration	30,000			(30,000)	
	$210,000	$ -o-	$ -o-	$ -o-	$210,000

Exhibit 7–17. Distribution of commercial standby costs to product lines.

allocated, along with other general standby costs, on the basis of the long-term forecast of sales dollars by product line. The objective is to provide a measure of product line profitability by matching long-term fixed costs with the products which should be expected to support these costs in the long run.

ASSIGNING PROGRAMMED COSTS TO PRODUCT LINES

The planned amount of a programmed cost is determined by a management decision and thereafter treated as an appropriation or fixed budget. Programmed costs, like standby costs, are distributed to product lines in lump sum amounts.

Generally each program or project can be readily identified with a specific product line. For example, two of the most frequently occurring programmed costs are research and development and advertising. These expenditures are nearly always specific to a product line. Occasionally, however, a programmed cost will be general to several or all product lines, and the cost must be allocated using procedures similar to those used to allocate standby costs.

CONSTRUCTING A PROFIT PLAN

After planned variable, standby, and programmed overhead costs have been converted from a responsibility basis to a product line basis, they are assembled in the profit plan format by product line. Planned sales and planned direct costs by product line are also included in the profit plan. These items require no conversion, because they are originally planned by product line. Exhibit 7–18 is an example of a profit plan by product line which incorporates the illustrative cost data presented earlier.

The key to the development of the profit plan is the detailed planning or forecasting of sales by product line. Actually two kinds of sales forecasts are involved:

1. *Short-term sales forecast.* This is the forecast for the period covered by the profit plan, usually the coming year. It is used to plan the profit contribution based on expected sales volume and

| | Total | Product Lines | | |
	Company	X	Y	Z
Gross sales	$2,850,000	$1,250,000	$800,000	$800,000
Variable costs				
Specific sales deductions:				
Trade discounts	227,500	187,500	40,000	
Commissions	118,500	62,500	32,000	24,000
Freight out	33,000	25,000	8,000	
Cash discounts allowed	8,000			8,000
Direct materials	768,500	312,500	240,000	216,000
Direct labor	300,000	100,000	80,000	120,000
Manufacturing overhead	297,700	102,500	80,800	114,400
Commercial overhead	199,500	87,500	48,000	64,000
Total variable costs	$1,952,700	$ 877,500	$528,800	$546,400
Profit contribution	$ 897,300	$ 372,500	$271,200	$253,600
Standby and programmed costs:				
Manufacturing - general	300,000	100,667	70,083	129,250
Commercial - general	162,000	77,000	34,000	51,000
Commercial - specific	48,000	23,000	10,000	15,000
Programmed - specific	130,000	50,000	21,000	59,000
	$ 640,000	$ 250,667	$135,083	$254,250
Planned operating earnings before taxes	$ 257,300	$ 121,833	$136,117	$ (650)

Exhibit 7–18.   The profit plan.

mix, standard direct costs, and budgeted variable overhead cost. The forecast must be sufficiently detailed as to mix of products within lines to permit reasonably accurate planning of direct costs and variable overhead costs.

2. *Long-term forecast.* This is a forecast of the expected trend of sales by product line over the next three to five years, after elimination of annual fluctuations. It is often used to allocate some general standby and programmed costs to product lines. The intent is to relate long-term fixed costs to the product lines which are expected to support them in the long run rather than to shuffle the cost around each year in an attempt to match cyclical volume fluctuations.

It should be noted that the short-term sales forecast is used to plan the amounts of variable costs and profit contributions. The long-term forecast, on the other hand, is used merely as a basis for allocating general standby and programmed costs to product

	Product Lines		
	X	Y	Z
Variable costs as a percentage of sales:			
Trade discounts	15.0%	5.0%	
Commissions	5.0	4.0	3.0%
Freight out	2.0	1.0	
Cash discounts allowed			1.0
Direct materials	25.0	30.0	27.0
Direct labor	8.0	10.0	15.0
Manufacturing overhead	8.2	10.1	14.3
Commercial overhead	7.0	6.0	8.0
	70.2%	66.1%	68.3%
Profit contribution percentage	29.8%	33.9%	31.7%
Standby and programmed costs:			
Manufacturing - general	$100,667	$ 70,083	$129,250
Commercial - general	77,000	34,000	51,000
Commercial - specific	23,000	10,000	15,000
Programmed - specific	50,000	21,000	59,000
	$250,667	$135,083	$254,250
Total standby and programmed costs	$250,667	$135,083	$254,250
Divided by profit contribution percentage	29.8%	33.9%	31.7%
Equals	=	=	=
Break-even point	$841,100	$398,475	$802,000

Exhibit 7–19. Summary of variable rates, standby costs, and break-even points by product line.

lines. It is not used to determine the amount of these costs. That determination is made during the detailed budgeting of costs.

The mechanics presented here for the assembling of a profit plan by product line should not be confused with the *profit-planning* function. Profit planning consists of devising and evaluating alternative courses of action with regard to sales, research and operating programs, marketing strategies, product volume and mix, and facilities; and ultimately deciding upon and adopting a specific plan for the coming year. It is essentially an evolutionary process involving many revisions. (See Chapter 9, for more on this.)

To assist in the evaluation phase of the profit-planning function, the profit plan is often re-stated in terms of cost factors, that is, with variable costs and profit contribution expressed as percentages of sales. This is illustrated in Exhibit 7–19. It facilitates the comparison of the financial consequences of alternative plans and the calculation of break-even points.

PROBLEMS IN MECHANICS

In the preceding sections, the illustrations were purposely kept simple so that the basic theory and techniques involved in the construction of a profit plan by product line would not be obscured by complicating factors. In practice, of course, more complex situations are often encountered. The cost groupings which will produce the most accurate product costs may not be the groupings of costs by departments. Even where separate cost control centers exist within departments, product cost centers may not conform to either the departmental or the cost control center organization. The common measure of volume may not be the same in all direct manufacturing departments, which complicates the task of assigning indirect department overhead costs to direct departments. In some cases, indirect manufacturing overhead costs are more easily related to product lines without the intervening distribution to direct cost centers.

These conditions make the mechanical development of a profit plan by product line somewhat more complex, but no more so than normal cost accounting in a similar situation. The problems can be handled quite readily in the memorandum determination of product and product line costs and cost rates. They do not affect the formal accounting records or the day-to-day accounting routines.

Product Cost Centers

A product cost center consists of a group of overhead costs whose variable elements tend to vary with, and can be related to, a particular measure of the volume affecting those costs. The resulting variable overhead rate can be applied selectively to the specific products which represent the volume affecting the group of overhead costs.

The concept of a product cost center was developed under traditional cost accounting to permit greater flexibility and thereby greater accuracy than would otherwise be possible in the assignment of overhead costs to products. The concept does not preclude the use of plant-wide or departmental overhead rates when such rates provide the desired accuracy in product costing. In these cases, an entire plant or one or more departments or cost control centers are considered to be a single product cost center.

The use of memorandum product cost centers in Profitability Accounting ensures that both cost control by responsibility and accurate product costing can be achieved without increasing the routine accounting workload. Costs are recorded in the accounts by responsibility so that they may be used directly for control purposes. No re-classifications or transfers of costs to product cost centers are required in the formal accounting records at any time. The grouping of planned overhead costs by product cost center and the development of product cost rates are accomplished on a memorandum basis in the course of developing the profit plan.

Establishment of a product cost center is essentially a matter of selecting a group of overhead costs which vary with a similar measure of volume and which can be associated with specific products. Product cost centers which differ from cost control centers are usually established when no single common measure of volume can be found which will accurately reflect the incidence of cost for all products within a cost control center.

For example, a machine shop which is a single cost control center may include large machine tools such as planers, milling machines, and boring bars; small machine tools such as drill presses and grinders; and automatic or semi-automatic machines such as gear cutters and screw machines. The common measures of volume typically available in such a department would be machine hours, direct labor dollars, and direct labor hours. However, it might well be found that none of these measures accurately reflect the incidence of overhead costs in the entire department. Consider the simplified data in Exhibit 7–20, which might be obtained from a machine shop such as the one described above.

If an over-all average variable overhead cost per machine hour were used to assign all costs to products, the products manufactured on the small machine tools, and especially on the automatic machines, would be assigned too much cost. The incidence of variable overhead cost per hour of operation of these machines is less than the average cost per machine hour for the entire department. If the average variable overhead cost per direct labor hour or dollar were used, products manufactured on the large and small machine tools would be assigned too much cost.

	Large Machines	Small Machines	Automatic and Semi-automatic Machines	(2) Department Average
Standard direct labor cost per machine hour	(1) $4.000	$2.000	$ .500	$2.167
Standard direct labor cost per direct labor hour	(1) $2.000	$2.000	$2.000	$2.000
Variable Overhead Costs Incurred Per Standard Machine Hour				
Indirect labor	$4.000	$2.000	$1.000	$2.333
Fringe benefits (on direct and indirect labor)	1.200	.600	.225	.675
Power	.500	.300	.500	.433
Total	$5.700	$2.900	$1.725	$3.438
Variable Overhead Costs Incurred Per Standard Direct Labor Dollar				
Indirect labor	$1.000	$1.000	$2.000	$1.333
Fringe benefits (on direct and indirect labor)	.300	.300	.450	.350
Power	.125	.150	1.000	.425
Total	$1.425	$1.450	$3.450	$2.108
Variable Overhead Costs Incurred Per Standard Direct Labor Hour				
Indirect labor	$2.000	$2.000	$4.000	$2.667
Fringe benefits (on direct and indirect labor)	.600	.600	.900	.700
Power	.250	.300	2.000	.850
Total	$2.850	$2.900	$6.900	$4.217

(1) Standard direct labor manning of each large machine is:
One machinist at standard rate of $2.50 per hour.
One helper at standard rate of $1.50 per hour.

(2) Department average is calculated assuming equal volume on each of
the three categories of machines.

Exhibit 7–20. Cost data in a machine shop.

The calculation of a single average variable overhead cost rate
for the entire department, on whatever basis, assumes a given
distribution of volume among the categories of machines. In
computing the department averages in Exhibit 7–20, it was assumed first that the machine hours were distributed equally
among the three categories of machine tools, and subsequently
that direct labor dollars and then direct labor hours were so distributed. As indicated by the three different answers, only one of

these conditions can be true at one time. If any of the three average variable overhead cost rates for the entire department is used to assign costs to products, a significant change from the anticipated distribution of volume by category of machine could result in a significant over- or under-absorption of variable overhead costs in the department.

The solution to this problem is to set up three separate product cost centers within the machine shop department, each with its own variable overhead rate. The volume basis may be machine hours or direct labor hours or dollars, but the overhead rate will include only those costs within the product cost center and will be applied only to the products which go through that cost center. Using machine hours, for example, a product which required four hours on a large planer would be assigned $22.80 in the machine shop variable overhead (4 × $5.700). Another product requiring four hours of machine time on an automatic gear cutter would be assigned $6.90 in machine shop variable overhead (4 × $1.725).

The individual cost center variable overhead rates in Exhibit 7–20 are obtained by analyzing budgeted costs and control factors for the machine shop department. They are incorporated in the profit plan by product line as illustrated in Exhibit 7–21. The planned volume of each product line in each cost center or department is obtained by exploding the forecast of product sales for the period of the plan.

The planned standby costs in the machine shop can be assigned to cost centers by making a separate allocation decision for each standby cost. They can then be assigned to product lines on the basis of the long-term expected usage of cost center facilities by each product line, in the manner illustrated in Exhibits 7–12, 7–13, and 7–14.

The actual accounting process for the machine shop does not recognize the cost center or the standby cost separations. Actual costs are recorded only by account and by departmental responsibility. Total planned costs in an account are affected by several factors—the standby cost plus planned variable costs determined by Control Factor Units. The latter, in turn, reflect the incidence of cost by cost center as well as the volume in the cost center. However, only the total planned cost in an account is compared with total actual cost in that account for control purposes.

Department or Cost Center	Variable Rate	Product Lines					
		X		Y		Z	
		Volume	Amount	Volume	Amount	Volume	Amount
Machine Shop							
Large machines	$5.700/Machine Hour	2,000 M.H.	$11,400	1,000 M.H.	$ 5,700	1,000 M.H.	$ 5,700
Small machines	2.900/Machine Hour	1,000 M.H.	2,900	500 M.H.	1,450	500 M.H.	1,450
Automatic machines	1.725/Machine Hour	1,000 M.H.	1,725	2,000 M.H.	3,450	3,000 M.H.	5,175
Fabricating shop	1.900/Direct Labor Dollar	6,000 D.L.D.	11,400	5,000 D.L.D.	9,500	8,000 D.L.D.	15,200
Assembly	1.600/Direct Labor Dollar	4,000 D.L.D.	6,400	3,000 D.L.D.	4,800	5,000 D.L.D.	8,000
			$33,825		$24,900		$35,525

Exhibit 7–21. Summary of variable manufacturing overhead costs by product line.

Distribution of Indirect Department Overhead Costs

It sometimes happens that not all direct cost centers which utilize the services of an indirect department have the same measure of volume for the absorption of their own variable overhead costs. Or two direct departments with the same measure of volume, such as direct labor hours, may not use the services of the indirect department in the same proportion to their respective volumes. These situations preclude the development of combined variable overhead rates for direct and indirect cost centers in the manner illustrated in Exhibit 7–5. However, the same result can be obtained by a different approach.

The common unit of volume in each direct cost center can be weighted to reflect the proportion of cost in an indirect department to the volume in each of the direct cost centers. Thus, for example, the machine hours in the small machine cost center may be assigned the weight "1" for purposes of absorbing tool room overhead. Because the large machines require about twice as much tool room service per machine hour, that direct cost center is assigned the weight of "2" for tool room overhead. This weighting process is performed separately for each indirect department.

The result of this kind of a process is summarized in Exhibit 7–22 for the three machine shop cost centers which use machine hours as a volume base and for two other direct cost centers with a base of direct labor dollars.

The volume base of the cost center which is assigned a weight of "1" for a particular indirect cost center becomes the equivalent unit for the overhead of that indirect cost center. The tool room cost, for example, is determined to be $.05 per machine hour of the small machine cost center (its equivalent unit). Multiplying this rate by the large machine center's weight of "2" results in a tool room cost of $.10 per machine hour in that direct cost center. The results of this process for the departments shown in Exhibit 7–22 are summarized in Exhibit 7–23, where the indirect department rates per equivalent unit appear in the first column of numbers to the left. The columns to the right are used for compiling the extension of the rate per equivalent unit by the appropriate weight, in order to determine the composite rate for each direct cost center.

Direct Cost Center	Raw Measure of Volume	Weights Applied to Direct Cost Center Units of Volume				
		Tool Room	Production Engineering	Material Handling	Maintenance	General Factory
Machine Shop						
Large machines	Machine hours	2	1	4	1	1
Small machines	Machine hours	1	1	2	1	1
Automatic machines	Machine hours	2	1	2	1	1
Fabricating	Direct labor dollars	0	.5	1	.5	.5
Assembly	Direct labor dollars	0	.5	1	.5	.5

Exhibit 7–22. Bases for distribution of indirect department variable costs.

| | | Own Department | Indirect Department Variable Rates Assigned to Direct Cost Centers | | | | | |
| | | | Tool | Production | Material | Main- | General | Composite |
Department or Cost Center	Basis for Overhead Absorption	Variable Rate	Room	Engineering	Handling	tenance	Factory	Rate
Machine Shop								
Large machines	Own machine hours	$2.10	$.10	$.20	$.32	$.50	$.60	$3.82
Small machines	Own machine hours	1.45	.05	.20	.16	.50	.60	2.96
Automatic machines	Own machine hours	1.35	.10	.20	.16	.50	.60	2.91
Fabricating	Own direct labor $	1.20		.10	.08	.25	.30	1.93
Assembly	Own direct labor $	1.10		.10	.08	.25	.30	1.83
Tool Room	Equivalent units	.05						
Production Engineering	Equivalent units	.20						
Material Handling	Equivalent units	.08						
Maintenance	Equivalent units	.50						
General Factory	Equivalent units	.60						

Exhibit 7–23. Composite variable overhead rates of direct cost centers.

In the example above, the tool room serviced only the machine shop cost centers. Most of the tool room labor and variable overhead was transferred to the machine shop cost centers on a requisition basis and was included in the direct cost centers' own variable overhead rates. It was the unabsorbed portion of tool room labor that was assigned to the direct departments in Exhibit 7–23, and it was assigned in proportion to the tool room services requisitioned.

In the production-engineering department, the variability of overhead cost was found to be related most closely to the total machine hours in the machine shop plus direct labor hours in the other direct departments. Although the addition of such dissimilar items results in a sort of "nonsense" statistic, it may still be useful. The common measure of volume in the fabricating and assembly department, however, was direct labor *dollars,* so a conversion was required. Since the standard labor rate in both departments was $2.00 per hour, the direct labor dollars were assigned a weight of ".5," half of a direct labor hour. The variable rate of the production-engineering department was calculated as $0.20 per equivalent unit. In accordance with the weight factors, a rate of $0.20 per machine hour was assigned to each machine shop cost center, and a rate of $0.10 per direct labor dollar was assigned to the fabricating and assembly departments.

In the material-handling department, overhead costs tended to vary with the purchase cost of materials processed in each direct cost center. The ratio of the cost of materials processed to the volume base in each direct cost was determined. The proportionate relationship of these ratios to each other were used to assign the weights for material-handling overhead to the direct cost centers. The material-handling variable rate, calculated as $0.08 per equivalent unit, was multiplied by the weights to determine the material-handling rate to be assigned to each direct cost center.

The maintenance and general factory variable overhead costs were found to vary with the total of machine hours in the machine shop cost centers plus direct labor hours in the other direct departments. The process of establishing weights and assigning rates to the direct cost centers is identical to that described for the production-engineering department.

The composite variable overhead rates determined for each direct cost center by the process described above are comparable to the composite variable rates developed earlier in this chapter by relating the variable overhead cost of each direct department to its own direct labor and relating all variable overhead costs in all indirect departments to total direct labor. This calculation of the composite variable rates is more complex, but, once the rates are obtained, their use is identical to that in the earlier, more simplified example.

The standby costs in direct and indirect cost centers are not affected by multiple bases of absorption of variable costs. The procedures described earlier already provide for complete flexibility in assigning standby costs to direct cost centers and to product lines.

In some cases it may be desirable to assign indirect department variable overhead costs directly to product lines without an intervening distribution to direct departments. This is appropriate when the services or cost incidence of the indirect cost center is more closely and easily associated with product lines than with direct cost centers. For example, material-handling overhead costs may tend to vary with pounds of material processed. The material-handling variable cost could be charged to products directly on the basis of the weight of the material in the product. In development of the profit plan, the forecast weight of material in each product line would be used to determine the planned variable cost of material handling.

Organizational Complexities

The pattern in which plans are developed and information is gathered and reported should conform to the organizational structure and conditions existing in the particular company. If the company is organized on a functional basis, as in the examples presented earlier in this chapter, information is gathered and reported by responsibility and by product line and summarized for the entire company. If the company is organized in divisions, with each division forming a distinct profit center and containing one or more product lines, it merely means that one more level is added to the planning and reporting pyramid. Information is gathered and reported by responsibility and by product line, summarized by profit center, and then summarized for the total company.

A more complex problem arises when sales responsibility extends across product lines, for example, where sales divisions are established on a regional basis and each sales division has sales responsibility for several or all product lines. In this situation, it is usually desirable to develop plans and gather and report information by responsibility and by product line within each sales division, by sales division in total, by product line in total, and in summary for the entire company. However, all of these arrangements can be obtained by applying one or another of the techniques described earlier in this chapter. The flexibility provided by the application of the building block principle makes it possible to pattern the information system around nearly any organization structure without undue effort.

SUMMARY

In Profitability Accounting, the same planned costs used to control performance by responsibility are converted to product costs and matched with revenues to determine product line profitability. Information by product line is particularly useful in making marketing and other operating decisions and in converting sales forecasts into a formal profit plan. The techniques illustrated here for developing overhead costs by product line are used only once each year, and on a memorandum basis, apart from the formal accounting records and routines.

The variable overhead rates for product-costing purposes may "absorb long-range variable costs" based on the long-range budgets described in Chapter 6, or they may "absorb short-range variable costs" based on short-range budgets or even historical cost behavior.

Manufacturing overhead costs of indirect cost centers are usually distributed to products and product lines by a three-stage process in which standby and variable costs are separately handled:

1. Costs are collected and summarized in the indirect manufacturing cost center.

2. They are incorporated in direct cost center variable rates and standby amounts.
3. The composite variable cost rates of the direct cost centers are applied to products on the basis of volume, and standby costs are allocated to product lines in lump sum amounts.

Distribution of commercial overhead costs to product lines can usually be made directly. The commercial variable costs so distributed are used to determine profit contribution, but they do not become a part of the variable cost of products in inventory. Lump sum amounts of programmed costs can be identified with a specific product line in most cases. Otherwise they are distributed to product lines, using procedures similar to those used to allocate standby costs.

Chapter 8

Return on Capital Employed and Capital Budgeting

THE RATE of return on capital has long been familiar to financial executives and investors as a measure of investment performance. A similar measure is used by managers to evaluate profit performance and to aid in decision making.

From the point of view of the manager, the rate of return on capital is one of the most important measures of profitability. As the agent of the investor, the manager is entrusted with capital for the purpose of earning a return on it. The ratio of the amount of the annual return to the amount of capital is the rate of return on capital. It is a measure of the profitability of the enterprise, and it is the measure of the effectiveness with which capital is being utilized, because the supply of capital is limited and investors have alternative investment opportunities.

The concept of return on investment is used for at least three general purposes:

1. Evaluating over-all company results
2. Evaluating results for segments of the business, such as profit centers or divisions, product lines, and market outlets
3. Measuring the anticipated return from proposed projects which require capital expenditures

The early part of this chapter is devoted to a discussion of the first two uses of rate of return. The latter part deals with the third use, evaluating the desirability of proposed capital investments.

RETURN ON CAPITAL EMPLOYED

First, let us define some of the terms we will be using. *Return on investment* is another way of saying "rate on capital," and capital must be considered under two fundamentally different concepts:

1. *Capital invested* relates to the equity capital which the shareholders have invested in the business and is particularly useful for financial management.
2. *Capital employed* relates to the money tied up in all the assets of the business.

It is the return on capital employed which is of principal interest to the operating manager. He is concerned with the effective utilization of all funds. For him, it is much more useful to look at the left side of the balance sheet, the asset side, rather than the capital side. It is much easier for managers to visualize resources in terms of the assets represented than in terms of the source of funds.

In the remainder of this chapter, capital will be used to mean total assets and the term *return on capital* will be used to describe the rate of return based on assets. When a different basis is intended, a specific description will be used.

There are several different methods of determining rate of return on capital, reflecting different kinds of performance measurement. Within a single enterprise, the rate of return on capital may be developed in several different ways, depending upon the purpose of the measurement. Rate of return for a division or a product line may be developed differently from the rate of return for the total company. The rate used for measurement internally may be on a different basis than the rate used for comparisons with other companies.

Assets To Be Included in the Investment Base

Although the investment base on which rate of return is calculated will include all assets, there are circumstances in which the rate of return calculation is better served by excluding or offsetting certain assets. The major purpose of such a calculation in most companies is to measure the performance of managers and to assist them in making decisions. Thus it is important to include those assets over which a manager has control and exclude those not controlled by him. It is also important to ensure consistency between the investment base used for planning performance and that used for measuring actual performance.

In many companies, the assets controlled at the corporate level are not allocated to divisions or product lines. Frequently, allocations would be quite arbitrary and would not make the rate of return measure any more useful at the divisional level. When the objective is to compare divisional performance with that of an outside competitor, however, the division's "capital" should include all that would be required to operate as an independent company.

Rate of return comparisons with outside companies, industry statistics, or general business statistics usually call for specific adjustment for any known differences in the asset bases in order to develop a rate of return which will give a meaningful comparison. The unadjusted balance sheets do not provide the proper basis for comparison between one company with extensive long-term leased facilities and another that completely owns all its facilities. Or one company may have a sizeable investment in a field in which the other company is not active.

When the objective is to compare the rate of return of a product line, division, or company against an alternative use of funds, the appropriate measure is usually the absolute rate of return on capital. This can seldom be obtained from the financial records, because it requires a determination not only as to whether, but at what values, assets should be included in the investment base.

Valuation of Assets

The use of assets as an investment base necessitates policies and decisions on asset valuation. Should assets be valued at cost, cost less depreciation, or replacement value? Should allowances and provisions be deducted from receivables and inventories? Again, the solution depends in part on the purpose for which the return on capital is being measured, but the same treatment may be used throughout the company for comparable purposes.

Generally, net book values must be used for measuring return as between companies, owing to inability to convert cost values of outside companies to any other basis. For internal purposes, where trends and greater accuracy are needed, it may be desirable to adjust the carrying basis of some of the assets.

Inventories are generally not adjusted from the book basis except where the "LIFO" method is used. The difference between the recorded value of the LIFO base inventory and the current value is usually available, or can be determined, as a part of the normal accounting procedure.

Property, plant, and equipment can be valued on any one of several different bases for measuring return on capital. The bases often suggested are historical cost, depreciated cost, replacement value, and historical cost adjusted to current dollars. Since internal planning is a main point of our theme, perhaps it might be well to point out that the appropriate value for any decision in this area is the current market value of the asset. Decisions for the future invariably involve the alternate use of funds. The amount which could be released for an alternative use is the market value of, or opportunity cost associated with, the asset. It is not original cost, net book value, or even replacement value.

Unfortunately, market values for many fixed assets either are not available or are extremely difficult to obtain. The problem can be overcome, however, by constructing a synthetic market value. The synthetic value is obtained by applying a price index to the original cost to convert it into dollars and then applying a realistic depreciation rate to the current dollars to arrive at a current value.

Objective and appropriate price indexes are available from several sources. The American Appraisal Company publishes price indexes for construction costs. E. H. Boeckh and Associates, Consulting Evaluation Engineers, likewise publish construction indexes. *The Monthly Labor Review*, published by the U.S. Department of Labor, Bureau of Labor Statistics, contains price indexes for a wide variety of commodity groups and sub-groups. Two other sources, though they do not provide the most recent statistics, cover a greater time span. These are the *Statistical Abstract of the United States*, published annually by the U.S. Department of Commerce, Bureau of Census, and *Business Statistics: A Supplement to the Survey of Current Business*, published by the U.S. Department of Commerce, Office of Business Economics.

Realistic depreciation rates for specific assets are necessarily less objective than price indexes, but they are seldom very difficult to obtain. Usually it means substituting the judgement of the plant engineer for that of the accountant or tax specialist. A qualified plant engineer can make sufficiently reliable estimates of the rate of technological change and the useful life of the asset in its particular application to set a realistic rate for depreciation.

The calculation of synthetic market values for assets, using price indexes and realistic depreciation rates, is illustrated in Exhibit 8–1. Once calculated, the synthetic market values are easily updated each year by applying a factor for the annual change in the price index and re-calculating the realistic depreciation.

Assigning Assets to Segments of the Company

Use of the asset side of the balance sheet for defining investment creates the problem of how to allocate assets to operating units. Allocation may be made

Type of asset	Metal-working machinery and equipment
Date of acquisition	June, 1953
Cost of acquisition	$100,000
Depreciation rate	15-year life, sum-of-the-years digits method
Accumulated depreciation to January 1, 1962	$79,580
Net book value January 1, 1962	$20,420
Price index - January, 1962 A	185.2*
Price index - June, 1953 B	131.1*
Multiplier (A÷B)	1.414
Acquisition value in current dollars	$141,400
Realistic depreciation rate - annual	6-2/3%
Realistic depreciation accumulated to January 1, 1962 (8-1/2 years)	$80,109
Current value in current dollars	$61,291

*Source: Monthly Labor Review, United States Department of Labor, Bureau of Labor Statistics, Table D-3, Index of Wholesale Prices by Group and Sub-group of Commodities, Metal working machinery and equipment.   1947-49=100.

Exhibit 8–1. Constructing a synthetic market value.

1. By profit-responsible divisions or centers
2. By markets or distribution centers
3. By product and product lines
4. By plants

Normally these will be the same segments of the business for which profits are measured, as was discussed in Chapter 7. Measuring performance by rate of return pre-supposes some control over revenues, costs, and resources. The technique is seldom applied below the level of division, plant, or product, because such control does not exist at the lower levels.

Decentralized divisions often maintain complete sets of records, including all assets except central office facilities and corporate cash balances. In other cases, property, plant and equipment, and inventories are specific to a plant, product, or division and can be coded directly in the accounting records. However, when these or other assets are shared by more than one segment, or are not segregated in the accounts, some allocation must be made. The appropriate basis for the allocation will depend upon the peculiar circumstances. Possible bases can only be suggested here.

In many companies the allocation of general corporate assets to divisions, product lines, or other segments would necessarily be on an arbitrary basis, as mentioned earlier. For most purposes it is better not to make this kind of an allocation. Without it, the rate of return will be just as useful and much more sensitive in measuring those factors which constitute managerial performance. If an absolute measure of rate of return is required, some allocation of these items to segments is essential, just as general standby costs must be allocated. Rate of return can be calculated on one bais regularly as a measure of management performance, taking into account only the costs and resources over which the manager has control. It may be calculated at longer intervals on another basis, using total costs and total resources, to be used for over-all planning purposes.

Property, plant, and equipment involved in production can usually be allocated fairly on the basis of usage in terms of hours, area occupied, or a similar statistic. The assets of service departments such as material handling and maintenance departments can also be allocated on the basis of some measure of usage of the services. Very often the basis used to allocate costs to segments or the amount of cost assigned to a segment will also serve as the basis for allocating service department assets.

When accounts receivable are not segregated in the records, they can be allocated on the basis of sales weighted for differences in the payment terms granted.

Finished inventories are usually specific to divisions, products, and plants. If an allocation is necessary, it can be based on the forecast demand in succeeding periods. A similar basis can be used to allocate work in process and raw materials inventories.

Cash may be assigned to a division or other segment in an amount related to the out-of-pocket costs and expenses forecast for the succeeding period. Usually any excess or shortage between the actual cash balance and the amount allocated is treated as part of the corporate investment and not allocated further. When the only objective is to measure performance against planned performance, the best approach is to treat cash as a general corporate asset and not allocate it at all.

In some companies, set policies govern working capital requirements, and managers of segments are not expected to concern themselves with the levels of current assets and current liabilities. Rather than allocate cash, receivables, and inventories, an amount of working capital can be assigned to a segment which approximates the amount that would be required if the segment were an independent company.

It should be mentioned that the asset balances as of the end of a period may not be representative of the assets employed during the period, in which event some sort of average balance should be used.

Measuring Earnings

As we have seen, return on capital is an appropriate measure of performance only at levels where some control over earnings and resources is exercised, which will normally be at the company, division, plant, or product level. It should be viewed as one of several measures which can help in comparing actual performance with planned and in comparing varying profit centers with each other.

In Profitability Accounting, specific and general standby and programmed expenses as well as specific variances are deducted from profit contribution to arrive at the earnings of a division, product line, or plant. While general standby and programmed expenses are allocated, and are not necessarily controlled by the manager whose performance is being measured, the allocation is always of a standard predetermined amount. The reported earnings of a segment of the company, such as a division, can be used directly in the rate of return calculation for a measure of performance against plan. The reported earnings can also be used to determine an absolute rate of return on capital for the segment, subject to possible adjustments to reflect current, realistic depreciation, and to eliminate interest on debt, where this may be considered as a return to suppliers of capital in the same sense as dividends.

Rate of Return in Management Reports

A typical format for reporting return on capital in an abbreviated form on the financial statements is illustrated in Exhibits 2–6, 10–5, and 10–7. Generally, the manager responsible will want more detailed information for purposes of analysis. Exhibit 8–2 contains all of the planned and actual data that would normally be developed for a division or a company. This type of a report would normally go only to the manager responsible. Exhibit 8–3 is a format for summarizing on one page the rate of return for all divisions in comparison with plan.

Note the classification "Corporate Pool" near the bottom of Exhibit 8–3. This is the category which will include all assets and earnings not allocated to the separate divisions, plants, or product lines. It may include excess facilities, or, on the other hand, these may be treated as a separate classification.

Note also that rate of return on capital and capital turnover are always expressed as annual rates, even when they apply to only one month. Thus, in Exhibit 8–2 the actual rate of return for May is 29.6% on an annual basis. Actual earnings of $178,000 divided by total assets of $7,090,000 result in a monthly rate of approximately 2.5%, which, multiplied by 12, is approximately 29.6%. An annual rate is used because managers are used to dealing with rates of return and turnovers on the basis of an annual rate. A monthly capital turnover of .25, for example, while equivalent to an annual rate of 3.0, will not be meaningful to a manager until he mentally makes the conversion.

Using the Rate of Return on Capital Measurement

The rate of return on capital could be simply computed by dividing income by capital. However, in order to clearly understand all of the forces at work, it is better to break the formula into its two components, a rate of return on sales and a capital turnover ratio, as follows:

$$\text{Return on Capital} = \frac{\text{Earnings}}{\text{Capital}} = \frac{\text{Earnings}}{\text{Sales}} \times \frac{\text{Sales}}{\text{Capital}}$$

By examining the formula in these components, it is possible to show that the factor accounting for the difference between return on sales and return on capital is the rate of capital turn-

1960	NOTES AND A/C REC FCST	NOTES AND A/C REC ACT	AVG MONTHLY INVENTORY FCST	INVENTORY ACT	OTHER ASSETS FCST	OTHER ASSETS ACT	PROP PLT AND EQPT FCST	PROP PLT AND EQPT ACT	TOTAL ASSETS FCST	TOTAL ASSETS ACT	GROSS SHIPMENTS FCST	GROSS SHIPMENTS ACT	STANDARD EARNINGS BEFORE TAXES FCST	STD EARN ACT	RETURN ON GROSS SHIPMENTS % FCST	RET GROSS % ACT	ANNUALIZED CAPITAL TURNOVER FCST	CAP TURN ACT	RETURN ON CAPITAL % FCST	RET CAP % ACT
JAN	1878	2249	2025	2175	618	778	960		5481	6162	1372	1276	60	36	4.4	2.8	3.0	2.5	13.2	7.0
FEB	1974	2280	2121	2207	556	822	960		5611	6269	1749	1728	59	54	3.4	3.1	3.7	3.3	12.6	10.2
MAR	2222	2484	2129	2300	560	740	960		5851	6484	1707	1550	129	155	7.6	10.0	3.5	2.9	26.6	29.0
APR	2416	2767	2082	2355	595	778	960		6053	6860	1714	1790	131	123	7.6	6.9	3.4	3.1	25.8	21.4
MAY	2678	3052	2027	2024	678	1,054	960		6343	7090	2101	2286	172	178	8.2	7.8	4.0	3.8	32.8	29.6
JUNE	2729		2168		720		960		6577		1469		80		5.4		2.7		14.6	
JULY	2675		2462		686		960		6783		1925		184		9.6		3.4		32.6	
AUG	2819		2585		610		960		6974		2459		235		9.6		4.2		40.3	
SEPT	3207		2445		621		960		7233		2089		203		9.7		3.4		33.0	
OCT	3217		2226		746		960		7149		1864		100		5.4		3.1		16.7	
NOV	2855		2031		820		960		6666		1532		102		6.7		2.8		18.8	
DEC	2428		1937		744		960		6069		1395		60		4.3		2.8		12.0	
YEAR TO DATE	2233	2566	2077	2212	597	834	960		5867	6752	8643	8629	551	546	6.4	6.3	3.5	3.2	22.4	20.2
ORIGINAL FORECAST	2592		2186		660		960		6398		21376		1515		7.1		3.3		23.4	
3-MONTH MOVING AVERAGE	2768		2226		857		960		6811		1875		152		8.1		3.3		26.7	

Exhibit 8–2. Statement of return on capital.

(MONTHLY OR YEAR TO DATE)   (IN THOUSANDS OF DOLLARS)

DIVISIONS	AVERAGE TOTAL ASSETS		GROSS SHIPMENTS		STANDARD EARNINGS BEFORE TAX		RETURN ON GROSS SHIPMENTS %		ANNUALIZED			
									CAPITAL TURNOVER		RETURN ON CAPITAL %	
	FCST	ACT	FCST	ACT	FCST	ACT	FCST	ACT	FCST	ACT	FCST	ACT
CORPORATE POOL												
CONSOLIDATED												
CONSOLIDATED AFTER VARIANCES OF $												
CONSOLIDATED INCLUDING EXCESS FACILITIES												

Exhibit 8–3. Summary statement of return on capital.

over. It is clear that, while return on sales is an important factor in profitability, it is only half the story. Capital turnover is just as important. In the examples in Exhibit 8–4, a 10% profit margin for Company A with a capital turnover rate of .5 will produce a return on capital of 5%. However, a 10% profit margin for Company C with a capital turnover rate of 2.0 will produce a return on capital of 20%.

	Company A	Company B	Company C
Sales	200,000	100,000	100,000
Income	20,000	10,000	10,000
Capital	400,000	100,000	50,000
Income as a % of sales	10%	10%	10%
Turnover	.5	1.0	2.0
Return on capital	5%	10%	20%

Exhibit 8–4. Varying returns on capital for a constant return on sales.

It can be seen that return on capital can be improved in three different ways, as follows:

1. By increasing sales revenue
2. By reducing costs
3. By reducing capital requirements

Looking at profitability in these terms enables managers to focus on the three separate factors of volume, cost, and capital. Just as the supermarket meets its profit objective with a low profit margin and a high rate of capital turnover, and the drugstore with a high margin and a low turnover, each company or division manager can tailor his action to fit his peculiar circumstances. He can

1. Measure the gaps between his performance and his objective by comparing his own ratios to industry statistics
2. Define the problems which cause the gaps
3. Develop corrective programs
4. Set forth the expected results in terms of the effects upon earnings and assets
5. Follow up to see that the results are achieved

If the problem is low volume, it may be necessary to re-design the product to make it competitive in performance and selling features, increase either the amount or the effectiveness of advertising and promotion, or make improvements in workmanship or punctuality in meeting scheduled delivery dates. If the problem is high cost, the solution may lie in re-designing the product to cut labor or material costs, in eliminating short runs and multiple set-ups, or in tightening labor standards and improving methods. If the problem is excess capital requirements, it may be the result of excessive inventories, over-extended credit terms, or excess manufacturing capacity. A manager can build into his plan the anticipated effects of the programs he undertakes and then measure his progress as he goes along.

EVALUATING PROPOSED CAPITAL EXPENDITURES

Making capital expenditure decisions is an essential function in long-range planning for profit. Moreover, it ranks as one of the most important of all management activities, for the very success of the company may be at stake, and long-range decisions, once made, can be changed only at great expense in terms of time and money.

The capital-budgeting process as a whole takes four elements into account. It considers

1. The manner in which the company is organized to perform the capital-budgeting functions
2. The analysis of investment proposals
3. The selection of projects to be undertaken
4. Follow-up and evaluation of results

Organization for Capital Budgeting

The manner in which capital spending is administered depends on the size of the company, the industry in which it is operating, and the peculiarities of its internal organization. Large companies may require an elaborate organization to determine where and how much to invest. In a small company, the task may be handled by one man, perhaps the top operating officer. Decentralized companies may delegate some responsibility for capital spending to division managers. In some industries such as oil and steel, a high investment rate is common; in others, capital spending may be quite limited.

The mechanism which a company may set up for capital budgeting depends on all these factors. No single system will work for all companies. But, regardless of how capital spending is administered, the same basic information and analysis are required in every case to make a sound investment decision.

One facet of administration which is commonly overlooked, especially in some of the smaller companies, is the coordination of capital-spending decisions with the long-range objectives of the company. Concentrated capital expenditures which do not reflect long-range objectives may seriously impair opportunities for growth.

Coordination of capital expenditures can be achieved by a specially organized planning group or by a committee of top management. One prerequisite, of course, is a generally agreed upon statement of the long-range objectives of the company. Against this can be ranged the current year's capital-spending proposals, as well as the capital expenditures of other years, and a summary of the investment remaining in the various areas of the business.

The ingredient which is most important to the success of a capital-spending program, however, is one which cannot be established by edict—a constant flow of good ideas for promising new projects. Ideas can and should come from all levels in every part of the organization, and promotion of the flow of ideas should be the objective of every manager. However, many of the nation's leading corporations no longer leave the matter to chance. They set up an organized planning group close to top management, responsible for innovations in marketing, product development, distribution, and other vital functions.

The Present Value Concept

The basis for modern capital budgeting is the present value concept, and progressive businessmen have long recognized it either explicitly or implicitly. This concept can be simply stated:

A dollar received today is worth more than a dollar to be received at a future date, because of the earnings that dollar can generate in the interim. Conversely, a sum of money to be paid today is a greater burden than the same sum to be paid at a future date, because of the earnings which must be foregone in the interim.

The present value concept is of special importance in capital spending, because of the relatively long period between the investment of the funds and the realization of the return. The effect of the timing of cash flows is so significant that failure to take it into account in evaluating a project's profitability can easily lead to a wrong decision.

ANALYSIS OF THE PROJECT

Management must conduct a searching analysis of every spending proposal to determine

1. The investment required
2. The economic life of the project
3. The earnings of the project
4. The risk involved

These estimates require engineering, marketing, and financial analysis as well as a high degree of management judgement. The project's characteristics ultimately determine its profitability, and it is in the assessment of these that management judgement plays its most vital role. The more penetrating the analysis at this point, the better will be the final decision, and the more explicit the data that can be brought to bear, the better will be the judgement.

Investment Required

The investment can generally be considered as the net cash outlay needed to realize the benefits of a project. Cash outlay is computed without regard to the accounting treatment of funds spent. Uncapitalized expenses and net increases in working capital are cash outlays, as are funds spent for land and depreciable assets. If the project will free funds now invested in assets, the return of these funds is properly treated as a reduction of the investment required.

Sometimes the net cash outlay does not adequately reflect the necessary investment. For example, if the project will utilize plant space now vacant, no cash outlay is required for buildings. However, if this space is used, it will not be available for other projects or for meeting the requirements of normal growth in a year or two.

If the space can profitably be utilized for something else, the *opportunity cost* of this space should be added to the investment needed. This cost is the outlay required to provide equivalent plant space when the currently vacant area is utilized for the later project. This is only one of several types of non-cash outlay which may properly be added to the investment. Considerable ingenuity must be exercised here in order to obtain an accurate measure of profitability.

A determination must also be made of when the funds are to be invested in whatever project is considered. All outlays, in cash or opportunity cost, as well as all returns of investment in terms of funds released by the project, should be arranged on a time schedule so that they may be related to a base point in time. The time value of money is sometimes as important a consideration in the investment as it is in the earnings of the project.

Life and Earnings of the Project

The *economic life* of a project is the period during which it produces earnings, and determination of earnings rests mainly on estimates of economic life. The economic life need not, and probably will not, be equal to the physical life of the assets, and an estimate of economic life is always subject to error because of the unpredictable factors involved. However, engineering, marketing, and financial analysis, dealing with both factors simultaneously, can provide a good estimate of earnings and the timing of them.

The earnings of a project may take one or both of these forms:

1. Savings due to a reduction in operating costs
2. Additional profits due to increased sales

Both types of earnings have the same effect, namely, an increase in net profit. The applicable earnings of a project are the after-tax savings that result. Since it is the net cash flow which is of interest, depreciation is not an expense. However, since depreciation is deductible for income tax purposes, its effect as a tax shield must be taken into account when determining net cash flows. Interest on any borrowings for the project is not considered an expense, because the method of financing is a separate decision based on desired capital structure, internal sources of funds, the condition of the money market, etc.

It is always the future income and expense of a project that management must consider. In most decision-making situations, however, there is an alternative to the project. Where a choice exists, the most useful measure of the project's earnings may be the difference between the cash flows of the alternatives.

Risk

Risk can be defined as the possibility that the benefits of the project will not be realized, and it can result from a variety of factors. Sales may fall short of their projected level, unanticipated technological changes may shorten economic life, or forecast savings may not be realized because of unforeseen expenses.

Another type of risk is inherent in the project itself. This can be illustrated by comparing investment in a project involving special purpose equipment and relatively high fixed costs with investment in a project involving general purpose equipment and relatively low fixed costs. An error in the utilization forecast in the former instance will have a much greater effect on the project's profitability than will an error of the same magnitude in the latter.

Several methods of considering risk have been proposed. One is to establish a risk factor for each proposal, ranging from 1.0 for no risk to .1 for a very high risk, and to multiply the return for each project by its risk factor to arrive at equivalent "riskless" returns.[1] However, the shortcomings of this approach are evident. By lumping all elements of risk together, the manager is unlikely to apply the risk factors to all proposals in a reasonably consistent manner.

Another approach suggested for measuring risk is to use the payback period as a secondary factor alongside of the return of the project.[2] This method also has limitations. It measures only

[1] Robert H. Baldwin, "How To Assess Investment Proposals," *Harvard Business Review*, May–June 1959.
[2] *Ibid.*

one element of risk, the period when the investment is at stake. It does not take into account the time pattern of risk, the inherent risk of the project, or the reliability of the earnings and investment estimates. For some proposals (for example, the introduction of a new product), management might find the payback period completely misleading as far as any evaluation of risk is concerned. Although the payback period may be only two years, which indicates no appreciable risk, all the risk may come in the first year, when the product is either accepted or rejected in the market. On the other hand, an improved production process may have a relatively long payout, say, four or five years, with no appreciable risk of obsolescence of either the product or the process until well after the payback period.

Sometimes managers use another approach to measure risk. They vary the critical estimates of a project's characteristics within the range of reasonable probability to arrive at an array of possible returns. This method only provides proof that risk is present and indicates the range of possible returns from the project. Only if all the possible returns are higher than the lowest acceptable return does the manager know it is a desirable investment opportunity. Even then he does not know which return properly evaluates the risk and whether investment in the project is better or worse than alternative uses of funds.

The best hope for a comprehensive appraisal of risk which could be applied to a majority of investment situations appears to lie in the area of probability statistics and expected values. These concepts and some practical applications of them are described by Robert O. Schlaifer.[3]

SELECTION PROCEDURES

Managers are often reluctant to employ the more sophisticated techniques for evaluating return on capital investments, because of their seeming complexity. Actually, only an understanding of arithmetic and the basic concept of compound interest is necessary. A word of caution is in order, however, because managements' mechanistic use of these techniques without a basic

[3] Robert O. Schlaifer, *Probabilities and Statistics for Business Decisions* (New York: McGraw-Hill Book Co., Inc., 1959).

understanding of them and their limitations could lead to serious mistakes.

Payback Method

The payback method does not give a rate of return figure for the investment opportunity. Rather, it reveals how many years it will take for a project to earn enough to return the original outlay.

Suppose a company has an opportunity to purchase certain automatic welding equipment which will save labor costs of $.13 per unit in the manufacture of a product. The cost of the equipment is $50,000 today and $50,000 to be spent on installation over a one-year period. The equipment has an economic life of ten years, and it will be depreciated by the straight-line method over the ten-year period. The estimated earnings of the investment are calculated in Exhibit 8–5.

Several variations of the payback method are possible. For example, average earnings could be used:

$$\frac{\text{Net Investment}}{\text{Average Earnings}} = \frac{\$100,000}{\$13,950} = 7.17 \text{ years}$$

More likely, if management had taken the time to develop the figures in Exhibit 8–5, the actual savings after taxes would be

Year		Forecast production in thousands of units	Annual savings	Depreciation	Taxable savings	Income taxes at 52%	Savings after tax
At	0						
0 to	1						
1 to	2	120	$15,600	$10,000	$ 5,600	$ 2,900	$ 2,700
2 to	3	160	20,800	10,000	10,800	5,600	5,200
3 to	4	200	26,000	10,000	16,000	8,300	7,700
4 to	5	240	31,200	10,000	21,200	11,000	10,200
5 to	6	280	36,400	10,000	26,400	13,700	12,700
6 to	7	320	41,600	10,000	31,600	16,400	15,200
7 to	8	360	46,800	10,000	36,800	19,100	17,700
8 to	9	400	52,000	10,000	42,000	21,800	20,200
9 to	10	440	57,200	10,000	47,200	24,500	22,700 ←
10 to	11	480	62,400	10,000	52,400	27,200	25,200

Payback in 8.4 years from completion of installation

Exhibit 8–5. Analysis of investment opportunity payback method.

cumulated to find the year in which they aggregated $100,000. In this case the payback would be about 8.4 years from the time the installation was completed.

The several other variations of the payback method need not be discussed here. All are unsatisfactory as an ultimate means of evaluating proposed capital expenditures, because (1) they ignore the time value of money and (2) they ignore any earnings after the investment has been recovered. The payback method, subject to these limitations, may be useful in evaluating risk in particular situations. Management may also use it as a simple screening device to eliminate unprofitable projects from further consideration.

Average Investment Method

The average investment method relates average earnings to average investment over the life of the project. It does not properly reflect total earnings of the project or the time at which these earnings are realized. With the same example as was used earlier, the formula and solution would be

$$\frac{\text{Average Annual Earnings After Depreciation and Taxes}}{\text{Average Book Investment}} = \frac{\$13,950}{\$100,000 \div 2} = 27.9\%$$

There are several possible variations of this method, but they all fail to take account of the time value of money. Hence they are unacceptable as sound criteria for evaluating the profitability of a project.

Interest Tables

Before considering the more advanced techniques for evaluating capital-spending proposals, it is worthwhile to discuss the interest tables used to compound and discount earnings and investment. Any compound interest tables can be utilized which provide the necessary range and coverage. They will be accurate enough for most practical purposes.

However, J. C. Gregory, assistant treasurer of the Atlantic Refining Company, has developed a set of tables particularly useful in capital budgeting.[4] Exhibit 8–6 is an abbreviated illustration.

[4] J. C. Gregory, *Interest Tables for Determining Rate of Return,* private paper, The Atlantic Refining Company.

COMPOUNDING PERFORMANCE BEFORE
REFERENCE POINT WHICH OCCURS:

A. IN AN INSTANT

	5%	10%	15%	20%	25%	30%	35%	40%	45%	50
1 MONTH BEFORE	1.0042	1.0084	1.0126	1.0168	1.0211	1.0253	1.0296	1.0339	1.0382	1.04
2 MONTHS "	1.0084	1.0168	1.0253	1.0339	1.0425	1.0513	1.0601	1.0689	1.0779	1.08
3 " "	1.0126	1.0253	1.0382	1.0513	1.0645	1.0779	1.0914	1.1052	1.1191	1.13
6 " "	1.0253	1.0513	1.0779	1.1052	1.1331	1.1618	1.1912	1.2214	1.2523	1.28
9 " "	1.0382	1.0779	1.1191	1.1618	1.2062	1.2523	1.3002	1.3499	1.4014	1.45
12 " "	1.0513	1.1052	1.1618	1.2214	1.2840	1.3499	1.4191	1.4918	1.5683	1.64
1½ YEARS BEFORE	1.0779	1.1618	1.2523	1.3499	1.4550	1.5683	1.6905	1.8221	1.9640	2.11
2 " "	1.1052	1.2214	1.3499	1.4918	1.6487	1.8221	2.0138	2.2255	2.4596	2.71
2½ " "	1.1331	1.2840	1.4550	1.6487	1.8682	2.1170	2.3989	2.7183	3.0802	3.49
3 " "	1.1618	1.3499	1.5683	1.8221	2.1170	2.4596	2.8577	3.3201	3.8574	4.48

B. UNIFORMLY UNTIL REFERENCE POINT

	5%	10%	15%	20%	25%	30%	35%	40%	45%	50
FROM 3 MONTHS BEFORE TO 0	1.0063	1.0126	1.0190	1.0254	1.0319	1.0385	1.0451	1.0517	1.0584	1.06
" 6 " " " 0	1.0126	1.0254	1.0385	1.0517	1.0652	1.0789	1.0928	1.1070	1.1214	1.13
" 9 " " " 0	1.0190	1.0385	1.0584	1.0789	1.0999	1.1214	1.1435	1.1662	1.1895	1.21
" 12 " " " 0	1.0254	1.0517	1.0789	1.1070	1.1361	1.1662	1.1973	1.2296	1.2629	1.29
FROM 2 YEARS BEFORE TO 0	1.0517	1.1070	1.1662	1.2296	1.2974	1.3702	1.4482	1.5319	1.6218	1.71
" 3 " " " 0	1.0789	1.1662	1.2629	1.3702	1.4893	1.6218	1.7692	1.9334	2.1166	2.32

DISCOUNTING PERFORMANCE AFTER
REFERENCE POINT WHICH OCCURS:

C. IN AN INSTANT

	5%	10%	15%	20%	25%	30%	35%	40%	45%	50
1 YEAR LATER	.9512	.9048	.8607	.8187	.7788	.7408	.7047	.6703	.6376	.60
2 YEARS "	.9048	.8187	.7408	.6703	.6065	.5488	.4966	.4493	.4066	.36
3 " "	.8607	.7408	.6376	.5488	.4724	.4066	.3499	.3012	.2592	.22
4 " "	.8187	.6703	.5488	.4493	.3679	.3012	.2466	.2019	.1653	.13
5 " "	.7788	.6065	.4724	.3679	.2865	.2231	.1738	.1353	.1054	.08
10 " "	.6065	.3679	.2231	.1353	.0821	.0498	.0302	.0183	.0111	.00
15 " "	.4724	.2231	.1054	.0498	.0235	.0111	.0052	.0025	.0012	.00
20 " "	.3679	.1353	.0498	.0183	.0067	.0025	.0009	.0003	.0001	
25 " "	.2865	.0821	.0235	.0067	.0019	.0006	.0002	-	-	
30 " "	.2231	.0498	.0111	.0025	.0006	.0001	-	-	-	
35 " "	.1738	.0302	.0052	.0009	.0002	-	-	-	-	
40 " "	.1353	.0183	.0025	.0003	-	-	-	-	-	
45 " "	.1054	.0111	.0012	.0001	-	-	-	-	-	
50 " "	.0821	.0067	.0006	.0000	-	-	-	-	-	

D. UNIFORMLY OVER INDIVIDUAL YEARS

	5%	10%	15%	20%	25%	30%	35%	40%	45%	50
FROM 0 TO 1 YEAR	.9754	.9516	.9286	.9063	.8848	.8640	.8438	.8242	.8053	.78
" 1 " 2 YEARS	.9278	.8611	.7993	.7421	.6891	.6400	.5946	.5525	.5135	.47
" 2 " 3 "	.8826	.7791	.6879	.6075	.5367	.4741	.4190	.3703	.3274	.28
" 3 " 4 "	.8395	.7050	.5921	.4974	.4179	.3513	.2953	.2482	.2088	.17
" 4 " 5 "	.7986	.6379	.5096	.4072	.3255	.2602	.2081	.1664	.1331	.10
" 5 " 6 "	.7596	.5772	.4386	.3334	.2535	.1928	.1466	.1115	.0849	.06
" 6 " 7 "	.7226	.5223	.3775	.2730	.1974	.1428	.1033	.0748	.0541	.03
" 7 " 8 "	.6874	.4726	.3250	.2235	.1538	.1058	.0728	.0501	.0345	.02
" 8 " 9 "	.6538	.4276	.2797	.1830	.1197	.0784	.0513	.0336	.0220	.01
" 9 " 10 "	.6219	.3869	.2407	.1498	.0933	.0581	.0362	.0225	.0140	.00
" 10 " 11 "	.5916	.3501	.2072	.1227	.0726	.0430	.0255	.0151	.0089	.00
" 11 " 12 "	.5628	.3168	.1783	.1004	.0566	.0319	.0180	.0101	.0057	.00
" 12 " 13 "	.5353	.2866	.1535	.0822	.0441	.0236	.0127	.0068	.0036	.00
" 13 " 14 "	.5092	.2593	.1321	.0673	.0343	.0175	.0089	.0045	.0023	.00
" 14 " 15 "	.4844	.2347	.1137	.0551	.0267	.0130	.0063	.0030	.0015	.00

E. UNIFORMLY OVER 5 YEAR PERIODS

	5%	10%	15%	20%	25%	30%	35%	40%	45%	50
FROM 0 TO 5 YEARS	.8848	.7869	.7035	.6321	.5708	.5179	.4721	.4323	.3976	.36
" 5 " 10 "	.6891	.4773	.3323	.2325	.1635	.1156	.0820	.0585	.0419	.03
" 10 " 15 "	.5367	.2895	.1570	.0855	.0469	.0258	.0143	.0079	.0044	.00
" 15 " 20 "	.4179	.1756	.0742	.0315	.0134	.0058	.0025	.0011	.0005	.00
" 20 " 25 "	.3255	.1065	.0350	.0116	.0038	.0013	.0004	.0001	-	
" 25 " 30 "	.2535	.0646	.0165	.0043	.0011	.0003	.0001	-	-	
" 30 " 35 "	.1974	.0392	.0078	.0016	.0003	.0001	-	-	-	
" 35 " 40 "	.1538	.0238	.0037	.0006	.0001	-	-	-	-	
" 40 " 45 "	.1197	.0144	.0017	.0002	-	-	-	-	-	
" 45 " 50 "	.0933	.0087	.0008	.0001	-	-	-	-	-	

F. DECLINING TO NOTHING AT CONSTANT RATE

	5%	10%	15%	20%	25%	30%	35%	40%	45%	50
FROM 0 TO 5 YEARS	.9216	.8522	.7906	.7358	.6867	.6428	.6033	.5677	.5355	.50
" 0 " 10 "	.8522	.7358	.6428	.5677	.5063	.4555	.4131	.3773	.3468	.32
" 0 " 15 "	.7906	.6428	.5355	.4555	.3945	.3468	.3088	.2779	.2525	.23
" 0 " 20 "	.7358	.5677	.4555	.3773	.3205	.2779	.2449	.2188	.1975	.18
" 0 " 25 "	.6867	.5063	.3945	.3205	.2689	.2311	.2026	.1800	.1620	.14
" 0 " 30 "	.6428	.4555	.3468	.2779	.2311	.1975	.1723	.1528	.1372	.12
" 0 " 35 "	.6083	.4131	.3088	.2449	.2026	.1723	.1499	.1327	.1189	.10

Exhibit 8–6. The Atlantic Refining Company continuous interest table.

The ordinary compound interest and discount tables assume that interest will be computed at discrete time intervals, such as a month or a year. But Mr. Gregory's tables assume the compounding or discounting is done continuously during any specific time period. In some situations, this continuous compounding will more closely approximate the way earnings actually occur and how funds are invested in a business. Six separate tables are designed for use with various patterns of cash flow, and each relates cash flow to a reference point.

Tables A and B provide the factors for compounding cash flow to a reference point in the future for various interest rates and elapsed times. Tables C to F provide factors for discounting cash flow to a reference point in the past. These tables can shorten considerably the calculation time required for use of any of the more sophisticated techniques of evaluating capital investment opportunities.

In the example used to illustrate the payback method, part of the investment is made at a specific point in time, while another part is made over a period in advance of the point where the inflows of cash begin. Earnings occur over periods, but they could also occur at specific points in time. By using appropriate compounding and discounting factors, the analyst can relate all investments and earnings to any reference point in time at a given rate. The specific reference point or points employed will depend upon the techniques employed.

Discounted Cash Flow Method

Most proponents of a sophisticated, or more disciplined, approach to capital budgeting usually advocate and use the discounted cash flow method. It is more complex than the methods that have been discussed, but it is also more precise, primarily because it recognizes the effect of the time value of money. Results of the valuation of a project are expressed as a rate of return, the rate at which the project's total earnings, discounted from the time they occur to the present, equal the original investment.

Besides recognizing that time is worth money and that a dollar today is worth more than the promise of a dollar at some time in the future, this method stresses the flow of cash. It also provides the flexibility to meet almost any conceivable investment and earnings pattern. Accounting policy with regard to capitalization and depreciation has no effect except as it affects income taxes. The effect of income taxes is taken into account in all facets of the calculation.

To illustrate the discounted cash flow method, we will re-use the earlier example, although some adjustments are necessary. To determine the cash flow in each year, current depreciation must be added to savings after taxes, since depreciation is a non-cash expense and acts merely as a tax shield. This is illustrated in Exhibit 8–7. A trial rate of return of 16% for the investment opportunity is selected, and the present value of the cash flows is computed by discounting them to time zero at the trial rate. The discount factors used in the illustration are from the complete set of Mr. Gregory's tables.

The object is to select a rate that will make the cash flows, discounted to present value, equal to the present value of the investment. Generally, the analyst will require only two or three trials to determine the correct rate to the nearest percent. In our example, a 16% rate resulted in a net present value of minus $7,864, shown as ($7,864) in the exhibit. To put it another way, the net cash outlay would have to be $7,864 less in terms of value at time zero if this series of cash inflows were to earn exactly 16%. Since the actual investment is higher, it is obvious the correct rate is something less than 16%. The process is repeated with a 13% rate. Since this results in a net present value of $7,984, the conclusion is that the correct rate is about midway between the two, or 14.5%.

To determine whether this return is satisfactory and the project should be accepted, management must adjust for risk and then compare the return to the *cut-off rate*. This is the rate below which no projects will be accepted. Theoretically, this cut-off rate should be the actual cost of capital, because the wealth of the stockholders is only increased when a company accepts projects that provide returns greater than this cost. Economists have given a great deal of attention to the cost of capital, but they have not been able to agree on precisely how to measure it, nor have they been able to agree on what it should measure. As a practical matter, management may set the cut-off rate for optional

Year		Savings after taxes	Add back depreciation	Total cash flow	Discount factors @16%	Present value @16%	Discount factors @13%	Present value @13%
At	0			$(50,000)	1.0000	$(50,000)	1.0000	$(50,000)
0 to 1				(50,000)	.9241	(46,205)	.9377	(46,885)
1 to 2		$ 2,700	$10,000	12,700	.7875	10,001	.8234	10,457
2 to 3		5,200	10,000	15,200	.6710	10,199	.7230	10,990
3 to 4		7,700	10,000	17,700	.5718	10,121	.6349	11,238
4 to 5		10,200	10,000	20,200	.4873	9,843	.5575	11,262
5 to 6		12,700	10,000	22,700	.4152	9,425	.4895	11,111
6 to 7		15,200	10,000	25,200	.3538	8,916	.4299	10,833
7 to 8		17,700	10,000	27,700	.3015	8,352	.3775	10,457
8 to 9		20,200	10,000	30,200	.2569	7,758	.3314	10,008
9 to 10		22,700	10,000	32,700	.2189	7,158	.2910	9,516
10 to 11		25,200	10,000	35,200	.1866	6,568	.2556	8,997
						$ (7,864)		$ 7,984

Indicated rate of return = 14.5%

Exhibit 8–7. Analysis of investment opportunity: discounted cash flow method.

projects somewhat above the actual cost of capital in an effort to counterbalance those investments which must be made but will provide little or no return.

Some adjustment for the risk inherent in different types of projects may be introduced by setting different cut-off rates for the different types. For an oil company, for example, a 30% return may be required for drilling projects, while a 20% return is satisfactory for transportation and refining projects, and only 15% is required for marketing projects.

The discounted cash flow method is a vast improvement over the payback and average investment methods. It produces the interest rate of return on the funds which are invested in the project, while they are invested. The manager can use it to determine correctly whether a given project is acceptable or unacceptable by comparing the project's rate of return to the cut-off rate.

In capital budgeting, however, a decision is sometimes required as to which of several conflicting opportunities is the most desirable. *Conflicting opportunities* are mutually exclusive projects the acceptance of one of which dictates the rejection of the others. An example of this would be a choice between the purchase of automatic equipment and the purchase of manual equipment to perform a specific job. In this type of situation, the discounted cash flow method is inadequate and may produce results which are quite misleading.

Present Value Method

The present value method of evaluating investment opportunities is not widely used. It is not to be confused with the present value concept, which is basic to all of the techniques that recognize the time value of money. When the analyst uses the present value method, he expresses the results of the evaluation as dollars of return per dollar of investment, all in present value. He obtains these figures by discounting the investment to the present and dividing it into earnings, also discounted to the present. The rate used for discounting is the expected earnings rate of capital or cost of capital. This is the average rate which management expects to earn in the future on all funds invested.

Exhibit 8–8, an illustration of the present value method, uses the same basic data as do the previous examples. The expected

Year	Cash flow	Discount factors at 8%	Present value of cash flow
Investment			
At 0	$50,000	1.0000	$ 50,000
0 to 1	50,000	.9610	48,050
			$ 98,050
Return			
1 to 2	$12,700	.8872	$ 11,270
2 to 3	15,200	.8189	12,450
3 to 4	17,700	.7560	13,380
4 to 5	20,200	.6979	14,100
5 to 6	22,700	.6442	14,620
6 to 7	25,200	.5947	14,990
7 to 8	27,700	.5490	15,210
8 to 9	30,200	.5068	15,310
9 to 10	32,700	.4678	15,300
10 to 11	35,200	.4318	15,200
			$141,830

$$\frac{\text{Present value of return}}{\text{Present value of investment}} = \frac{\$141,830}{\$\ 98,050} = \begin{array}{l}\$1.45 \text{ return per} \\ \$1.00 \text{ of investment}\end{array}$$

Exhibit 8–8. Analysis of investment opportunity: present value method.

earnings rate of capital is taken as 8% in this case, because the company is earning 8% on investment values, expects to continue earning at this rate, and does not wish to accept projects promising to earn less.

The present value of the cash flows is $141,830, which means that investment in this project is worth $1.45 for each dollar invested. To put this in slightly different terms, an investor who expected to earn 8% on his money would be willing to pay $141,830 at time zero for this opportunity. Since the present value of the investment required is only $98,050, it is obvious the return is greater than 8%. If the present value of the return were less than $98,050, it would indicate the project's rate of return to be less than 8%.

The projects with the highest present value of return per dollar of investment will have the greatest earning power. When the analyst determines the dollars of return per dollar of investment for each investment proposal, he will have an array of alternatives adjusted for the time pattern of investment and earnings, and for the expected earnings rate of capital. With this information, the manager is able to select the most desirable projects.

It is unfortunate that results are not in terms of a percentage rate of return, because most people are accustomed to viewing investment in the light of such a rate. This probably accounts for the limited use of this method.

Applicability of the Various Selection Procedures

The serious deficiencies of the payback and average investment methods, if used for anything beyond rough estimates, have already been pointed out.

The discounted cash flow method may prove unsuitable as a measure of investment worth. It does not always rank projects properly or consistently. In Exhibit 8–9 the earnings of Project A equal the investment when the earnings are discounted to the present at 26%. For Project B the comparable rate is 19.5%. Therefore, according to the discounted cash flow method, Project A is better than Project B and management will select it if the two are mutually exclusive alternatives. Since this method does not take into account the expected earnings rate of capital, the results will be the same no matter what this rate actually is.

However, when we analyze the same two projects by employing the present value method, and use an expected earnings rate of 10%, we find that Project B is better than Project A. What is the source of the conflict between the result of the discounted cash flow method and that of the present value method?

Cash flow	Year	Projects	
		A	B
Investment	0	$100	$100
Earnings	1	100	
Earnings	2		
Earnings	3	50	180
Method of Evaluation		Evaluation	
		Project A	Project B
Discounted cash flow rate of return		26%	19.5%
Present value dollars of return per dollar of investment*		$1.275	$1.333

* Expected earnings rate 10%

Exhibit 8–9. Comparison of discounted cash flow and present value methods (evaluating two mutually exclusive capital expenditure proposals).

By employing a discount rate which equates the earnings and investment at a point in time, the discounted cash flow method disregards the rate at which funds released by the project can be re-invested. In making decisions on projects which are not mutually exclusive from either an operating or a financial point of view, this is of little consequence, since all projects whose true rate of return is higher than the cut-off rate can and should be accepted in order to maximize the profits of the company.

In evaluation of mutually exclusive investment opportunities, however, selection of the project which yields the highest interest rate of return will not necessarily maximize company profits. This is true because the interest rate of return measures only the rate of earnings on the amount invested, while it is invested in the project. Funds released by the project before the end of its life can be expected to earn only at the average re-investment rate for the company as a whole. Thus a project which has a lower interest rate of return than another conflicting project, but which holds funds longer, could result in greater profit to the company. This is the situation illustrated in Exhibit 8–9. The funds released by Project A at the end of the first year are re-invested at 10%. Meanwhile, the full amount of the investment in Project B continues to earn at the interest rate of 19.5%. At the end of three years, with the same outlay of funds, the company would accumulate more dollars if it chose Project B than if it chose Project A.

The present value method properly ranks mutually exclusive projects as well as providing correct decisions about accepting or rejecting a project. The manager can always rely upon the discounted cash flow method to produce a correct decision if the question is merely whether to accept or reject a given project, but he cannot rely on it to properly rank mutually exclusive projects.

EXAMPLE OF USING THE TECHNIQUES FOR DECISION MAKING

An important feature of using the discounted cash flow and present value techniques for evaluating capital investment opportunities is their complete flexibility. Either can be used in a variety of situations. On the next page are examples of situations in which these techniques were applied.

- A company with a product line that was gradually losing sales because of technological changes had several possible alternatives. It could allow the line to run out at its own pace; it could develop and introduce new products to make the line competitive; or it could sell the line. The present value method was used to determine which alternative was best if the line were kept and what selling price was required if the company were to be as well off selling the line as keeping it.

- A small company considered building a new plant to consolidate operations performed in two buildings, both quite old. Management used the present value method to decide whether to build a completely new plant or a partially new plant to replace the older of the buildings, or to repair and modernize the present buildings.

- A company with a small subsidiary engaged in a business undergoing substantial changes used the present value method to determine its course of action when the subsidiary's plant was condemned as part of an urban redevelopment project.

- One company that had not previously employed any of the sophisticated techniques of capital budgeting used the present value method to evaluate an earlier decision. In order to obtain sales that could not otherwise have been obtained in a particular area of the country, this company had built a plant in that area before an addition to total company capacity was actually required. No freight or other savings were involved. Management wished to know if, on the basis of original estimates and the results to date, its decision to use plant location as a sales tool had been correct.

- A company which closed a plant used the present value method to determine whether to sell the machinery and equipment or to use the newer items to replace older machinery and equipment in other plants.

These samples illustrate the wide variety of decision situations in which management can employ return on investment calculations to evaluate opportunities.

The capital-budgeting problem has come in for a great deal of attention in the last few years. As a result, better techniques have been developed, and the applicability and limitations of these new methods have been defined.

But despite this progress, the time is not yet here when managers can make capital expenditure decisions by any automatic process which relieves them from exercising their judgement. It will always be management's task to discover investment opportunities and utilize judgement to describe their cost, the benefits to be gained, and the risks involved. The new techniques are merely devices for systematically measuring the characteristics of investment proposals in numerical terms which can assist in making a decision. The techniques cannot suggest a proposal, nor can they estimate costs or savings, risks or economic life. But they can, combined with good management judgement, contribute to more effective capital budgeting.

SUMMARY

Rate of return on capital employed is one useful measure for evaluating performance against plan and for comparing planned performance of various segments of a company. The investment base used internally should be restricted to the valuation of assets over which the manager has some control. This base usually has to be adjusted if return is to be compared with that of outside companies.

Sophisticated techniques which recognize the time value of money are very helpful in evaluating capital expenditure proposals, and can be understood by businessmen with relatively little effort. They do not eliminate the need for management judgement in making decisions, in these areas, but they do provide a disciplined framework within which to make them.

Chapter 9

Communication and Coordination Through Formal Profit Planning

INTRODUCTION

THE PREVIOUS chapters contain discussions of individual managerial accounting techniques which are widely used by modern businesses. The decision-making implications inherent in the ability to differentiate between variable and fixed costs were discussed (Chapters 2 and 3), as was the importance of building a responsibility-accounting structure which conforms to the organization structure (Chapter 4). Techniques which provide both control over the cost of production operations and knowledge of the cost of finished products were demonstrated by the use of cost standards for direct labor and material (Chapter 5) and flexible budgets for overhead expenses (Chapter 6). Memorandum accounting for product line cost and profit relationships was presented in Chapter 7 along with illustrative use of these relationships for converting a sales forecast into a profit plan. The use of return on investment measures with the profit plan was discussed in Chapter 8. The reporting of actual performance against such a plan is described in the following chapter.

This chapter is directed toward an understanding of the profit-planning process out of which a profit plan evolves. The *profit plan* is the mechanism for integrating the individual accounting techniques into a coordinated management information system, and *profit planning* is the management function of devising and evaluating alternative courses of action and ultimately deciding upon a specific plan. The arithmetic calculations required to quantify the monetary effects of a particular plan have been illustrated previously and will not be elaborated upon here. This chapter is concerned with what management can expect from profit planning and what it must do in order for these expectations to be realized.

The First Profit Plan Is Tentative

Exhibit 9–1 is a somewhat simplified version of the typical kind of profit plan which might result from accounting mechanics such as those described in the latter portion of Chapter 7. It is introduced to illustrate the tentative nature of such initial results and the kind of management evaluation which should follow. The

	PRODUCT LINE			TOTAL COMPANY
	A	B	C	
SALES	1,000,000	800,000	600,000	2,400,000
SPECIFIC SALES DEDUCTIONS	120,000	144,000	60,000	324,000
STANDARD VARIABLE MFG. COST	500,000	464,000	372,000	1,336,000
STANDARD VARIABLE COMM. EXPENSE	80,000	64,000	48,000	192,000
PROFIT CONTRIBUTION	300,000	128,000	120,000	548,000
P.C. % TO SALES	30.0%	16.0%	20.0%	22.8%
SPECIFIC PROGRAMMED	20,000	40,000	110,000	170,000
SPECIFIC STANDBY	80,000	60,000	–0–	140,000
GENERAL PROGRAMMED	20,000	16,000	12,000	48,000
GENERAL STANDBY	70,000	50,000	20,000	140,000
EARNINGS BEFORE TAXES	110,000	(38,000)	(22,000)	50,000
EARNINGS % TO SALES	11.0%	(4.7%)	(3.7%)	(2.1%)

Exhibit 9–1. A tentative profit plan.

profit plan in Exhibit 9–1 immediately raises questions about the two product lines which show net losses but contribute revenue in excess of their variable costs. Can all of the programmed marketing and equipment conversion costs specific to Product Line C be eliminated by not producing this line? Might the forecast sales for Line C be over-estimated by 10%, in which case its profit contribution would not cover these specific programmed costs? At first glance, Line B shows up poorer in terms of profit contribution percentage and net earnings than Line C, but it is a less likely prospect for elimination, partly because the standby costs identified with it cannot be easily eliminated and partly because its profit contribution would exceed its specific programmed and standby costs even if forecast sales were reduced by 20%. Other questions occur concerning the possibilities of increasing total sales or reducing over-all expense levels. The point of Exhibit 9–1 is that the first draft of a profit plan merely provides management with a vehicle for analyzing the quantitative effects of contemplated courses of action. It focuses attention on potential problems and provides a framework for selective revisions of particular segments of an initial plan in order to derive a satisfactory and realistic final plan.

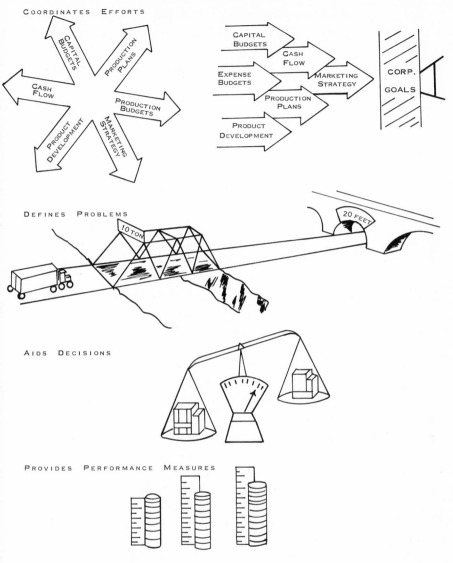

COORDINATES EFFORTS

CAPITAL BUDGETS

CASH FLOW

PRODUCTION PLANS

PRODUCTION BUDGETS

PRODUCT DEVELOPMENT

MARKETING STRATEGY

CAPITAL BUDGETS

CASH FLOW

EXPENSE BUDGETS

MARKETING STRATEGY

PRODUCTION PLANS

PRODUCT DEVELOPMENT

CORP. GOALS

DEFINES PROBLEMS

20 FEET

10 TON

AIDS DECISIONS

PROVIDES PERFORMANCE MEASURES

Exhibit 9–2. The reasons for formal profit planning.

THE REASONS FOR FORMAL PROFIT PLANNING

Having mentioned the possibility of sales-forecasting errors as an illustration of the uncertainties inherent in any plan for future events, it is worthwhile to review the reasons for expending effort on the development of a formal profit plan which will be admittedly imperfect. These reasons are presented pictorially in Exhibit 9–2 and discussed briefly below.

Formal profit planning helps to direct and coordinate the efforts of the separate organizational components of a company toward the attainment of common corporate goals. Accounting plans for controlling cash flow and performance against expense budgets are related to the planned activities of the various marketing, manufacturing, and engineering groups. Production plans are shaped to support marketing strategies. Divisional plans are aligned toward corporate objectives. As the pressures of competition and specialization increase the number of activities requiring explicit managerial attention within each organizational function, they also complicate the problem of coordinating these functions. Without a formal profit-planning procedure, it is nearly impossible to ensure explicit consideration of all the important relationships among the many various activities within a company.

The development of a formal profit plan helps to define problems more explicitly and to provide more advanced warning of their potential existence. Only by detailed quantification of the expected monetary effects of initial plans can the over-all financial results of these plans be evaluated with any precision, and this may give the first indication that the tentative plans are unsatisfactory. If so, the cost building blocks defined in Chapter 2 (and the standards which they incorporate) facilitate the revision of selected segments of the initial plan in a realistic manner. Attention is directed toward those programmed costs most responsive to change by management decision and to product lines where unsatisfactory profit contribution indicates a need for action. The net effect on profit of any change in forecast sales volume or mix can be readily computed. Only the systematic construction of a detailed corporate profit plan is likely to uncover potential conflicts among individual sub-plans and to provide measures of the relative importance of various potential problems.

By providing measures of the probable effects of alternative courses of action, formal profit planning assists management in the making of decisions. Not all management decisions can be reduced to simple quantitative comparisons, but a properly prepared profit plan can provide an objective basis for many decisions.

While profit contribution data are useful for short-range decisions about adding, dropping, or promoting particular products, product line data which include the effect of programmed and standby costs are available for making similar but longer-range decisions. The marketing costs of opening a sales territory can be considered in terms of the profit contribution and the corresponding sales required to cover these costs. The production costs and the related levels of customer service for alternate production plans can be compared. The range of profit dollars associated with the possible range of error in a particular plan helps to define the comparative risks of various plans. Although nothing can eliminate the need to apply sound business judgement in arriving at correct management decisions, the profit plan can greatly increase the opportunities for applying it and reduce the risks inherent in its application.

Once developed, a formal profit plan provides the basic measures by which subsequent actual performance can be evaluated. The planned sales and profit contributions are set out for each month of the year along with the planned lump sum expenditures for programmed and standby costs. Although the reported performance in controlling variable costs will be based on the actual volumes and operating conditions experienced during the year, the standards used for this purpose are directly related to those used in developing the profit plan. Thus any difference between planned and actual profit can be reconciled completely in terms of variances from planned performance. This includes the effect of sales price, volume, and mix variances on the amount of profit contribution, as well as the effect of variances from standard and budgeted amounts of cost.

A Plotted Course by Which To Steer

The benefits obtainable from the profit plan having been restated, one point about its proper use deserves clarification and emphasis. Although the annual profit plan provides a useful basis from which to measure performance during the year, it is still a plan. It will not prove satisfactory if used merely as a rigid yardstick against which performance can be automatically and mechanically measured throughout the year. Events will force changes in plans. Sales forecasts will prove inaccurate. Business

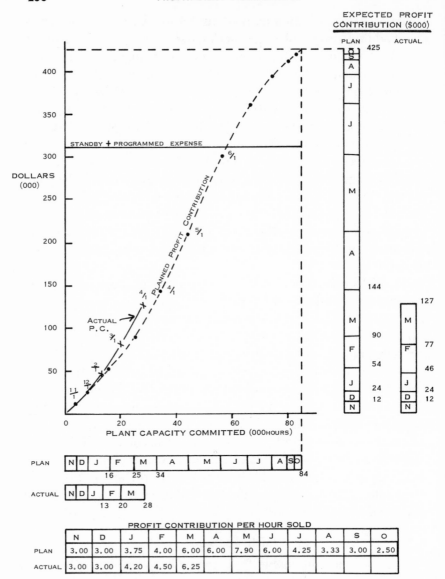

Exhibit 9–3. Planned profit contribution from customer orders placed.

conditions will change, presenting unexpected opportunities and unforeseen problems. The annual profit plan is presumably the best plotted course, as of the beginning of the year, for reaching a year-end profit goal. As actual progress during the year deviates from this plotted course, either the company must steer on revised course headings for the remainder of the year or it must steer for a revised profit goal.

Exhibit 9–3 illustrates graphically how one job-shop type of company made literal use of this "plotted course" philosophy in monitoring its bids for customer orders, probably the most important single function affecting its profits. Because of its essentially fixed annual standby and programmed costs, the management viewed the company as starting the year with a $310,000 loss which was continuously reduced as profit contribution was earned from the sale of plant hours. The time between the placing and filling of a customer's order averaged about two months, and management focused its attention on the placing of these orders. Approximately 80% of the business was placed during six months of the year.

It was the expected profit contribution from orders placed that management plotted as a guide to its bidding policies. The profit plan indicated the plant capacity which was to be committed by receipt of customer orders each month as well as the profit contribution dollars expected from these orders. Thus, Exhibit 9–3 shows that the orders placed through the end of March accounted for only 28,000 plant hours while the plan called for 34,000. Although actual profit contribution rates per hour sold were running higher than planned, this favorable price variance was more than offset by the unfavorable volume variance. With the peak business months just ahead, management had to decide whether to return to its planned pattern of bid prices or to go to some higher or lower level. Whatever the decision, the extent to which it seemed to result in narrowing or widening the gap between planned and actual profit contributions would be closely watched for any indication that another pricing policy should be adopted. This simple example typifies the proper use of the profit plan as a plotted course by which to steer. It provides the reference points needed, not only for establishing the current position but also for evaluating various courses for the remainder of the year.

THE MANAGEMENT APPROACH TO
PROFIT PLANNING

In order to be successful, profit planning must be approached as an evolutionary process which requires the personal participation of all levels of management and which results in explicit assignment of responsibility for carrying out each segment of the plan.

Management Participation

The significance of middle- and lower-level management participation in the development of their own plans is fairly well understood. The manager closest to an operation is usually in the best position to set attainable goals for it, although these goals must be subject to independent review to ensure that they are not too easily attainable. The plan which the manager has participated in formulating is more likely to be effective than one which has merely been imposed on him from above. He feels a greater responsibility for its successful execution and is likely to expend more effort on trying to make it work and less effort on explaining why it won't work.

The need for, and the kind of, top management participation required for successful profit planning is perhaps not so clearly understood. If top management participation is limited to specifying the dates on which their subordinates will submit detailed forecasts and budgets, the preparation of the latter will eventually become an academic exercise. If their participation is extended only to adding the detailed plans together and then imposing "across-the-board" increases in forecast sales and decreases in budgeted costs, the exercise will become a game in which their subordinates attempt to gauge how much "fat" they should include in preliminary plans. In guiding the preparation of preliminary plans, top management should summarize the major elements of each manager's performance against plan for the current year and specify those elements in which improvement is most expected during the next year. In reviewing the preliminary plans, top management must go into sufficient detail to be able to request revision of selected segments of these plans or the preparation of particular alternative plans. They must also satisfy themselves that revised and alternative plans have been prepared realistically before they can finally decide that a particular plan is most desirable.

Explicit Assignment of Responsibility

As emphasized pictorially in Exhibit 9–4, for a functionally organized company, the effectiveness of any profit plan which is finally evolved depends upon the ability to assign explicit responsibility for various segments of the plan to particular individuals within the organizational structure. The over-all responsibilities for carrying out marketing, manufacturing, engineering, and financial plans are assigned to the respective managers of these functions. These broad plans, however, must be supported by integrated subsidiary plans which cover narrower areas in increasing detail at successively lower levels of responsibility. A marketing vice-president's responsibility for producing a total amount of profit contribution is translated into each product line manager's planned sales prices, volumes, and mix and finally into detailed sales quotas. A manufacturing vice-president's planned production volumes are converted into a factory manager's planned sequence of various levels of production and then into detailed production schedules and departmental manning charts. In each case, the detailed plans should be fed back to confirm or to revise the top-level plans, and, insofar as possible, responsibility for executing each segment of the final plan should be assigned to an individual.

An Evolutionary Process

In order to do an intelligent job of profit planning, management must approach it as an evolutionary and to some extent a circular process, as was illustrated for the reader in the simple schematic diagram of Exhibit 2–2. The first attempt at detailing the profit plan will usually raise problems. If problems are not obvious, they should be looked for. A few possible alternatives will be suggested: some conflicts of interest will appear; certain planned performance will seem unsatisfactory. The purpose of the first plan is to provide a comprehensive and tangible basis for review, challenge, and eventual agreement on realistic revisions. Certain segments of the plan may go through several revisions as is illustrated in the example of Exhibit 9–5, where the flexible manpower budget for a production control department is twice

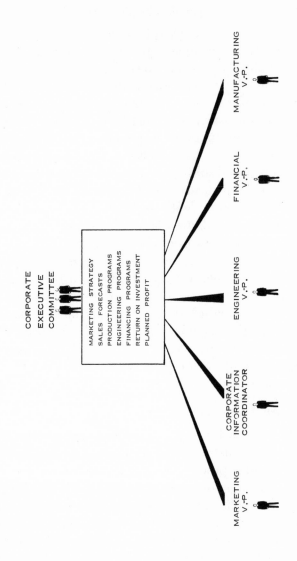

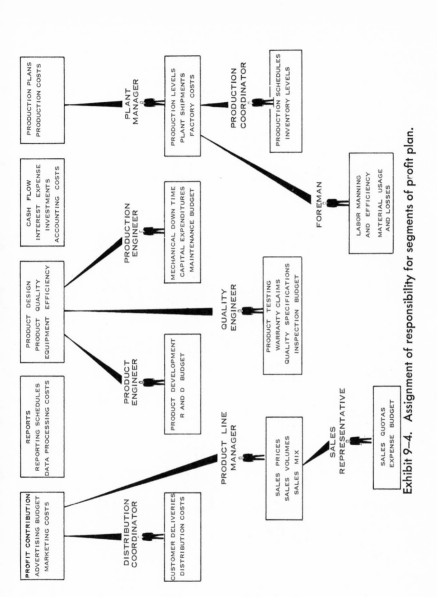

Exhibit 9–4. Assignment of responsibility for segments of profit plan.

MANPOWER BUDGET — PRODUCTION CONTROL DEPT.

FIRST STAGE

LEVEL OF ACTIVITY / DIRECT LABOR HOURS	STANDBY	40% 8,000	60% 12,000	80% 16,000	100% 20,000	120% 24,000
MANAGER - H.R. WALTERS	1	1	1	1	1	1
ASST. MANAGERS	2	2	2	2	2	2
PLANNERS	4	4	4	4	4	4
Record Clerks	6	6	8	8	8	8
Stock Controllers	5	5	5	5	5	5
Key Punch Operators	3	4	5	5	5	5
TOTAL PLANNED MANPOWER	21	22	25	25	25	25
TOTAL SALARY EXPENSE	$105,000	108,600	118,800	118,800	118,800	118,800

SECOND STAGE

LEVEL OF ACTIVITY / DIRECT LABOR HOURS	STANDBY	40% 8,000	60% 12,000	80% 16,000	100% 20,000	120% 24,000
MANAGER - H.R. WALTERS	1	1	1	1	1	1
ASST. MANAGERS						
PLANNERS	3	3	2	3	3	3
Record Clerks	4	6	7	8	8	8
Stock Controllers	2	3	4	5	5	5
Key Punch Operators	2	3	4	5	5	5
TOTAL PLANNED MANPOWER	12	17	20	23	24	24
TOTAL SALARY EXPENSE	$66,000	83,400	95,100	106,800	111,600	111,600

APPROVED PLAN

LEVEL OF ACTIVITY / DIRECT LABOR HOURS	STANDBY	40% 8,000	60% 12,000	80% 16,000	100% 20,000	120% 24,000
MANAGER - H.R. WALTERS	1	1	1	1	1	1
ASST. MANAGER						
PLANNERS		1	1	2	2	2
Record Clerks	2	2	2	2	2	2
Stock Controllers	2	3	4	6	6	6
Key Punch Operators	2	2	3	4	4	5
TOTAL PLANNED MANPOWER	7	11	14	17	19	20
TOTAL SALARY EXPENSE	$38,400	57,600	67,800	82,800	89,400	93,000

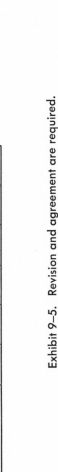

RESULTING SALARY EXPENSE (THOUSANDS OF DOLLARS) — LEVEL OF ACTIVITY (0 to 120%); NORMAL OPERATING RANGE.

Exhibit 9–5. Revision and agreement are required.

reduced rather drastically. Such dramatic revisions, although not typical, are possible when management considers existing policies as integral parts of the plans which are subject to revision. In the example, full employment and order-processing time policies limited flexibility. Several revisions may be required in order to evaluate alternatives, resolve conflicts, and refine planned performance. The work involved is justified if it results in agreement on a revised plan which the operating manager considers attainable and his superiors consider acceptable.

THE ACCOUNTANT'S ROLE IN PROFIT PLANNING

The accountant's primary contribution to the profit-planning process is the providing of quantitative information to management so that planning can be done in the most effective and objective manner. This broad definition encompasses at least two distinct responsibilities. The accountant is responsible for summarizing the over-all effects of various programs, forecasts, and opinions and presenting these in the common business language of cost and profit dollars. This includes, of course, the responsibility for ensuring that the mechanical details of preparing such presentations are properly integrated and consistently handled so that the dollar comparisons which are likely to be made can be made with validity.

The accountant, however, also has a very important responsibility for providing accounting data in the form which is most informative for particular decisions. He should recognize, even if management does not, that different decisions require different accounting data. He should know that there is no such thing as "true cost," but rather a variety of costs, each of which is most useful for a particular purpose. The accountant has a duty to determine the planning decisions which management is contemplating before he attempts to provide the quantitative data which will help to guide those decisions. He also has a responsibility to point out the limitations of those data if used for other purposes.

The Dual Function of the Accountant

The preceding discussion helps to delineate the dual function which the accountant should perform in the profit-planning process. Although the two functions are related, failure to distinguish their separate requirements and mutual importance can greatly reduce the effectiveness of profit planning. The two functions are

1. Constructing a complete profit plan so that the over-all results for the year can be evaluated in the financial-accounting terms of profit and return on investment (This is done for an initial plan, which, if unsatisfactory, helps to point out problems and areas for potential revision. It is also done for a final plan, which establishes the financial goals for the year and assists in the measurement of performance toward these goals during the year.)

2. Aiding particular planning decisions by providing the particular arrangement of quantitative data most useful for evaluating each decision (This may require different arrangements of similar data for different decisions, arrangements which may differ from that used later for reporting financial performance against the profit plan.)

Both of the above functions must be performed, but not necessarily by way of a common set of procedures. The procedures for constructing an entire plan should not be unduly complicated by attempts to incorporate all of the data which might possibly be useful for planning decisions. Usually, the decisions can best be facilitated by special data preparation as required. It is important, however, that accounting data be used, insofar as possible, to evaluate the quantitative aspects of these decisions and that the data used in arriving at an eventual decision be consistent with those reflected in the final version of the profit plan.

The key to successful profit planning lies in incorporating accounting disciplines into management communications—in coordinating the preparation of the appropriate data from the accounting system with the managerial decisions which have to be taken. Not only should the quantitative data be tailored to fit the decision, but they must be available in time to aid the decision, and such data should be prepared with the systematic discipline which is more characteristic of accounting than of any other organizational area of a company. For best results, management should foster reliance on its accounting organization for quantitative evaluations and should provide it with sufficient advance notice of the decisions to be evaluated. Satisfactory results will only be obtained, however, if the accounting organization is sufficiently flexible to provide a variety of special quantitative analyses which are integrated with, but not limited to, traditional financial-accounting results and which can be prepared in a reasonably short period of time.

Examples of Accounting Communication Failures

The above emphasis on the importance of accounting as a medium of communication for managerial planning may seem obvious and elementary to many readers. Satisfactory communication is unlikely to occur, however, without a continuing, conscious, and systematic effort to maintain and improve it on the part of both the manager and the accountant. In real business situations, communication of accounting data frequently fails. The following few actual examples of such communication failures are not rare occurrences.

- A small tool and die manufacturer was operating at about 50% of capacity and showing continuing small losses. In the product line income statement which was prepared on the basis of full absorption of overhead costs, one line, which accounted for 30% of the sales, showed a net loss. Management dropped this line and then began to experience losses of such magnitude that they seriously considered going out of business.
- A metal extruder and fabricator developed standard operation costs per piece as a guide to sales estimating. These costs, or "prices," included an allocation of machine depreciation and other fixed costs based on forecast volumes through each operation. Thus, an automatic buffing operation with lower variable costs than the manual buffing operation was assigned a higher "price" because of high fixed costs and low forecast volumes. This led to sales insistence on routing even more jobs through the less efficient but lower-priced manual operation.
- A medium size engine manufacturer had an opportunity to bid on a contract which would add 50% to its forecast volume for the coming year and which would probably be followed by further contracts. The company could estimate direct costs accurately but did not know how overhead varied with volume. It relied on re-forecasting a full overhead absorption rate to labor. This rate, which was 370% without the contract, was estimated at a minimum of 330% with the contract, and an even lower rate was used in preparing the bid. The company did not get the contract. A post-mortem analysis of fixed and variable overhead indicated that a rate of 270% would have provided full overhead absorption.

- A large, multi-division manufacturer of consumer durable goods had substantial corporate expenses which were charged against divisional operations. These charges were allocated monthly in proportion to actual sales. In a year when all other divisions were falling substantially below their planned sales, one division was breaking all sales records. For some time, however, the relative profitability of the various divisions was largely obscured by an accounting system which in effect was charging the bulk of a volume variance against the division which was doing the most to eliminate that variance.

- In a small paint-manufacturing company, a particular product might be made by any one of several alternative processes, depending upon order size and existing workloads. A memorandum cost system was designed primarily to obtain product costs which could serve as a basis for pricing. Since production options existed and volume through each operation fluctuated, the actual production mix for a "typical period" was used to relate costs to products. This resulted in unrealistic cost variations between similar products, variations which could not be reflected in the sales prices, and the cost system was abandoned. Without a cost basis, however, pricing solely "to meet competition" eventually led to net losses for the company.

The cases cited above illustrate the variety of ways in which accounting communications can and do fail in actual business situations and with serious consequences. The remainder of this chapter is devoted to elaborating upon ways in which the risk of such failures can be minimized by ensuring that the accountant performs both of his profit-planning functions. The first of these functions, the construction of a complete profit plan, will be summarized rather briefly, since it was discussed in considerable detail in Chapter 7. The second function, aiding particular planning decisions, will then be illustrated by considering a number of specific examples.

CONSTRUCTING A COMPLETE PROFIT PLAN

One of the accountant's two main functions in profit planning is to combine all of the individual programs and predictions and summarize them in a comprehensive forecast, or complete plan, of profit for the year. He has to construct the various chains of quantitative relationships which link a single corporate profit

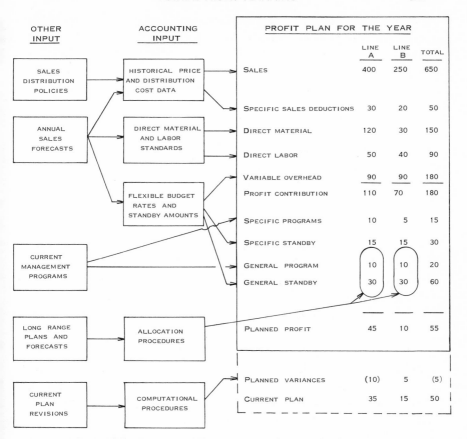

Exhibit 9–6. Constructing a complete profit plan.

figure to a number of subsidiary plans. As was indicated in Exhibit 9–1, the first such plan for a year is subject to revision, but without it the need for revision might escape notice. And, unless the initial plan is carefully constructed in detail, revisions directed at improving the plan may not be realistic. Without detailing of any of the extensive arithmetic calculations which may be required, the major steps in constructing a complete profit plan are summarized schematically in Exhibit 9–6 and discussed briefly in the following paragraphs.

Using a Formal Forecast of Annual Sales

From a narrow accounting point of view, profit planning starts after receipt of a forecast of annual sales. From a broader management point of view, however, determining forecast sales is the most difficult and the most important element of profit planning. There are at least five frequently used and significantly different methods of making sales forecasts. Arranged in rough order by frequency of use among businesses, these five are as follows:

1. Projection of past patterns in company sales
2. Compilation of sales force estimates
3. Projection of past sales correlations with other economic data
4. Jury of corporate executive opinion
5. Surveys of opinion outside the company

There are also variations in the way in which one or another of these methods may be applied. It might be used to first forecast industry sales and then the company's share; it might be used to first forecast the sales of the company's potential customers; or it might be used to forecast directly sales of the company's individual product lines. Many companies use more than one of the five methods listed above, either to provide cross-checks or because different methods are best suited to different product lines. Although methods 2 and 4 were once predominant in the sales-forecasting area, there has been an increasing tendency to supplement sales force estimates by methods 1 and 3 and to restrict the "executive jury" to reviewing the forecasts which are prepared initially by other means.

In terms of effect on profit planning, the most important aspect of the current trends in sales-forecasting practices is not so much the increasing use of scientific techniques as the increasing formality with which forecasts are being prepared. Use of sophisticated techniques does not prevent forecasting errors, although it tends to reduce them. But the formal preparation of explicit and detailed forecasts can provide the basic data on unit volumes which are a prerequisite to the computation of a meaningful profit plan.

A forecast of total dollar sales is obviously inadequate for projecting production costs. On the other hand, forecast unit volumes must be supplemented by other sales information on prices, commissions, discounts, and other direct distribution costs before forecast sales can be expressed in terms of realizable revenue. While proper segregation of price variances and specific sales deductions in the accounts can provide data on their historical relationships to the sales of various product groupings, distribution policies are sufficiently volatile in most companies to require a detailed review of current policies before projecting past relationships.

Once supplied with a detailed forecast of unit sales and supplemental data on distribution plans, the accountant can complete the profit plan down through the level of profit contribution. He can do this by applying the forecast data to the first three of the "cost building blocks" presented in Chapter 2. Thus, planned sales can be expressed in dollars and then reduced by (1) specific sales deductions, (2) specific material and direct labor costs, and (3) variable overhead costs, in order to arrive at planned profit contribution. This is usually summarized for each major product line. It should also be summarized by division, if there are divisional profit centers, and should be converted into units of workload, such as labor or machine hours, by productive department in order to determine the planned utilization of existing facilities.

Handling Programmed and Standby Costs

To reduce planned profit contribution to planned profit, it is only necessary to introduce the remaining two standard "cost building blocks." These are (4) programmed costs established by management decisions and (5) standby or fixed costs of being in business. The proper handling of each of these two types of cost in the profit plan is the result of a two-stage process of determining costs and then allocating costs.

The first stage, that of determining the total amount of planned lump sum costs, is fairly straightforward, although it may involve considerable work. For programmed costs, which tend to be fixed for some limited period such as a year, cost determination is essentially the recording of managerial decisions as to how much money will be spent on various advertising, engineering, research, and maintenance projects. Although the specified results to be obtained from these projects may be somewhat vague, the amount of costs to be incurred is likely to be specified rather precisely. These costs are also likely to be most subject to revision when an initial profit plan proves unsatisfactory. Determination of standby costs is an integral part of developing flexible budgets as described in Chapter 6. These costs are available in memorandum form from the initial budgetary worksheet calculations and are reviewed annually.

The second stage, the allocation of the total amount of programmed and standby costs in the profit plan, is not quite so straightforward. Typically, these costs are allocated to product lines in an effort to focus attention on relative product profitability. There may also be merit in allocating corporate costs to operating divisions in order to emphasize the total costs which have to be recovered out of the earnings of profit centers. In either case, the amounts allocated should be fixed at the beginning of the year. They should not be changed during the year to conform with actual sales volumes or actual cost levels. These allocations should not be directed at merely "spreading" fixed costs in proportion to actual sales in order to prepare reports after the fact. Rather they should be directed at specifying fixed costs in groupings which facilitate planning and in amounts which reflect planned activity and are fixed in advance for purposes of performance measurement.

The particular details of the proper allocation of programmed and standby costs will vary from company to company, depending upon the various planning considerations which are most important. Two general rules should be followed, however. First, specific costs which can be definitely identified with a particular profit center or product line should be shown separately from general allocations of cost which cannot be so identified. Second, if standby costs are allocated on the basis of forecast sales, long-range forecasts covering several years should be used in preference to a forecast of current annual volume.

- For example, one company that basically made and sold paint developed paint-mixing equipment which it sold to its retail outlets. Although this product was expected to account for 10% of current annual sales, it was charged with less than 1% of the standby costs. Management knew that these sales would drop to nearly nothing after another year or so, and wanted to focus attention on the costs which the other products had to support in the long run.

This is merely one example drawn from the many various planning considerations which may affect the allocation of programmed and standby costs.

Fixing the Plan at a Date

The steps described above lead to the preparation of a complete profit plan, although it may be a tentative one. Review of this initial plan and evaluation of alternative planning decisions will usually result in a series of revisions. As individuals spend time on the details of the profit plan, more alternatives can be seen, more refined quantitative measures can be devised, and more current forecasts can be made. As the fiscal year approaches, a decision must be made similar to that which "freezes" engineering changes on a new product in order to get it into production.

The profit plan should be fixed at a date and published within the company before the year begins. The sales, production, and cost plans which various individuals are expected to fulfill during the year should be set out explicitly at the beginning of the year along with the profit which will result if these plans are fulfilled. The cost and other standards incorporated in these plans should be "frozen." If these steps are not taken, the plan becomes a flexible yardstick and deviations which occur at different times during the year are not comparable, nor is their effect on the initially planned profit measurable. As mentioned earlier, the profit plan is a plotted course by which to steer. Managerial flexibility can be retained with a minimum of confusion by fixing on one such course for the year and continuing to relate the most current position to that original course by measurements which reflect both planned and unplanned deviations. Even after fixing on a particular formal plan, the effect of subsequent planning information can continue to be recognized by forecasting variances from the initial plan. But, the profit plan must be fixed at a date in order to provide the firm base of reference which is necessary for measuring performance and useful for revising plans.

AIDING PARTICULAR PLANNING DECISIONS

The accountant's second major function in the profit-planning process is to provide the particular arrangements of quantitative data which are most useful for evaluating the probable effects of specific planning decisions. The proper kind and arrangement of data depend upon the particular decision under consideration, and the variety of possible decisions is practically endless. The diverse areas in which management planning decisions may be required include methods of financing, allocation of research effort, design of products, and specification of systems for reporting information. The bulk of the profit-planning decisions are concerned, however, with marketing or production alternatives. It is from these two areas, therefore, that the examples presented in the remainder of this chapter are drawn.

Some Marketing and Production Decisions

Planning decisions are required on a wide variety of marketing problems. Although any one of these problems may be fairly complex by itself, it is usually rendered even more complicated because of interaction with other problems. Thus, the planned sales for each product depend upon price relationships within and between a company's own product lines and on its competitors' prices and also depend upon the volume and composition of both its own and its competitors' advertising. In bidding for a potential customer's contract, the amount quoted depends not only on the company's estimated costs and the probable quotations of its competitors but also on the volume and profitability of the company's existing business and the possible effect of the current bid on other future business. A decision to introduce a new product is interdependent with other marketing decisions, not only about price and advertising but also about distribution channels and sales territories, and with decisions in other areas, particularly in the production area.

The planning process may require a variety of production decisions about manufacturing methods and schedules and about plant capacity and equipment. These decisions are likely to be related to each other and to one or more of the kinds of marketing decisions which were referred to above. A decision to produce a product in a particular manner imposes constraints upon the way in which other products can be produced, and the forecast volume, timing, and location of sales introduce further restrictions on the manner in which each product should be produced. Decisions to increase the size of the plant or modernize the equipment within it may be affected, not only by forecast sales, estimated costs, and required investment, but also by possible alternative uses of existing facilities. Thus a proposed capital expenditure may involve an evaluation of make or buy alternatives.

The few general references above serve to indicate the variety and the complexity of the marketing and production decisions which may be required in the process of profit planning. In order to illustrate how accounting data can be useful in aiding such decisions, the following few specific examples are discussed in greater detail.

The area of product pricing requires perhaps the most important marketing decisions made in the entire profit-planning process, and it is an area in which accounting data should have a significant, although not necessarily a decisive, effect. Some specific examples in this area are contained in Chapter 11, which is devoted solely to the subject of pricing. The particular example which is included here has to do with bid pricing in a somewhat specialized field, namely, a government contract with provision for price re-determination. It is included here for two reasons. It emphasizes the need for evaluating potential new business in relation to existing business. It is also an example of an actual business problem which can be completely described in relatively few words but which was not fully understood until the quantitative evaluation shown in Exhibit 9–7 was performed.

This company, which was operating well below capacity, was doing one-half of its existing business ($500,000 of direct labor costs which totaled $1,000,000) in price-re-determinable contracts with the United States government. These contracts limited profit to 10% of total cost and defined total contract cost to include full absorption of overhead based on direct labor. In other words, the portion of the company's total fixed costs which could be allocated to government contracts depended solely on the ratio of the direct labor in those contracts to the total direct labor. Under existing conditions, 50% of the total fixed costs of $3,000,000 were allocable to the government contracts. The profit contribution from these contracts was limited, therefore, to allocable fixed costs plus 10% of total contract costs. This amounted to $1,950,000, a rate of 65% to total variable costs (or 39% to sales).

The company had an opportunity to bid on another price-re-determinable contract with direct labor estimated at an additional $500,000. As shown in Exhibit 9–7, this would increase the

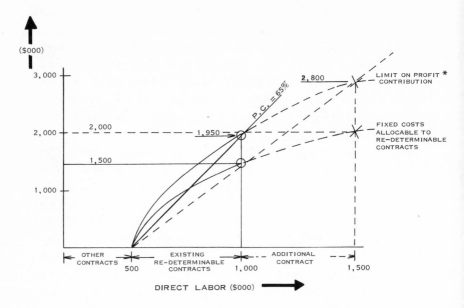

Cost And Profit Analysis Of Price-Re-determinable Contracts (in $000)

Existing Contracts		With Added Contracts
1,500	Material	3,000
500	Direct Labor	1,000
1,000	Variable Overhead	2,000
3,000	Total Variable Costs	6,000
1,500**	Allocable Fixed Costs	2,000**
4,500	Total Costs	8,000
1,950	Profit Contribution Limit	2,800
65%	P.C. % to Variable Costs	47%

* Limit = allocable fixed costs + 10% of total costs

** Allocation of $3,000,000 total fixed costs based on relative direct labor.

Exhibit 9–7. Evaluating contract bidding (effect on profit contribution of adding another price-re-determinable contract).

total amount of fixed costs allocable to government contracts. It would also, however, decrease the ratio of allocable fixed costs to variable costs and consequently would reduce the profit contribution limit from 65% to 47% of total variable costs (or 32% of sales). Thus, obtaining the new contract would increase the company's total profit, but it would decrease the over-all profit ratio for the company.

Although, upon reflection, the calculations in Exhibit 9–7 seem rather elementary, it was only after they had been performed that management had a clear and precise understanding of the effect of new business on existing contracts, and this effect was independent of whether or not the new business was price-re-determinable. The management also recognized, of course, that additional profit contribution, even at a reduced rate, was preferable to making no use of the idle capacity. But the fact that the addition of business, which seemed to be as profitable as the existing business, would actually yield a reduced rate of profit contribution was only recognized when the calculations shown here were put down on paper.

In addition to being useful as an aid to pricing and bidding, accounting data can assist decisions on the desirability of producing a new product when the probable price is fairly well established. A simple example of the evaluation of the profitability of a potential new product is shown in Column 1 of Exhibit 9–8. If idle plant capacity is available, the profit contribution and its proportion to sales (20.9%) is a valid measure of desirability. The accountant has also computed the investment in working capital which would be required to support production of this product, and, after deducting income taxes, shows a profit which amounts to a 50.3% return on this investment. Fixed costs, which are not a factor in this decision, are not considered in the calculation.

Column 2 of the exhibit shows how the evaluation changes when idle capacity is not available and new equipment is required in order to make the product. For simplicity, the investment in equipment is considered here as the average of the $1,000,000 initial cost and the $20,000 recoverable costs at the end of four years, and the annual allowable depreciation is assumed to equal the annual loss in recovery value. (In a real problem, the time value of money would be recognized by some method of discounting cash flow in future periods as was discussed in Chapter 8. This would reduce the rate of return on investment shown here.) The fixed costs are now considered, since they are a factor in the decision. Their inclusion reduces profit and increases investment, with the result that the return on investment is now reduced to 17.5%. Although the profit contribution is unchanged, the desirability of the new product is much less obvious, particularly in

	1	2	3
	MAKE NEW PRODUCT		BUY NEW PRODUCT
	HAVE IDLE CAPACITY	NEED NEW EQUIPMENT	
PROFIT			
SALES	300,000		300,000
MATERIAL	66,000		265,000
DIRECT LABOR	48,000		-0-
VARIABLE OVERHEAD	123,200		12,000
TOTAL VARIABLE COSTS	237,200		277,200
PROFIT CONTRIBUTION	62,800	62,800	22,800 ⇐
% TO SALES	20.9%	20.9%	7.6%
LESS DEPRECIATION *	-0-	20,000	-0-
LESS TAX AT 50%	31,400	21,400	11,400
PROFIT AFTER TAX	31,400	21,400	11,400 ⇐
% TO INVESTMENT	50.3%	17.5%	27.6% ⇐
INVESTMENT			
CASH	5,365		11,175
ACCOUNTS RECEIVABLE	30,000		30,000
INVENTORY – MATERIAL	2,750		11,050
" – IN-PROCESS	25,270		-0-
" – FINISHED	9,850		11,050
TOTAL CURRENT ASSETS	73,235		63,750
LESS – ACCOUNTS PAYABLE	8,835		22,100
LESS – ACCRUED PAYROLL	1,900		250
NET WORKING CAPITAL	62,500	62,500	41,400
FIXED ASSETS (AVERAGE VALUE) *	-0-	60,000	-0-
TOTAL INVESTMENT	62,500	122,500	41,400

* EQUIPMENT PURCHASED FOR $100,000 HAS ESTIMATED RECOVERY VALUE OF $20,000 FOUR YEARS LATER. ALLOWABLE DEPRECIATION = ANNUAL LOSS IN RECOVERY VALUE = $20,000.

Exhibit 9–8. Evaluating new product profitability under various production conditions.

view of the increased risk involved in making commitments based on a sales projection for a four-year period.

Column 3 of Exhibit 9–8 shows the evaluation of an alternative decision that may often be considered in conjunction with a decision to make a new product, namely, a decision to buy it. The profit contribution that results from buying major components of a new product is likely to be much less than that from making these components, but the rate of return on investment may be higher. In our example, the decision to buy yields a higher rate of return than the decision to make only if the latter required additions in capital equipment. Even in that instance, however, it produces less profit dollars. Therefore, a decision "to buy" implies that the additional investment which would be needed in order "to make" can be invested more profitably, or perhaps with less risk, elsewhere. The difference in relative rates of return on investment is useful for evaluating alternative decisions, but it may not be the decisive measure when the difference in total profits is in the opposite direction. This point is illustrated again in the last example.

The preceding example demonstrates three points in connection with the use of accounting data as an aid to planning decisions. Other data in addition to costs may be required from the accounting system. The kind of data which should be considered for different decisions may differ even when the decisions seem quite similar. In order to evaluate one decision, it may be necessary to prepare comparable data on a variety of alternative or interrelated decisions.

The last example in this chapter reflects, more clearly than the preceding ones, the complexity of detail which may be involved in evaluating planning decisions, although this example is a greatly simplified version of an actual decision which has to be made in many companies. It illustrates the interaction of marketing and production considerations in the planning process and also demonstrates again the dangers of sole reliance on a single measure, such as return on investment, as a guide to all planning decisions. It also illustrates one area in which more sophisticated mathematical techniques, such as linear programming, have actually been applied to accounting data to improve planning decisions.

Exhibit 9–9A summarizes the profitability of three products which are being manufactured under conditions where sales demand exceeds plant capacity. The data for Product A are the same as shown in Exhibit 9–8 except that machining labor is shown separately from other labor costs because the machining department is the "bottleneck" which limits production. Although Products B and C are being produced at an annual rate of 10,000 units apiece, the demand for each product is twice that large.

Exhibit 9–9B shows how total profit can be increased by buying Product A, and using the machining capacity thus released to first satisfy the total demand for Product B and then make as much more of Product C as capacity will allow. This results in a higher

A – ANNUAL RESULTS IF ALL PRODUCTS ARE MADE

	A	B	C	TOTAL
UNITS SOLD	12,000	10,000	10,000	32,000
UNIT SALES PRICE	$ 30.00	$ 45.00	$ 32.00	$ 33.40
SALES	$300,000	$450,000	$320,000	$1,070,000
MATERIAL	66,000	164,000	48,000	278,000
MACHINING LABOR	36,000	24,000	40,000	100,000
OTHER LABOR AND OH	135,200	190,000	152,000	477,200
TOTAL VARIABLE COSTS	$237,200	$378,000	$240,000	$ 855,200
PROFIT CONTRIBUTION	$ 62,800	$ 72,000	$ 80,000	$ 214,800
% TO SALES	(20.9%)	(16.0%)	(25.0%)	(20.1%)
$ PER MACH. LABOR $	$ 1.74	$ 3.00	$ 2.00	$ 2.15
INVESTMENT	$ 62,500	$110,800	$ 67,400	$ 240,700
% RETURN	(100%)	(65%)	(119%)	(87%)
PROGRAM AND STANDBY COSTS				144,800
NET PROFIT BEFORE TAX *Can be ignored for this decision*				$ 70,000

B – ANNUAL RESULTS IF PRODUCT A IS BOUGHT

	A	B	C	TOTAL
UNITS SOLD	12,000	20,000	13,000	45,000
SALES	$300,000	$900,000	$416,000	$1,616,000
MATERIAL	265,200	328,000	62,400	655,600
MACHINING LABOR		48,000	52,000	100,000
OTHER LABOR AND OH	12,000	380,000	197,600	589,600
TOTAL VARIABLE COSTS	$277,200	$756,000	$312,000	$1,345,200
PROFIT CONTRIBUTION	22,800	144,000	104,000	270,800
% TO SALES	(7.6%)	(16.0%)	(25.0%)	(16.7%)
$ PER MACH. LABOR $		$ 3.00	$ 2.00	$ 2.71
INVESTMENT	$ 41,400	$221,600	$ 87,600	$ 350,600
% RETURN	(55 %)	(65%)	(119%)	(77%)

Exhibit 9–9. Effect of multi-product competition for bottleneck facilities.

total profit than would be obtained from first satisfying the total demand for Product C, despite the fact that Product C shows higher rates of both profit contribution and return on investment. The reason for this lies in the varying amount of machining labor which is required for each product in order to produce the same amount of profit. The most useful measure for this decision is dollars of profit contribution per dollar of machining labor. Maximizing this ratio maximizes the total profit contribution, although it does not maximize its proportionate relationship to either sales or investment.

Many companies face a production-planning problem which is related to Exhibit 9–9. Although the problem may not include make or buy alternatives, it will require the assignment of each of a large number of products to one of a number of different machines on which it can be produced. The cost and, consequently, the profit contribution of a product will vary depending upon the machine on which it is produced, and each assignment of a product restricts the ability to assign other products. If more than a few products and machines are involved, trial and error solutions are unlikely to result in the most profitable set of assignments. Linear programming has been applied successfully to this problem in a variety of industries. Its success, however, depends on the existence of accurate data on the variable cost of producing a particular product on a specific machine. The compilation of such data often requires much more effort than does mathematical solution of the linear programming problem.

SUMMARY

The use of formal profit planning within a company can provide a disciplined method for more effective coordination of its various activities, and a basic language for more precise communication between its varied personnel. Profit planning is an evolutionary process which requires management to participate at each of several steps and requires accounting to provide quantitative information of two different kinds. It must provide a comprehensive summary of the effect of all of the sub-plans on total profit and also provide the particular arrangements of data which are most suitable for evaluating specific planning decisions. Profit planning should result in explicit assignment of the responsibility for implementing each element of the plan which is finally evolved. This "final plan" should be retained during the year in order to provide a firm base for measuring performance, but it should be interpreted as "a course by which to steer" as events indicate a need for planning revisions.

Chapter 10

Control and Feedback Through Management Reports

PRINCIPLES OF EFFECTIVE MANAGEMENT REPORTING

MANAGEMENT'S OPINION of the effectiveness of a management information system is based largely on the reports which they receive. No matter how effective the systems for profit planning, expense budgeting, and data processing may be, if the final results are presented in a poorly designed set of reports, management will consider the entire information system to be ineffective.

It is important to recognize that there is no "ideal" set of management reports for all companies. What is required in one company may be unimportant in another. Management reports must be tailored to the personnel, systems, and policies of each organization. However, in spite of the fact that reports must be tailored to the needs of each company, there are certain fundamental principles which should always be considered in designing the management reports for an organization.

Form of Presentation

It has been said that the amount of information contained in a report is often limited only by the size of the paper on which the report is presented. Although most companies undoubtedly use a more intelligent approach than this in deciding on the scope of the information presented on a report, it is true that the quantity of information presented as well as the format used to present the information often result in excessive time and effort being spent by executives in reading reports.

An example of a report which would be difficult for an executive to use is the comparative statement of net earnings shown in Exhibit 10–1. The net earnings statement is a high-level report directed at the senior executives of a company. However, most senior executives would object to the report in Exhibit 10–1 for the following reasons:

1. The amounts shown are carried out to the penny when rounding to the nearest thousand dollars would be just as meaningful and far more readable.
2. The account breakdowns are too detailed.
3. There is no indication of how the results to date compare with the profit plan and of how the results to date affect the annual plan for profit.

| | THIS YEAR | | LAST YEAR | THIS YEAR | LAST YEAR |
	APRIL	MARCH	APRIL	TO DATE	TO DATE
Gross sales	$13,675,657.40	$12,991,874.53	$11,624,308.45	$67,154,494.43	$65,796,769.33
Less:					
Returns and allowances	$ 88,664.10	$ 84,230.89	$ 75,364.44	$ 471,692.93	$ 448,107.47
Cash discounts	102,820.20	97,679.19	87,397.02	547,002.47	519,650.22
Freight and express allowed	93,961.43	89,263.36	79,867.41	499,874.82	474,880.24
	$ 285,445.73	$ 271,173.44	$ 242,628.87	$ 1,518,570.22	$ 1,442,637.93
NET SALES	$13,390,211.67	$12,720,701.09	$11,381,679.58	$65,635,924.21	$64,354,131.40
Costs and expenses:					
Cost of products sold:					
Inventory at beginning of period	$12,680,496.09	$12,546,471.20	$10,768,421.60	$11,030,237.64	$10,697,213.44
Purchased material	3,432,208.27	3,180,597.62	3,097,376.82	17,271,343.24	16,502,458.93
Direct labor	2,877,356.73	2,753,488.21	2,645,753.52	14,307,532.89	13,591,876.24
Indirect labor	2,657,832.40	2,533,549.74	2,359,157.22	13,299,874.46	12,634,849.23
Supervision	943,494.80	916,320.06	841,975.54	5,019,307.72	4,768,924.64
Other employee benefits	474,820.13	451,080.23	403,597.76	2,473,264.55	2,349,811.11
Small tools and shop supplies	87,436.26	93,058.75	73,155.62	465,124.87	441,897.62
Heat, light, and power	76,764.19	72,925.98	52,494.77	408,385.48	387,949.73
Traveling	30,124.30	28,618.09	25,605.47	160,260.81	152,441.18
Telephone and telegraph	13,086.87	12,431.70	11,123.49	69,617.84	66,124.98
Royalties	487.21	462.85	413.95	2,591.96	2,460.60
Property taxes	102,680.72	97,546.66	87,278.36	506,257.61	480,771.52
Pay roll taxes	75,749.40	71,961.93	64,382.81	402,394.72	261,387.94
Maintenance and repairs	570,280.00	574,162.37	484,501.11	3,047,307.21	2,894,076.53
Rent	23,455.20	23,455.20	19,947.62	131,348.01	124,782.44
Insurance	39,000.82	38,056.29	33,150.22	213,113.67	202,349.98
Miscellaneous	782,378.08	743,259.10	455,021.48	3,662,205.74	3,478,949.67
Scrap sales (credit*)	48,766.29*	46,327.97*	41,452.23*	259,391.62*	246,874.22*
	$24,818,879.18	$24,131,118.01	$21,381,905.13	$72,180,780.80	$68,791,451.56
Less inventory at end of period	12,977,200.03	12,680,496.09	11,030,601.49	12,977,200.03	11,030,601.49
TOTAL COST OF PRODUCTS SOLD	$11,841,679.15	$11,450,621.92	$10,351,303.64	$59,203,580.77	$57,760,850.07

Selling and advertising expense:					
Branch expense	$ 209,001.18	$ 198,552.23	$ 177,650.29	$ 1,111,189.24	$ 1,055,450.71
Advertising and promotion	125,002.62	118,763.47	106,257.43	665,072.94	631,752.25
Engineering and service	39,760.80	37,791.62	33,813.62	211,629.67	201,020.47
Home office sales	72,830.28	69,188.97	61,908.70	387,452.81	367,651.74
General	27,181.14	25,822.37	23,146.29	144,603.27	136,892.76
TOTAL SELLING AND ADVERTISING EXPENSE	$ 473,796.02	$ 450,118.66	$ 402,776.33	$ 2,519,947.93	$ 2,392,767.93
Administrative and general expense:					
Administrative expense	$ 45,505.64	$ 43,230.57	$ 38,671.92	$ 242,088.97	$ 229,987.69
General office expense	187,949.32	178,551.45	159,732.44	999,605.62	949,876.22
Tabulating	21,677.24	20,593.72	18,425.61	115,320.04	109,324.67
Legal	3,208.71	3,048.27	2,726.66	11,468.72	10,868.69
Public relations	27,480.20	26,106.21	23,359.14	146,130.82	138,764.77
TOTAL ADMINISTRATIVE AND GENERAL EXPENSE	$ 285,821.11	$ 271,530.22	$ 242,915.77	$ 1,514,614.17	$ 1,438,822.04
TOTAL COSTS AND EXPENSES	$12,601,296.28	$12,172,270.80	$10,996,995.74	$63,238,142.87	$61,592,440.04
NET OPERATING EARNINGS	788,915.39	548,430.29	384,683.84	2,397,781.34	2,761,691.36
Other income:					
Dividends	$ 37,082.00	$ 39,230.00	$ 31,450.00	$ 79,620.00	$ 75,051.00
Gain on sale of securities	46.25	-0-	-0-	46.25	24.80
Gain on disposal of property, plant, and equipment	3,127.08	5,820.10	5,207.08	32,592.04	30,960.21
Interest	1,180.00	1,121.00	1,003.00	6,446.00	6,123.70
Royalties	8,027.50	8,027.50	7,846.00	47,614.00	45,220.00
TOTAL OTHER INCOME	$ 49,462.83	$ 54,198.60	$ 45,506.08	$ 166,318.29	$ 157,379.71
Other expense:					
Interest	$ 108,233.33	$ 102,826.66	$ 91,982.67	$ 575,825.64	$ 547,621.42
Amortization of bond discount	17,300.00	15,469.00	14,762.00	86,626.42	82,267.41
TOTAL OTHER EXPENSE	$ 125,534.33	$ 118,295.66	$ 106,744.67	$ 662,452.06	$ 629,888.83
NET EARNINGS BEFORE TAXES ON INCOME	$ 712,843.89	$ 484,333.23	$ 323,445.25	$ 1,901,647.57	$ 2,289,182.24
Federal taxes on income	377,000.00	254,000.00	168,000.00	1,051,000.00	1,280,000.00
NET EARNINGS	$ 335,843.89	$ 230,333.23	$ 155,445.25	$ 850,647.57	$ 1,009,182.24

Exhibit 10–1. Old format for comparative statement of net earnings.

4. There is no indication of the monthly trends of sales, expenses, and profit.
5. In general, this report gives a crowded appearance and appears to be designed for a bookkeeper rather than an executive.

The above objections would suggest that a well-designed management report should have the following characteristics:

1. Amounts should be rounded to the nearest significant digit.
2. The amount of detail shown should be related to the management level at which the report is directed.
3. The results shown should be related to meaningful standards.
4. Where applicable, the impact of actual results upon the profit plan should be reported.
5. Information should be presented in trend form wherever possible.
6. In general, the report should be readable by being concise and avoiding a crowded appearance.

Use of Standards To Measure Performance

If reports are to be useful in providing management with the information necessary to control the operations of the organization, they must be directed toward performance measurement. However, performance can only be measured if meaningful standards of performance are available.

As evidenced by the report in Exhibit 10–1, many companies consider last year's performance to be a meaningful standard for judging current performance. This concept of performance measurement probably results from the emphasis which newspapers and financial journals place on the comparison of the sales and net earnings of a corporation with similar figures for the prior year. From the standpoint of stockholders and creditors who read these publications, comparisons with the prior year are very interesting.

However, the information required by operating management is quite different from the information desired by stockholders and creditors. A significant feature of Profitability Accounting is that the only standards used in reporting operating information are those which are directly related to the profit plan. This means that any standard which is shown on a report will be consistent with the corresponding dollars in the profit plan. In reporting of operating results to a plant foreman, for example, both standards and actual results may be expressed in man-hours, gallons, or pounds, while the same information would be expressed in dollar terms when being reported at higher management levels. By always relating operating results to the profit plan, management reports can be designed to continually focus management's attention on the impact of actual results on planned earnings.

Exception Reporting

The great volume of data which is available in most companies must be carefully condensed and summarized, if reports to busy managers are to be truly informative. The manager should not have to read through pages of data in order to determine if and where there is a need for action. In order to direct attention quickly to those areas where there is such a need, the principle of exception reporting should be followed in the design of management reports.

With the existence of performance standards and a profit plan, the reports should direct attention more toward the few significant exceptions, or variances, from planned performance which indicate a need for management action, rather than toward the bulk of the activities which are proceeding more or less according to plan. One of the main features of Profitability Accounting is that the actual earnings can be completely reconciled with the planned earnings in terms of a series of dollar variances which are separately identified by type and responsibility.

Integrated Reports Keyed to Organization Structure

Another major feature of an effective management reporting system is the integration of reports with each other in the context of a company's organization structure. On the principle of exception reporting, the reporting structure should be designed so that the chief executive has the over-all results of operations summarized for him on the top earnings statement in terms of deviations from planned performance. He should be able to quickly recognize any significant variances from planned performance and to "track" them through the various organization levels responsible for controlling the variances. If the reports are designed so that the results shown can be directly related to specific individuals, the executive can readily pinpoint responsibility for poor performance.

Exhibit 10–2 illustrates the integration of the various kinds of reports which may be of use in a company. Note that each figure on the top earnings statement can be followed into increasingly detailed reports. This applies not only to manufacturing expense variances by department, but also to sales volume, mix, and prices which can be traced to product line.

The reporting system should be designed so that each senior executive receives information concerning the performance of his immediate subordinates, who, in turn, receive information regarding each of their subordinates. This process continues down to the operating level so that each manager of a group of people receives information concerning the performance of each of his subordinates. At the lower operating levels, where control over costs is likely to be the primary measure of performance, both actual results and standards are often more effectively presented in non-dollar terms such as number of people or gallons of cutting oil. These measuring units are often more familiar to the operating supervisor than dollars and should be used as long as the physical units can be converted to dollar terms which tie into the profit plan.

Detailed information should be presented at lower levels of management, but there should be more summarization in the presentation of information at higher levels of management. At higher levels of management, the tendency should be to limit the scope of the information presented to that which highlights problems and pinpoints responsibility for their correction.

Reports should always be designed with the reader's scope of interest in mind. A shop foreman is not particularly interested in the level of advertising expense. Similarly, the advertising manager is not interested in seeing information regarding the efficiency of the maintenance department.

MODEL REPORTS FOR THE
VORTEX MANUFACTURING COMPANY

The type of reports generated by a Profitability Accounting system can best be visualized by considering a hypothetical company using Profitability Accounting. At this point, it is important

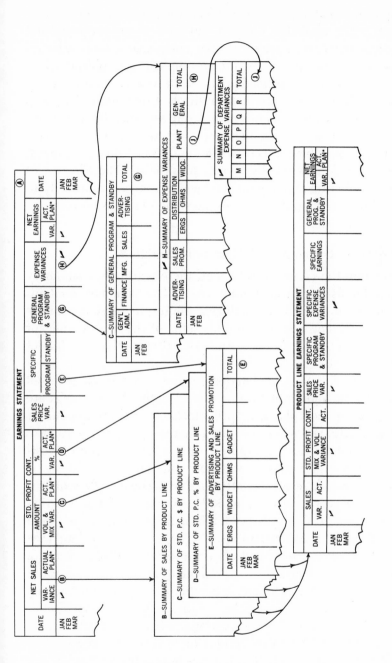

Exhibit 10–2. Integrated operating statements.

to emphasize that reports do not control performance or make decisions. The most that a report can do is reveal problems and guide the executive in taking proper corrective action. The reports which follow are designed to accomplish these objectives.

The reports to be described are from the Vortex Manufacturing Company. It is a multi-product, multi-plant operation. The firm manufactures refrigerators in a completely separate, integrated division according to the organization chart in Exhibit 10–3. This division is responsible for its own sales and its own manufacturing. It is comparable to a wholly owned subsidiary. The Electronics Division of the firm manufactures television sets and radios. Both product lines are manufactured in the same plant, using common processing facilities.

Statements of Earnings and Financial Condition

Preceding the earnings statement, there is usually a summary of highlights as shown in Exhibit 10–4. This summary contains comments by the controller analyzing the results presented in the earnings statement, and it highlights some of the most significant financial data on company performance. It is another example of exception reporting.

Exhibit 10–5 is a consolidated statement of net earnings for all divisions for the month of April, a good month. Net earnings are $258,000 better than plan for April, $622,000 better than plan for the year to date, and it is anticipated that the company will make $2.03 per share for the year, representing a 7.3% return on investment, which is also significantly better than plan.

These favorable results are attributable to the net effect of four factors. First, sales are running $974,000 ahead of those antici-pated this year to date. These additional sales, of course, yield additional profit contribution—some $234,000 year to date (see the box in the lower left-hand corner of Exhibit 10–5). Second, the company is selling a mix of products that has a higher profit contribution rate than the average anticipated. The rate is only two percentage points better than plan for the year, but that is equivalent to $514,000. Third, variations from established sales prices are unfavorable to the extent of $161,000 for the year to date. Fourth, over-all expenses have been running well below the

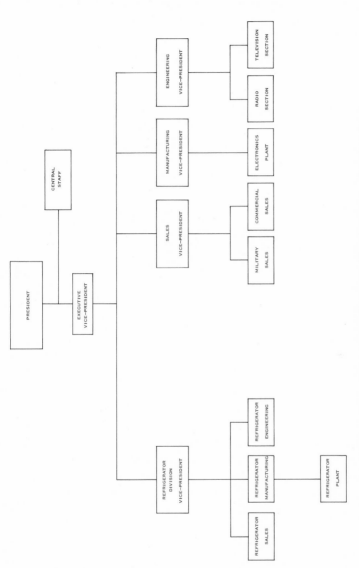

Exhibit 10-3. Vortex Manufacturing Company organization chart.

FIGURE 10 - 4

VORTEX MANUFACTURING COMPANY

HIGHLIGHTS

(DOLLARS IN THOUSANDS)

	ORIGINAL PLAN	CURRENT FORECAST
GROSS SALES	$71,012	$71,986
CAPITAL TURNOVER	2.06	2.09
RETURN ON SALES	2.7 %	3.5%
RETURN ON ASSETS EMPLOYED	5.5%	7.3%
EARNINGS PER SHARE	1.53	2.03
PROFIT CONTRIBUTION	26.5%	27.2%
NET EARNINGS	$ 1,894	$ 2,516

	APRIL	YEAR TO DATE
GROSS SALES	$8,155	$23,398
PLANNED PROFIT CONTRIBUTION	1,532	5,394
VOLUME VARIANCE	95 *	234 *
MIX VARIANCE	252 *	514 *
ACTUAL PROFIT CONTRIBUTION	1,879	6,142
EXPENSE VARIANCES	187 *	563 *
NET EARNINGS	337	832

GROSS SALES ARE OVER PLANNED VOLUME PRIMARILY AS A RESULT OF THE SUCCESS OF OUR NEW TELEVISION LINE. IN ORDER TO ACHIEVE THIS VOLUME, PROMOTIONAL PRICE CONCESSIONS HAVE BEEN GRANTED WHICH EXCEEDED THOSE PLANNED BY $119,000. RADIO SALES WERE AHEAD OF PLAN THIS MONTH, BUT STILL BEHIND YEAR TO DATE. REFRIGERATOR SALES ARE CONTINUING TO LAG. THIS CONDITION SHOULD IMPROVE IN MAY WITH AN INCREASE IN RESIDENTIAL CONSTRUCTION.

IN ADDITION TO A FAVORABLE VOLUME PICTURE, THE PROFIT CONTRIBUTION RATE IS RUNNING 2.2% OR $514,000 BETTER THAN PLAN. MOST OF THIS FAVORABLE MIX VARIANCE IS ATTRIBUTABLE TO THE NEW TELEVISION LINE.

THE FAVORABLE EXPENSE VARIANCE IS PARTIALLY DUE TO THE REDUCTION IN INDIRECT PERSONNEL IN ELECTRONICS MANUFACTURING. THE ADVERTISING PROGRAM IS ALSO BEING ACCOMPLISHED AT LESS THAN ANTICIPATED COSTS. EXPENDITURES FOR RESEARCH HAVE BEEN HELD BACK BY DELAYS IN THE COMPLETION OF NEW LABORATORIES. A VERY FAVORABLE PURCHASE OF ELECTRONIC COMPONENTS WAS MADE THIS MONTH WHICH ALSO ACCOUNTED FOR PART OF THE FAVORABLE VARIANCE.

THE REFRIGERATOR DIVISION IS CONTINUING TO TURN IN UNFAVORABLE PERFORMANCE VARIANCES PRIMARILY AS A RESULT OF EXCESSIVE LABOR ALLOWANCES. A SOLUTION IS BEING SOUGHT THROUGH THE APPLICATION OF OPERATIONS RESEARCH TO SCHEDULING PROBLEMS.

THE CURRENT FORECAST REFLECTS THE INCREASE IN VOLUME AND THE FAVORABLE RESULTS OF OPERATIONS WHICH HAVE BEEN REALIZED THIS YEAR TO DATE. OTHER FACTORS AND ASSUMPTIONS BASIC TO THE ORIGINAL FORECAST WERE EVALUATED IN THE LIGHT OF CURRENT KNOWLEDGE BUT NO EVENTS OR CHANGES IN TRENDS WERE NOTED OF SUFFICIENT MAGNITUDE TO WARRANT A CHANGE IN OUR FORECAST.

* FAVORABLE VARIANCE

Exhibit 10–4. Vortex Manufacturing Company summary of highlights.

( ) = UNFAVORABLE VARIANCE   (DOLLARS IN THOUSANDS)

MONTH	GROSS SALES OVER (UNDER)	GROSS SALES ACTUAL/PLAN*	STD PROFIT CONTRIB. AMOUNT OVER (UNDER)	STD PROFIT CONTRIB. AMOUNT ACTUAL/PLAN*	PER CENT SALES OVER (UNDER)	PER CENT SALES ACTUAL/PLAN*	SALES PRICE VARIANCES OVER (UNDER)	EXPENSES VARIANCES (OVER) UNDER	EXPENSES STANDBY PLAN	EXPENSES PRO-GRAMMED PLAN	OPER. EARN. BEFORE TAXES OVER (UNDER)	OPER. EARN. BEFORE TAXES ACTUAL/PLAN*	BONUS & PROFIT SHARING OVER (UNDER)	BONUS & PROFIT SHARING ACTUAL/PLAN*	NET EARNINGS OVER (UNDER)	NET EARNINGS ACTUAL/PLAN*	EARNINGS PER SHARE ACTUAL/PLAN*	MONTH
JAN	(225)	3,750	(190)	1,073	(3.2)	28.6	(59)	164	850	249	(85)	79	(17)	16	(34)	31	.02	JAN
FEB	237	5,035	205	1,432	2.8	28.4	(42)	140	852	284	303	394	21	79	143	160	.13	FEB
MAR	483	6,458	386	1,758	4.3	27.6	(10)	183	858	307	559	766	43	153	255	304	.24	MAR
APR	479	8,155	347	1,879	3.1	23.0	(50)	237	856	385	534	825	32	165	258	337	.27	APR
MAY		5,991*		1,617*		27.0*			855	245		517*		103*		211*	.17*	MAY
JUN		6,348*		1,775*		27.8*			855	50		870*		174*		343*	.28*	JUN
JUL		6,262*		1,712*		27.4*			855	277		580*		116*		209*	.17*	JUL
AUG		7,111*		1,927*		27.2*			856	324		747*		149*		292*	.24*	AUG
SEP		6,804*		1,854*		27.2*			856	372		626*		125*		225*	.18*	SEP
OCT		5,305*		1,527*		28.9*			855	237		435*		87*		158*	.13*	OCT
NOV		5,413*		1,511*		27.9*			856	276		379*		76*		139*	.11*	NOV
DEC		5,354*		1,498*		29.1*			858	327		313*		63*		107*	.09*	DEC
YEAR TO DATE	974	23,398	748	6,142	2.2	26.2	(161)	724	3,416	1,225	1,311	2,064	79	413	622	832	.66	
ORIGINAL PLAN	71,012	18,815		26.5					10,262	3,333	5,220		1,227		1,894		1.53	
CURRENT FORECAST	71,986	19,563		27.2			(161)	724	10,262	3,333	6,531		1,306		2,516		2.03	

	THIS MONTH	YEAR TO DATE
PLANNED EARNINGS BEFORE TAXES	291	753
SALES VOLUME VARIANCE	95	234
SALES MIX VARIANCE	252	514
SALES PRICE VARIANCE	(50)	(161)
EXPENSE VARIANCE	237	724
ACTUAL EARNINGS BEFORE TAXES	825	2,064

	ORIGINAL PLAN	CURRENT FORECAST
AVERAGE CORPORATE ASSETS	34,500	34,500
CAPITAL TURNOVER	2.06	2.09
X		
RETURN ON SALES	2.7%	3.5%
RETURN ON ASSETS EMPLOYED	5.5%	7.3%

Exhibit 10–5.   Vortex Manufacturing Company statement of net earnings.

budgeted and standard amounts as is indicated by the $237,000 favorable expense variance in April and an aggregate favorable variance for the year of $724,000. This indicates either unusually effective cost control or weakness in the standards and should be investigated.

This report is designed to emphasize deviations from plan. It keeps management thinking about the objectives that they have intended to accomplish. It shows clearly the present position relative to the desired goals. The current forecast for the remainder of the year is an index of the probability of reaching that goal. The information given in this report also suggests that perhaps management should look at current and projected economic conditions and revise their goals in the light of their findings. The position indicated in this report is certainly favorable, but it may not be as favorable as it really should be in relation to current economic conditions. It might also be that the favorable sales picture has been achieved by "appropriating" business from later in the year, in which case the current forecast of the profit plan may have to be revised downward.

The amounts shown on the summary statement of net earnings can be traced to various detailed analysis. Only one of these, the summary of variances in Exhibit 10–8, is illustrated in this chapter, but an idea of some of the other kinds of statements which support the top earnings statement can be gained from Exhibit 10–2. In the case of Vortex, there would be an analysis which showed how much of the sales and profit contribution was provided by the refrigerator division, military sales, and commercial sales. Underlying each of these would be product line earnings summaries. In each case the planned and actual performances would be compared.

The statement of financial condition shown in Exhibit 10–6 is a somewhat novel form of balance sheet presentation. The trend format, however, can be quite helpful for focusing attention on seasonal patterns in current assets and liabilities and as an aid to planning cash requirement.

Division (and Product Line) Statements of Earnings

Exhibit 10–7 is a Division Earnings Statement for the Refrigerator Division. As does the net earnings statement, this report

ASSETS

MONTH	NET WORKING CAPITAL Plan	Actual	CURRENT ASSETS CASH AND SECURITIES Plan	Actual	NET ACCOUNTS RECEIVABLE Plan	Actual	INVENTORIES Plan	Actual	NET PROPERTY, PLANT AND EQUIPMENT Plan	Actual	TOTAL ASSETS EMPLOYED Plan	Actual	MONTH
JAN	13,009	12,486	1,650	1,548	4,500	4,291	13,900	13,991	11,450	11,974	31,500	31,804	JAN
FEB	13,001	12,884	950	852	5,100	5,094	14,700	14,751	11,500	11,599	32,250	32,296	FEB
MAR	13,575	13,539	1,000	827	5,800	5,902	14,800	14,843	11,150	11,207	32,750	32,779	MAR
APR	12,948	13,737	850	973	6,000	6,072	15,000	15,179	11,650	10,897	33,500	33,121	APR
MAY	13,446		700		5,200		15,200		11,400		32,500		MAY
JUN	13,714		600		5,200		15,400		11,550		32,750		JUN
JUL	13,417		1,000		5,000		15,000		11,750		32,750		JUL
AUG	14,176		1,850		5,400		14,400		11,350		33,000		AUG
SEP	14,876		2,650		5,200		14,200		10,950		33,000		SEP
OCT	14,510		2,650		4,800		14,000		11,050		32,500		OCT
NOV	14,692		2,100		4,750		14,000		11,150		32,000		NOV
DEC	14,742		1,850		5,000		13,900		10,750		31,500		DEC

LIABILITIES AND STOCKHOLDERS' INVESTMENT

MONTH	CURRENT RATIO Plan	Actual	CURRENT LIABILITIES TRADE ACCOUNTS PAYABLE Plan	Actual	NOTES PAYABLE TO BANKS Plan	Actual	ACCRUED INCOME TAXES Plan	Actual	LONG-TERM DEBT Plan	Actual	STOCKHOLDERS' INVESTMENT Plan	Actual	MONTH
JAN	2.8	2.7	3,809	4,111	3,000	3,000	232	233	5,000	5,000	19,459	19,460	JAN
FEB	2.7	2.6	4,672	4,756	2,800	2,800	277	257	5,000	5,000	19,501	19,483	FEB
MAR	2.7	2.7	5,016	5,002	2,600	2,600	409	431	5,000	5,000	19,725	19,746	MAR
APR	2.5	2.6	5,824	5,371	2,400	2,400	678	716	5,000	5,000	19,598	19,634	APR
MAY	2.8		4,507		2,200		947		5,000		19,846		MAY
JUN	2.8		4,197		2,000		1,289		5,000		20,264		JUN
JUL	2.8		4,192		1,800		1,591		5,000		20,167		JUL
AUG	2.9		3,895		1,600		1,979		5,000		20,526		AUG
SEP	3.1		4,864		1,400		910		5,000		20,826		SEP
OCT	3.1		4,504		1,200		1,136		5,000		20,660		OCT
NOV	3.4		3,825		1,000		1,333		5,000		20,842		NOV
DEC	3.5		5,108		800		100		4,500		20,992		DEC

Exhibit 10–6. Vortex Manufacturing Company data with respect to financial condition.

() INDICATES UNFAVORABLE VARIANCE (DOLLARS IN THOUSANDS)

DATE	GROSS SALES OVER (UNDER)	GROSS SALES ACTUAL PLAN*	STD PROFIT CONTRIB AMOUNT OVER (UNDER)	STD PROFIT CONTRIB AMOUNT ACTUAL PLAN*	STD PROFIT CONTRIB PER CENT SALES OVER (UNDER)	STD PROFIT CONTRIB PER CENT SALES ACTUAL PLAN*	STANDBY EXPENSES SPECIFIC	STANDBY EXPENSES GENERAL	PROGRAMMED EXPENSES	STANDARD PRODUCT LINE EARNINGS	DIVISION SALES PRICE VARIANCES BETTER (WORSE)	DIVISION EXPENSE VARIANCES BETTER (WORSE)	DIVISION OPERATING EARNINGS OVER (UNDER)	DIVISION OPERATING EARNINGS ACTUAL PLAN*	ORDERS RECEIVED THIS YEAR	ORDERS RECEIVED THIS YEAR	ORDER BACKLOG THIS YEAR	ORDER BACKLOG THIS YEAR
JAN	(231)	1,266	(89)	328	(2.0)	25.9	54	270	90	(86)	(15)	(15)	(119)	(116)	371	601	1,315	749
FEB	(102)	1,830	(41)	490	(0.8)	26.8	54	270	114	52	(6)	2	(45)	48	972	1,100	1,511	1,269
MAR	(10)	2,609	(4)	749	(0.1)	28.7	57	273	116	303	8	(26)	(22)	285	1,241	1,301	1,427	527
APR	(45)	2,331	(16)	683	(0.1)	29.3	57	273	118	235	(2)	(13)	(31)	220	622	727	1,311	608
MAY		1,860*		489*		26.3*	57	273	84	75				75 *		711		371
JUN		2,193*		645*		29.4*	54	270	3	318				318 *		1,921		1,006
JUL		2,109*		591*		28.0*	57	270	96	168				168 *		1,875		1,137
AUG		2,145*		618*		28.8*	57	273	90	198				198 *		992		1,192
SEP		2,508*		708*		28.2*	54	273	108	273				273 *		1,176		1,187
OCT		1,932*		534*		27.6*	57	270	105	102				102 *		1,483		1,369
NOV		1,419*		417*		29.4*	57	270	81	9				9 *		1,519		908
DEC		1,290*		378*		29.3*	54	273	105	(54)				(54)*		1,633		1,579
YEAR TO DATE	(388)	8,036	(150)	2,250	(0.5)	28.0	222	1,086	438	504	(15)	(52)	(217)	437	3,206	3,729		
ORIGINAL PLAN		23,880		6,780		28.4	669	3,258	1,110	1,743				1,743				
CURRENT FORECAST		23,492		6,630		28.2	669	3,258	1,110	1,578	(15)	(52)		1,526				

VOLUME AND MIX VARIANCE

	THIS MONTH	YEAR TO DATE
PLANNED EARNINGS	251	657
VOLUME VARIANCE	(14)	(110)
MIX VARIANCE	(2)	(40)
SALES PRICE VARIANCE	(2)	(15)
EXPENSE VARIANCES	(13)	(52)
ACTUAL PROFIT CONTRIBUTION	220	437

RETURN ON ASSETS

	ORIGINAL PLAN	CURRENT FORECAST
AVERAGE DIVISION ASSETS	14,431	14,140
CAPITAL TURNOVER	1.65	1.66
RETURN ON SALES	7.2%	6.5%
RETURN ON ASSETS EMPLOYED	11.9%	10.8%

Exhibit 10–7. Vortex Manufacturing Company statement of earnings—Refrigerator Division.

presents information in columnar fashion so that trends are highlighted. An examination of this report will reveal that this division certainly is not experiencing the favorable variances being enjoyed by the company as a whole.

The division statement includes the four basic kinds of variances shown on the corporate net earnings statement and is carried to the level of operating earnings. Product line earnings statements, which are not illustrated here, are generally quite similar to the type of division statement shown in Exhibit 10–7, except that they usually do not include expense variances unless the latter can be specifically identified with a particular product line. Usually expense variances are only identifiable with operations, in which case an arbitrary allocation to product may serve no purpose.

Note that standby expenses on the division statement are divided into two categories—specific and general. The specific standby expenses include depreciation of plant and equipment, salaries of key supervisors, and other costs that would be incurred as long as the division is maintained in a ready-to-operate condition. The general standby costs, on the other hand, are the division's share of general corporate standby costs.

These standby costs are charged to the division on the basis of a planned allocation reflecting a long-term forecast, perhaps for five years, of its activity in relation to that of the total company. They are not lowered just because the division experiences a temporary decline in volume; nor are they raised if the division experiences a temporary improvement in volume. These costs are not allocated on the basis of the current sales volume, a mistake made by many companies. Charging a higher proportion of corporate standby costs to the division which increases its proportion of corporate sales distorts the reported comparative performance by diverting profits from the division which has done most to provide them to others less deserving.

The programmed expenses shown in the Division Earnings Statement are the costs of special projects undertaken by this division. They are not related to volume and do not recur regularly. A special advertising campaign for the division or a general plant improvement program would fall into this category.

Variance Reports

A summary of the variances from planned performance for the corporation is presented in the variance report in Exhibit 10–8. Notice that the total of variances shown on this report equals the total of the expense and sales price variances shown on the statement of net earnings, but does not include sales volume and mix variances. The first two kinds of variances are deductions from (or additions to) the standard profit contribution obtained; the latter two are deviations in standard profit contribution from the planned amount. This variance report serves to analyze variances by cause so that senior executives can determine the nature of the variance and, most importantly, begin to pinpoint responsibility for unfavorable variances so that corrective action can be taken. For further definition of responsibility for unfavorable variances, other variance reports, showing responsibility at lower management levels, should be examined.

Exhibit 10–9 shows who is responsible for the $13,000 unfavorable variance in the Refrigerator Division. Of the directors of the three major units in the Refrigerator Division, T. Sawyer, Director of Manufacturing, is responsible for both the largest amount and the largest percentage of variance from budget. Within his unit, it is the Plating Department that is the major culprit.

Notice that, in these reports, extraneous details that can interfere with communication have been eliminated. Each of the figures shown, for instance, is in terms of significant digits. The last three dollar digits and the cent digits are not reported. Because of the purpose of this report and the magnitude of the figures involved, the Plant Manager cares very little whether Mr. Wilde in the Plating Department is $11,714 or $12,356 in excess of his budget. The last three digits are not decision-making information.

Departmental Reports

Exhibit 10–10 is a detailed comparison of actual performance against allowable performance for the Plating Department. This report is prepared both for use by Mr. Wilde in evaluating his own position and also for the Plant Manager as an index of Mr. Wilde's performance.

( ) INDICATES UNFAVORABLE VARIANCE   (DOLLARS IN THOUSANDS)

| DATE | TOTAL | SPENDING PERFORMANCE | | | | | PROGRAMMED EXPENSE | | | DATE |
		CENTRAL STAFF	REFRIGERATOR DIVISION	ELECTRONIC SALES	ELECTRONIC MANUFACTURING	ELECTRONIC ENGINEERING	ADVERTISING	PRODUCT DEVELOPMENT	RESEARCH	
JAN	105	2	(15)	(17)	57	11	47	15	23	JAN
FEB	98	(6)	2	(6)	62	13	43	(17)	65	FEB
MAR	173	9	(26)	(2)	34	(2)	13	15	54	MAR
APR	187	3	(13)	(8)	45	4	10	(5)	76	APR
MAY										MAY
JUN										JUN
JUL										JUL
AUG										AUG
SEP										SEP
OCT										OCT
NOV										NOV
DEC										DEC
YEAR TO DATE	563	8	(52)	(33)	198	26	113	8	218	YEAR TO DATE

| DATE | SALES PRICE | PURCHASE PRICE | YIELD | MANAGEMENT DECISION | CONVERSION | SPECIFIC SALES DEDUCTIONS | | | | | DATE |
						TRADE DISCOUNTS	COMMISSIONS	FREIGHT OUT	ALLOWANCES	CASH DISCOUNTS ALLOWED	
JAN	(59)	19	12	(2)	(16)	6	2	7	2	11	JAN
FEB	(42)	(8)	8	(5)	(11)	(7)	1	5	(3)	4	FEB
MAR	(10)	27	(4)	(12)	18	15	3	22	1	18	MAR
APR	(50)	37	15	- 0 -	29	12	(4)	24	(1)	13	APR
MAY											MAY
JUN											JUN
JUL											JUL
AUG											AUG
SEP											SEP
OCT											OCT
NOV											NOV
DEC											DEC
YEAR TO DATE	(161)	75	31	(19)	20	26	2	58	(1)	46	YEAR TO DATE

Exhibit 10–8. Summary of variances by type.

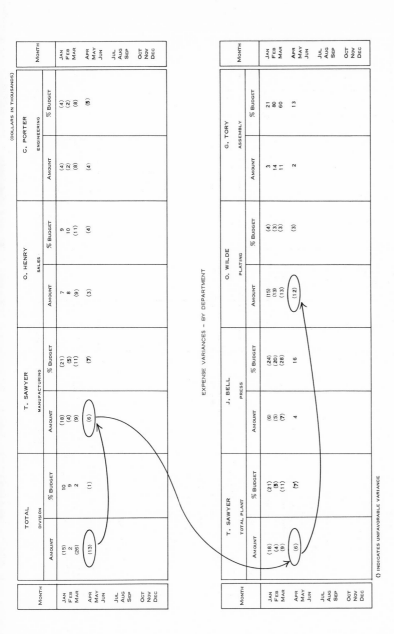

Exhibit 10-9. Variances, tracked to source—Refrigerator Division.

MONTH : APRIL
LEVEL OF OPERATION 80%

PLATING DEPARTMENT — O. WILDE

(DOLLARS IN THOUSANDS)

EXPENSE ITEM	MONTH			YEAR TO DATE		
	VARIANCE		ACTUAL EXPENSE	VARIANCE		ACTUAL EXPENSE
	AMOUNT	% TO BUDGET		AMOUNT	% TO BUDGET	
MANUFACTURING EXPENSE						
INDIRECT LABOR :						
SALARIES	(4)	(17)	27	(19)	(18)	122
MATERIAL HANDLING	3	25	9	6	13	40
SETUP	(2)	(100)	4	(7)	(64)	18
INSPECTION	2	40	3	3	19	13
MAINTENANCE	(11)	(17)	78	(29)	(7)	317
OTHER	(6)	(30)	26	(22)	(26)	107
TOTAL	(18)	(14)	147	(68)	(12)	617
OVERTIME PREMIUM	(2)	(40)	7	(7)	(29)	31
FRINGE BENEFITS	4	22	14	(22)	(61)	58
INDIRECT MATERIAL :						
PERISHABLE TOOLS	1	33	2	2	22	7
MAINTENANCE	11	14	70	24	8	286
OTHER	(2)	(50)	6	(9)	(50)	27
TOTAL	10	11	78	17	5	320
OTHER EXPENSE	9	23	29	39	25	117
TOTAL MANUFACTURING EXPENSE	3	1	275	(41)	4	1,143
DIRECT LABOR						
DIRECT LABOR VARIANCE	(18)			(8)		
OVERTIME	–			(6)		
TOTAL DIRECT LABOR VARIANCE	(18)			(14)		
DIRECT MATERIAL						
MATERIAL USAGE VARIANCE	1			2		
SCRAP VARIANCE	2			–		
TOTAL DIRECT MATERIAL VARIANCE	3			2		
TOTAL DEPARTMENTAL VARIANCES	(12)			(53)		

Exhibit 10–10. Departmental expense report.

This detailed report shows that the $12,000 unfavorable variance is the result of an unfavorable direct labor variance of $18,000, a favorable direct material variance of $3,000, and a $3,000 favorable manufacturing expense variance. Although the over-all variance is relatively small, individual items represent significant departures from allowable performance. Indirect salaries, maintenance labor, other indirect labor, and the direct labor variance are particularly out of line. Dollars of variance may not mean too much to Mr. Wilde; therefore, these dollar figures are supplemented by weekly labor efficiency reports expressed in man-hours and by weekly material usage and scrap reports expressed in physical units. These reports provide the kind of information upon which Mr. Wilde can act.

The Plant Manager wants to know what Mr. Wilde is going to do about these departures from acceptable performance. Exhibit 10–11 is an example of a variance letter prepared by Mr. Wilde to explain material departures from the flexible budget. The items that he decides to explain should be determined by company policy. For instance, he might be required to explain all variances in excess of $1,000, or he might be required to explain all variances in excess of a given percentage of the budget. In reviewing his report, it is noted that he does not explain any of the favorable variances. The Plant Manager may very well challenge this decision.

SUMMARY

Because management reports are the "finished product" of a Profitability Accounting system, it is important that all reports be carefully designed to meet the information requirements of management. The proper test of the adequacy of any report is whether it provides information that assists managers in controlling performance and in making sound decisions.

The form of presentation should make the report readable to the individual to whom it is directed. This can be accomplished by adjusting the amount of detail presented to the management level at which the report is directed, using trend format wherever possible, being concise, and avoiding a crowded appearance on the report.

EXPENSE ITEM	AMOUNT (IN THOUSANDS)	EXPLANATION OF VARIANCE	CURRENT CORRECTIVE ACTION
SALARIES	(4)	SALARY FORCE WAS INCREASED TO EXPECTED 100% LEVEL, BUT ACTUALLY OPERATED AT 80%.	SALARY FORCE CUT BACK TO OPERATING LEVEL TO FIT CURRENT OUTLOOK.
SETUPS	(2)	COST OF WORKING ALL SETUP MEN EVERY SATURDAY DURING MONTH FOR NECESSARY EXTRA LINES.	EXTRA WORK COMPLETED.
MAINTENANCE	(11)	PREMIUM DAYS WORKED TO REPAIR UNITS CAUSING DOWNTIME, THUS CREATING MORE BACKLOG ON BALANCE OF MAINTENANCE WORK.	THIS AREA IS BEING WATCHED CLOSELY.
OTHER	(6)	EXTRA MANPOWER NECESSARY TO REMOVE PURCHASED MATERIALS FROM FREIGHT CARS, AND MOVE MATERIALS INTO HOPPER.	TEMPORARY SITUATION, CORRECTED IN MONTH OF CHARGE.
OVERTIME PREMIUM	(2)	SETUP AND MAINTENANCE WORKED SATURDAYS DURING MONTH.	NO OVERTIME IS PERMITTED WITHOUT PROPER APPROVAL. EVERY ATTEMPT IS BEING MADE TO HOLD THIS CHARGE TO A MINIMUM.
OTHER INDIRECT MATERIAL	(2)	COSTS OF LUBRICATORS FOR CONVEYORS AND PRESSURE TANKS IN DEPT. 63.	NO HISTORICAL DATA WAS AVAILABLE TO SET BUDGET MORE ACCURATELY. NO ACTION PLANNED.
DIRECT LABOR	(18)	TRAINING OF APPRENTICE WORKERS INCLUDED IN DIRECT LABOR CHARGE.	APPRENTICE TRAINING OVERLOOKED IN SETTING STANDARDS LAST YEAR. EXPECT TRAINING TO STAY SMALL, WILL INCLUDE NEXT YEAR. NO STANDARD REVISION BELIEVED NECESSARY NOW.

SIGNED _____
SUPERVISOR, PLATING DEPT.

Exhibit 10–11. Supervisor's explanation (variance letter).

To facilitate performance measurement, actual results should always be expressed in relation to meaningful standards, and these should be tied to the profit plan. At lower operating levels, the most useful standard may be expressed in quantities other than dollars, but it should also be included in the profit plan in dollar terms. At all levels, management reports should focus attention on "exceptions" from planned performance.

The management reports should be integrated with each other, so that summary figures can be readily traced to the appropriate detail, and with the organization structure. Each executive should receive information pertinent to his area of responsibility, and helpful in evaluating performance of his subordinates.

Chapter 11

Using Profitability Data in Pricing Decisions

INTRODUCTION

DECISIONS as to product prices are probably the most important and most frequent decisions which businessmen must make in their efforts to earn a respectable return on investment.

At the same time, the product-pricing area is probably the one in which there are the least agreement on theory and the least consistency in practice. This lack of generally accepted "ground rules" is due to the variety of factors which influence the pricing decisions and to the difficulty of expressing these factors in precise, quantitative terms.

There are at least five basic considerations in a businessman's setting of his product prices. These are

1. The customers' demand curves, i.e., how much the customers would buy at any given price during a particular time period
2. The price and availability of competitive and substitute products
3. The legality of a price in terms of its effect on competition in any sector of economy
4. The cost and investment required to produce and sell at various volumes
5. The most profitable combination of price, volume, and cost

The emphasis given to each of the above considerations in the thinking of a particular individual is dependent upon his background. Thus, a marketing man is likely to think of the last two considerations together as "determining cost and desired profit," while an accountant is likely to combine the first two in his thinking as "estimating demand." Although this chapter is primarily concerned with the use of accounting, and particularly cost, data in pricing decisions, it is most important to emphasize that cost is only one element that affects a pricing decision.

The fact that product cost can be readily expressed in quantitative terms (which gives an impression of precision, however unwarranted) probably accounts for much of the exaggerated emphasis on cost as a final determinant of selling price. In practice, cost is probably the least important of the considerations mentioned above. Certainly it is not the sole consideration in pricing. Cost may set a lower limit on the price at which a particular producer will accept business, but this does not mean that he will do any business at that price. Furthermore, the cost which is used for setting such lower limits is not a precise, invariant figure for each product. Full product cost is at best an approximation based on a set of assumptions. The particular assumptions and the resulting product cost which determine a lower price limit should differ under different conditions of demand and unused facilities, as will be discussed later in this chapter. Rigid adherence to full cost-plus pricing tends to reduce profit when demand is high and prices can be raised, and it tends to cut off the profit contribution toward standby and programmed costs when demand is low and desirable prices cannot be obtained.

On the other hand, prices have to cover costs in the long run, and a company that does not give explicit consideration to costs when setting short-run prices is likely to find itself in serious trouble. This is particularly true where there is a dominant sales policy of shaving prices in order to increase volume. The bulk of this chapter is concerned with the kinds of cost considerations that should underlie pricing decisions.

Three Basic Uses of Costs

Joel Dean lists three valid uses of costs in the process of establishing prices:

1. To measure the effects of alternative prices upon profits
2. To guess what customers, competitors, and potential competitors will do in response to a proposed price
3. To justify a course of action that has already been decided upon by other means; here costs may be used to justify prices to the government (where the Robinson-Patman Act applies), to price regulatory commissions, or to customers and the general public [1]

The bulk of this chapter is devoted to the first of these three uses of cost, and the third use is discussed briefly in the section on the Robinson-Patman Act. Discussion of the second use of costs is limited to the immediately following paragraph.

Buyers' alternative costs are always important, particularly in the pricing of capital goods. The amount of cost savings that can be offered to the customer may be more important than the costs of the producer. Competitors' reactions can be guessed more accurately with knowledge of the competitors' costs. Where these cannot be obtained via "espionage," it may be worthwhile to use one's own costs merely as a point of departure for estimating competitors' costs. This may be particularly useful in deciding

---

[1] Joel Dean, "Cost Forecasting and Price Policy," *The Journal of Marketing*, Jan. 1949.

whether competitors will follow a price increase or decrease. Potential competition, or rather the desire to keep out potential competition, may be the reason for setting price based on cost. Here the producer's cost is actually serving as the estimated cost of unborn competitors.

Before proceeding to discuss some valid uses of cost for pricing purposes, it is worthwhile to elaborate briefly on some of the non-cost considerations. Considerations of demand and competition are too important to be ignored in any discussion of pricing. Consequently the next few pages are devoted to a brief, illustrative résumé of some economic theories, some pricing strategies, and some legal restrictions on pricing.

ECONOMIC THEORY OF MONOPOLISTIC COMPETITION

Up until the 1930's, the theories of the economist had little direct impact on the pricing practices of businessmen. The economist was heavily concerned with long-term balances between average revenues and average costs for an industry. The businessman was fully occupied in trying to set the current price for his own particular products. The economist elaborated on the best courses of action under "perfect competition," where no single buyer or seller could significantly affect market price, or "simple monopoly," where one seller was so dominant that he could safely set price without regard to the actions of competitors. Most businessmen faced practical pricing problems which did not seem to fit either category.

The economists of the day who elaborated on perfect competition were fundamentally correct in the direction of their efforts. They were trying to build a model which was simple enough to provide quantitative understanding of price-cost-volume relationships and general enough to permit application to a variety of special cases. The businessmen who tried to develop specific rules for their own pricing decisions usually bogged down in the complexity of actual factors and finally settled for simple empirical rules such as "follow the market," "all the traffic will bear," or "cost-plus." The simplicity of the perfect competition model was no more exaggerated than these. And the model did fit some actual situations rather well, although it was certainly not applicable to all. Still, it was the basis for building a subsequent model that has more general application.

In 1933, Joan Robinson and Edward Chamberlain came out in print with the theory of monopolistic, or imperfect, competition.[2] In essence, this theory states that each seller has a partial monopoly because of product differentiation. In other words, the seller's product is at least partially distinguished in the customer's mind from all competitive products, by selling and advertising effort. Thus, instead of a single demand curve for all companies in an industry, as under perfect competition, each company has its own demand curve. The shape of the curve (the extent to which demand changes with price) is affected by the prices of competitors, but it still is the company's demand curve, not the industry's.

The recommended pricing policy under monopolistic competition is essentially the same as under monopoly; i.e., set the price at the point where marginal (or incremental) costs equal marginal revenue. This is tantamount to setting selling prices based on maximizing short-run profits. Edward Hawkins and Joel Dean have shown how the conventional marginal cost and marginal revenue curves of the economist can be converted into a graph of total revenue and total cost, a graph which is generally more meaningful to businessmen because of its similarity to the breakeven chart.[3]

Exhibit 11–1 illustrates the conventional economic approach to price setting under monopoly or monopolistic competition. The demand curve shows the decreasing quantities that can be sold at increasing prices. It is also equal to the total revenue divided by the total units that can be sold at each price. The marginal revenue curve shows the net change in total revenue as a result of each additional unit to be sold. For example, if one unit could be sold at a price of $3.25 and two units could be sold at $3.24 each, the marginal revenue would be $3.23 (2 × $3.24 − $3.25). Note that this is made up of the $3.24 for the second

[2] Joan Robinson, *The Economics of Imperfect Competition* (London: Macmillan & Co., Ltd., 1933). Edward Chamberlain, *The Theory of Monopolistic Competition* (Cambridge, Mass.: Harvard University Press, 1933).

[3] Edward R. Hawkins, "Price Policies and Theory," *Journal of Marketing*, Jan. 1954, p. 233. Joel Dean, *Managerial Economics* (Englewood Cliffs, N.J.: Prentice-Hall, Inc., 1951), p. 405.

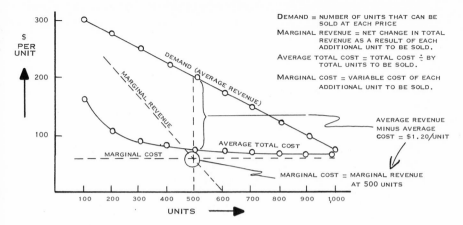

Exhibit 11–1. Equating marginal costs and revenues—the classical approach to pricing under monopoly or monopolistic competition.

unit minus the $0.01 decrease which results from also having to sell the first unit at $3.24 instead of $3.25. Average total cost is merely total cost divided by total units. It approaches marginal cost (variable cost per unit) as standby costs are spread over more and more units. The pricing rule implied by the model is to set price (and presumably volume) where marginal revenue equals marginal cost.

Exhibit 11–2 shows essentially the same thing in different form. The graph shows a series of curves that represent potential total revenues at different prices, where TR_{10} represents a price of $3.00, TR_9 a price of $2.75, and so on. A total demand curve is shown by connecting the various total revenues which could be obtained at each price, and this curve is related to a total cost curve which begins at a level of standby costs and increases linearly with volume. Presumably the $2.00 price ($TR_6$) would be selected in order to maximize the difference between total revenue and total cost, resulting in sales of 500 units and revenue of $1,000. This gives maximum profit, even though it results in less total revenue than would be obtained at lower prices, because the increase in total revenue at the lower prices would be less than the increase in total cost.

It is worth emphasizing that this method ignores the per unit value of standby costs when setting short-run prices. To this

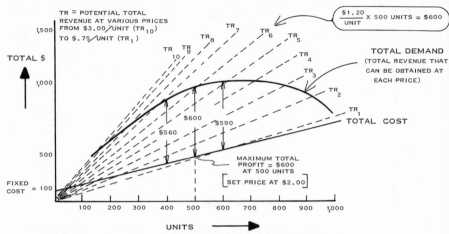

Exhibit 11–2. Maximizing total profit—the classical approach to pricing in a form which is more meaningful to businessmen.

extent the economists have probably been ahead of the cost accountants. In 1950, Carl Devine pointed out that most cost accountants seem to misapply the rules for long-run cost recovery to short-run pricing problems.[4] He basically supports the marginal approach to pricing, which is embodied in the theory of monopolistic competition. He also points out some of the great obstacles to its general use. One of the greatest is the difficulty of estimating either the demand curve or the response of the demand curve to selling effort. As a practical matter, the demand curves in Exhibits 11–1 and 11–2 are only estimates and merely indicate that the price should probably be set somewhere in the range from $1.75 to $2.25.

Another problem is the long-range repercussions from a policy of short-range profit maximation. This policy tends to increase the businessman's own future costs, and it encourages both competition and substitution for his products.

The point of all this is not that use of this model for pricing under monopolistic competition is the universal answer, which it is not, but that the economic theories are beginning to exercise a definite effect on business pricing practices and vice versa.

[4] Carl Thomas Devine, "Cost Accounting and Pricing Policies," *The Accounting Review*, Oct. 1950.

People like Joel Dean, who is both a teacher and a practical problem solver, have begun to bridge the gap between theory and practice. It is even beginning to look as if the accountant, the economist, the marketing analyst, and the businessman may all be working their way toward an area of agreement and common understanding.

PRICING STRATEGIES

No brief discussion can do more than highlight a few of the myriad considerations which influence pricing policies. It is worthwhile, however, to cite a few examples of pricing strategy, that is, the use of price as an instrument for developing markets or combating competition.

Skimming vs. Penetration

The choice of a new product price is usually made from a wide range of possible prices. The market considerations are best illustrated by the two strategies which result in prices at the opposite ends of this range. The two strategies are commonly referred to as "skimming" and "penetration."

Under the skimming strategy, the initial price is set high to skim off the most profitable business before competition arises. This is followed by subsequent price reductions to reach other customers, who will only buy at successively lower prices. The skimming strategy is an attempt to move down the demand curve in steps over a period of time. Theoretically each decrease picks up new business at the highest obtainable price after exhausting the market at the previous higher price. As a practical matter the policy often results in holding a "price umbrella" over competitors until they are strongly entrenched.

Under the penetration strategy, the initial price is set relatively low to get early access to a wide market, even though this results in selling to many customers at a price below that which they would be willing to pay. This policy makes possible the spreading of standby costs over greater volume, and it also tends to discourage competition. It may even engender demand which permits subsequent price raises.

Either of the above policies may prove highly profitable, but, as Alexander Duncan points out,[5] the most successful examples of each have been accompanied by heavy promotional expenditures. As an example of successful skimming, he cites the ballpoint pen, which Reynolds originally sold for $12 and which was sold by most pen manufacturers a few years later for 98¢ or less. As an example of successful penetration, he cites the Toni home permanent wave, which originally sold for $1.50 with applicator and curlers. Several years later the same combination sold for about twice the price. Both products were launched with a great advertising campaign.

Some Other Pricing Policies

There are a number of other forms of special price policies which imply some very interesting and rather odd demand curves, as is indicated in Exhibit 11–3. These include:

1. *Odd number or psychological prices,* where odd number prices are believed to result in higher unit sales than a lower even numbered price (e.g., unit sales might be higher at 69¢ than 60¢) or where unit sales are believed to drop sharply at critical points (e.g., sales at $1.00 might drop sharply from sales at 99¢)
2. *Customary prices,* where it is believed that demand will drop sharply with any price raise, and therefore price is maintained and quality or quantity is adjusted (e.g., the diminishing size of the 5¢ candy bar)
3. *Prestige prices,* where customers judge quality by price and buy more at higher prices (e.g., aspirins which sold better at 49¢ than at 19¢, 29¢, or 39¢)

There are other pricing theories which state that quantity discounts and transportation allowances should be based not on quantity or distance but on the demand curve of individual customers. Neither the theories nor the Robinson-Patman limitations on their application will be discussed here.

There is one rather fundamental pricing policy that is worthy of mention here and that will be elaborated upon in the following section on cost. This is the policy that prices should fluctuate over time in response to cyclical fluctuations in demand. In es-

[5] Alexander D. Duncan, "How To Price a New Product Realistically," *AMA Management Report Number 17—Competitive Pricing,* 1958, p. 92.

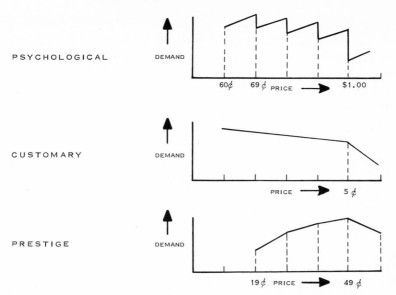

Exhibit 11–3. Demand curves implied by certain pricing policies.

sence, this policy is a sophisticated version of "all the traffic will bear," and it gives the proper long-run perspective on recovery of full cost. In periods of low demand, business may be taken at a loss if it provides revenue above variable cost. In periods of high demand, prices should not only provide a desirable profit for that period but they should also provide recovery of earlier losses.

THE ROBINSON-PATMAN ACT

Few businessmen today can set prices without giving at least some thought to the various legal restrictions on this process. The passage of the Sherman Anti-Trust Act in 1890 made it illegal for competitive companies to enter into any agreement or understanding to fix prices. Because of a feeling that this Act failed to protect small competitors from the discriminatory pricing practices of large national manufacturers, the Clayton Act was passed in 1914. This Act outlawed geographical price discrimination (undercutting a competitor's prices in one locality until he was driven out of business), by providing that a company's price for its product must be the same everywhere in the country if the product is sold in similar quantities. It did not restrict price differentials where the quantities sold were different. As the large chain stores and other mass retail distributors grew, they were able to put considerable economic pressure on suppliers to give them discounts, brokerage fees, advertising allowances, and other price concessions which the independent retailers could not obtain. This resulted in the passage in 1936 of the Robinson-Patman Amendment to the Clayton Act.

It is the Robinson-Patman Act which most affects business pricing decisions. The most significant provision of this Act renders it illegal to charge different prices to different customers for products of like grade and quality if this differential tends to injure competition. Other provisions ensure that discounts, advertising allowances, etc., are included in the determination of price differences.

The Act does not restrict price differences to customers who are not in competition with each other, but, where customers are in competition, any price difference which tends to injure competition is illegal. It is not necessary to prove intent to injure on the part of the seller or actual injury to one of the competing customers. The seller has two acceptable defenses: He must be able to prove that his lower price to one customer was made in good faith in order to equal the lower price of a competitor of his, or he must be able to prove that the price differential reflects an actual difference in costs. It is the cost defense which is of interest in this chapter.

There have been very few instances of successful cost defense in the courts during the first 25 years of the Act's existence, although there have been a number of cases where action did not reach the courts, because the seller had cost support for his pricing policies. Cost defense has proven quite expensive for most companies, because their normal accounting records do not provide costs in the detail required under the interpretation of the Act by the Federal Trade Commission (FTC) and the courts. Defendants have had to make intensive special cost analyses or have become involved in lengthy arguments over cost allocations between rival batteries of accountants. Companies have not been permitted to allocate overhead costs to customers at different per unit rates merely because of differences in total sales to those customers. A company is fairly well limited to providing cost differences on an order-by-order basis, and the costs which can differ are largely restricted to production set-up costs and, more importantly, distribution costs.

Distribution Costing

The typical methods of accounting for the cost of distributing a company's products do not result in specific identification of these costs with particular customers. Many attempts to give volume discounts to customers have been ruled illegal by the FTC because of inability to prove that the unit costs of distribution were in fact different for customers who were buying in different volumes. The following example shows a method of justifying volume discounts, the use of which, although not formally approved by the FTC, has been permitted without challenge by the FTC in a number of instances.

The first part of Exhibit 11–4 shows a producer's weekly costs of operating one of a fleet of trucks which deliver his products to the customer's door, and the relation of these costs to the productive time during which the truck is actually used for driving to and from customers and making deliveries. The proportion of productive time was determined by a time study analysis. Note that the total cost of operating the delivery service is reflected by inclusion of truck depreciation, garage rental, etc., since these are costs which should be paid for by customers who use the delivery service. In other words, the programmed costs of operating a delivery service are included along with the directly variable costs of making each delivery. The second part of the exhibit shows the other results of the time study analysis in determining the extent to which productive time per delivery varied with the size of the order delivered. This shows that productive time is basically related to the number of deliveries and varies only slightly with the size of the order (in this case about 1 minute for each $10.00 over the minimum delivered order size of $10.00).

The last part of Exhibit 11–4 summarizes the extent to which profit contribution after deduction of delivery costs varies with order size if the pricing policy is set to obtain a profit contribution of 40% on list price before consideration of delivery costs. The minimum order size of $10.00 requires 16 minutes of delivery time, which, at $0.20 per minute, amounts to $3.20. The compa-

A. AVERAGE COST PER UNIT OF PRODUCTIVE TRUCK TIME

AVERAGE COST PER WEEK		TRUCK UTILIZATION IN MINUTES PER WEEK	
DRIVERS WAGES	$130	TOTAL WEEKLY USE (5 DAYS X 8 HOURS) =	2,400 MINUTES
FUEL, OIL TIRES	190	LESS. NON-PRODUCTIVE TIME FOR PICK-UP AND LOAD TRUCK, FUEL, RETURN TO GARAGE AND UN-LOAD, ETC. =	420 MINUTES
TRUCK DEPRECIATION AND MAINTENANCE	36		
GARAGE RENTAL, SERVICE AND SUPERVISION	40		
TOTAL	$396		1,980 MINUTES

AVERAGE COST PER PRODUCTIVE MINUTE ($396 ÷ 1,980) = $.20/MINUTE

B. VARIABILITY OF PRODUCTIVE TRUCK TIME WITH ORDER SIZE

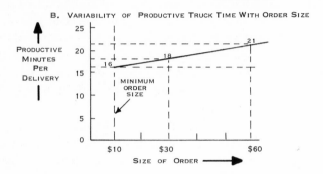

PRODUCTIVE TIME = 16 MINUTES/MINIMUM ORDER + 1 MINUTE/ADDITIONAL $10

C. VARIABILITY OF PROFIT CONTRIBUTION WITH ORDER SIZE

SIZE OF ORDER	P.C. @ 40% OF LIST PRICE	DELIVERY COST *	P.C. LESS DEL. COST	% TO LIST PRICE	DISCOUNT WHICH GIVES 25% P.C. AFTER DEL. COST
$ 10	$ 4.00	$3.20	$ .80	8.0%	–
20	8.00	3.40	4.60	23.0	–
23	9.20	3.43	5.77	25.1	0.1%
30	12.00	3.60	8.40	28.0	3.0
40	16.00	3.80	12.00	30.7	5.7
50	20.00	4.00	16.00	32.0	7.0
60	24.00	4.20	19.80	33.0	8.0

*NUMBER OF PRODUCTIVE MINUTES X $.20/MINUTES

Exhibit 11–4. Delivery cost support for volume discounts.

rable cost for a $60.00 order is only $4.20. Thus, the profit contribution after deduction of delivery costs ranges from 8% to 33%.
If the producer wishes to obtain a profit contribution of 25% after
delivery costs, he must average almost $23.00 of sales per order.
On the basis that each customer should provide this 25% profit
contribution, the producer is justified in offering discounts for
orders over $23.00, ranging up to the 8% shown for a $60.00 order.
A more detailed discussion of this type of discount is available,
illustrating differences between "inside versus platform delivery"

and relating the discounts to total variable costs rather than list prices.[6]

LIMITATIONS OF COST-BASED PRICING

It should be apparent from the earlier discussion that costs do not determine long-run prices in all instances, as evidenced by companies which go bankrupt and industries which sustain non-profitable operations for prolonged periods.

Impact of Cost on Price by Industries

Howard Greer has mentioned how the influence of cost on price tends to vary by type of industry, as indicated in the following three paragraphs.[7]

In industries which perform the initial processing of primary raw materials (such as grain into flour, livestock into meat), cost has little effect on price. In fact, demand-fixed prices are more likely to determine costs. When flour sales slump, wheat prices drop, and higher milling costs are more likely to depress the prices of wheat than to raise the price of flour.

In industries which perform secondary processing or final fabrication, cost becomes a more important factor in pricing. Even here, cost is not the sole determinant. A brand name or the price of possible substitutes may have more influence on price than the producer's costs. The fact that a producer was able to recover all costs in his price when he started in business does not mean that this condition will continue.

The one type of business in which cost-plus is the common and proper method of pricing is the individual bid project. Here the vast bulk of the costs are incurred solely in connection with performance of the project. And competitive bidding is likely to ensure that the contract price is not inordinately higher than estimated costs.

What Product Cost?

Another factor which weakens the cost-plus method of pricing is the difficulty of determining a specific product cost. As has

[6] Albert Bergfield, James Earley, and William Knobloch, Chapter 10 in *Pricing for Profit and Growth* (Englewood Cliffs, N.J.: Prentice-Hall, Inc., 1962).
[7] Howard Clark Greer, "Cost Factors in Price Making," *The Harvard Business Review*, July–Aug. 1952.

been mentioned, full product cost is rather meaningless for pricing purposes. Any assignment of standby costs to units of product is correct only for a specific volume of that product. Yet how can this be the basis for pricing, if the volume is heavily influenced by the price?

Chapter 9 contained several references to cases in which the use of full absorption costs led to unwise pricing decisions. One of the major problems in such cases is that use of full overhead absorption rates is very likely to be accompanied by a lack of knowledge as to just how overhead costs vary with volume. Thus, when a company's volume is subject to fluctuations, the resultant variation in overhead costs per unit, or in overhead absorption rates, may be based on rather poor estimates of the variation in total costs. Even when overhead variability is known fairly accurately, however, it is confusing to work with continually changing unit costs or overhead rates. In addition, the use of full absorption unit costs or rates obscures the extent to which the price of a product covers its directly variable costs and provides a contribution toward programmed and standby costs.

Entirely apart from standby costs, many variable costs can only be assigned to individual products by rather arbitrary allocations. Joint products are a case in point. Suppose the variable costs of separately producing either Product A or Product B are $15, but the two can be produced simultaneously for a total variable cost of $20. If Product A sells for $16 and Product B sells for $8, what is the cost of each?

The accountant who apportions $10 of cost to each product must conclude that Product B shows a $2 loss. If Product B is dropped, however, the cost of A increases to $15 and a profit of $4 on A and B together is reduced to a $1 profit on A alone. The accountant who apportions the joint costs on the basis of the relative selling prices may get a less misleading answer. There is, however, no unique product cost for either product. We can only say that the cost of either should be no less than the $5 which could be saved by eliminating the product and no more than the $15 cost of making it separately.

Varying Cost Recovery with Market Conditions

One of the most readable and sensible discussions of product cost in relation to price was presented over 20 years ago by E.

CLASS OF COST		BY ORDER AND UTILIZATION						BY PRODUCT **			
		CAPACITY EXCEEDS DEMAND		DEMAND BALANCES CAPACITY		DEMAND EXCEEDS CAPACITY		STRONG	SELF-SUP-PORTING	WEAK	PROB-LEM
		EVERY ORDER	AVERAGE ORDER	EVERY ORDER	AVERAGE ORDER	EVERY ORDER	AVERAGE ORDER				
PROVIDING THE CAPITAL	RETURN FOR R AND D RISK & EFFICIENCY					////	////	////			
	RECOVERY OF PRIOR LOSSES					////	////	////	////		
	RETURN ON FIXED ASSETS					////	////	////			
	RETURN ON WORKING CAPITAL					////	////	////			
OBTAINING THE ORDER	GENERAL ADVERTISING & SELLING (SLOWLY VARIABLE			////	////	////	////	////			
	VARIABLE COST OF CALLS ON CUSTOMERS / MARGINAL CUSTOMERS		////	////	////	////	////	////			
	SPECIFIC PRODUCT ADVERTISING					////	////	////		////	////
FILLING THE ORDER	DISTRI-BUTION * & : STANDBY AND PROGRAM			////	////	////	////	////			
	INDIRECT MFG. : VARIABLE OVERHEAD	////	////	////	////	////	////	////			
	DIRECT MFG. : MATERIAL & LABOR	////	////	////	////	////	////	////	////	////	////

RECOVER AT LEAST THE SHADED COSTS AND AS MUCH MORE AS THE MARKET PERMITS

AUCTION PLANT HOURS TO HIGH-EST BIDDER AND CONCENTRATE SELLING EFFORT ON PRODUCTS WITH HIGHEST PROFIT CONTRI-BUTION PER HOUR.

* DISTRIBUTION INCLUDES :
  ORDER HANDLING
  WAREHOUSING
  SHIPPING
  & FREIGHT OUT

** STRONG –   VERY PROFITABLE, BUT EXAMINE TOTAL PROFIT AT VARIOUS PRICES AND CONSIDER HOW CURRENT PRICE IS AFFECTING COMPETITION.

SELF-SUPPORTING –   ADEQUATE PROFIT, BUT LOOK FOR WAYS TO IMPROVE.

WEAK –   INSUFFICIENT CONTRIBUTION TO JOINT COSTS; FIND WAYS TO IMPROVE OR ELIMINATE DURING PERIODS OF HIGH CAPACITY UTILIZATION OR BY RETRENCHING.

PROBLEM –   DOES NOT COVER COSTS WHICH COULD BE SAVED BY ELIMINATING IT; IMPROVE OR ELIMINATE.

Exhibit 11–5. Relating selling prices to costs under various conditions (shaded area represents the minimum costs that should be recovered in net sales price).

Stewart Freeman.[8] "There is really no need," he said, "for the accounting system to distribute all the joint costs by product currently." He maintained that the important short-run considerations are whether prices are adjusted to the market and whether costs are under control, not whether each product is yielding a desirable profit. In the long run, he preferred to determine what

[8] E. Stewart Freeman, "Pricing the Product," *Year Book 1939—National Association of [Cost] Accountants*, 1939.

contribution to joint costs could be expected from each product rather than to attempt to allocate joint costs to product.

Mr. Freeman pointed out that the distinction in overhead costs was not so much between fixed and variable as it was between slowly variable and quickly variable, or, as we might say, among variable, programmed, and standby. He emphasized the use of costs as only a lower limit on the price at which business should be accepted. And he spelled out how this lower limit should include a greater portion of costs in periods of high demand than in slack periods.

He also discussed the life cycle concept of products and illustrated the typical variations of products within a company by use of an "industrial family" of products ranging from those with a strong profit position to those which were a profit problem. Exhibit 11–5 is quite similar to one used by him to illustrate the relation of costs to short-run prices under differing conditions of demand and for different members of the "industrial family." The shaded sections represent the minimum portion of cost which should be recovered in the price under each condition. Naturally the price may be set as far above this minimum as the market will permit.

ACCOUNTING SYSTEM PRINCIPLES FOR PRICING

The previous discussion in this chapter has emphasized the important effects of various non-accounting considerations on pricing decisions and has pointed out some of the limitations of the use of cost-accounting data in making these decisions. The remainder of this chapter is devoted to a discussion of how accounting data can be used to measure the effect of pricing on profits. It shows how the accounting system can be designed, and how the accounting data can be prepared and used, in a manner that will aid pricing decisions. The key principles that should usually be followed in the design of such a system are listed on page 321, accompanied by a brief mention of the objectives these principles are intended to accomplish.

The application of these principles is illustrated in the remainder of this chapter with the help of a number of specific examples. The use of profit contribution analysis as a means of comparing

System Principles	*Objectives*
1. Use only variable costs in determining a product's unit cost and its profit contribution toward programmed and standby costs.	1. Focus attention on profit contribution for short-range pricing decisions and avoid the confusing use of full unit costs that change with volume.
2. Establish lump sum amounts of programmed and standby costs in pools which can be realistically related to classes of products.	2. Ensure that non-variable costs are not ignored in setting pricing policies and that important differences between products in the relation of these costs to variable costs are recognized.
3. Establish explicit, cost-based pricing formulas as guides to pricing.	3. Induce consistency in pricing practices and ensure that cost considerations are not overlooked in pricing practice.
4. Report separate sales variances in terms of effect on profit contribution because of price, volume, and mix variances.	4. Segregate effect of pricing practices on profits from effect of other sales and cost variances.
5. Adapt system to pricing problems of particular company.	5. Emphasize the most pertinent principles and balance effort against utility of information.

the relative profitability of a limited number of pricing alternatives is illustrated first, and its possible use as a guide to selective selling effort is discussed briefly. The desirability of establishing the proper pools of non-variable costs is demonstrated along with the importance of differentiating costs which can be specifically identified with product classes from costs which are general to all products. The value of pricing formulas as a check against overemphasis on the policy of pricing to meet competition is illustrated along with the possible need for distinguishing between material and conversion costs when applying mark-up percentages. Finally, a method of reporting on various aspects of sales performance in terms of their respective effects on profit contribution is demonstrated by the use of separate sales volume, sales mix, and sales price variances.

PROFIT CONTRIBUTION ANALYSIS
OF PRICING PROBLEMS

As mentioned early in this chapter, the primary use of cost-accounting data in the pricing area is to measure the effect of alternative prices upon profit. Because of the interaction among price, volume, and full product cost, the effect can be measured

	PRODUCT LINE			
	A	B	C	TOTAL
SALES	$500,000	$300,000	$200,000	$1,000,000
VARIABLE COSTS	350,000	180,000	100,000	630,000
GROSS PROFIT CONTRIBUTION	$150,000	$120,000	$100,000	$ 370,000
% TO SALES	30%	40%	50%	37%
SPECIFIC PROGRAMMED COSTS	100,000	36,000	14,000	150,000
NET PROFIT CONTRIBUTION	$ 50,000	$ 84,000	$ 86,000	$ 220,000
% TO SALES	10%	28%	43%	22%
GENERAL PROGRAMMED COSTS				40,000
STANDBY COSTS				120,000
OPERATING PROFIT BEFORE TAX				$ 60,000
% TO SALES				6%

Exhibit 11–6. Analysis of product line profit contribution.

most readily by the use of profit contribution analysis. In addition, the determination of profit contribution by product line for both management reporting and profit planning helps to focus attention on areas where pricing alternatives should be considered. The following simple example illustrates both of these points.

Exhibit 11–6 summarizes the results of an initial profit plan for a company with three product lines. It shows the gross profit contribution of each product line after deduction of only variable costs, and then it proceeds to show deduction of advertising and other programmed costs which can be specifically identified with a product line in order to determine a net profit contribution by line. The attention of management, who are not satisfied with the planned results, is drawn to the low profit contribution from Line A, which accounts for half of the dollar sales. For simplicity, assume that Line A consists of a single product with planned sales of 5,000 units at a price of $100 each.

In a search for a way of improving the profitability of Line A, management asks their marketing analysts to estimate the effect of different prices on sales of that line. In theory, the company should try to formulate the demand curve for the product, but, the practical difficulties in making such estimates being known, only two questions are asked. With no change in marketing expense, what volume of Line A could be sold at a 10% higher price and what volume at a 10% lower price? The analysts estimate that the present sales volume of 5,000 units would decrease by 20% at the higher price and increase by 40% at the lower price. A comparison of the estimated profitabilities of these two alternative

	PRESENT PRICE	10 % HIGHER PRICE	10 % LOWER PRICE
UNIT SALES	5,000	4,000	7,000
UNIT PRICE	$100	$110	$90
VARIABLE UNIT COST	$ 70	$ 70	$70
SALES	$500,000	$440,000	$630,000
VARIABLE COSTS	350,000	280,000	490,000
GROSS PROFIT CONTRIBUTION	$150,000	$160,000	$140,000
% TO SALES	30.0%	36.4%	22.2%
SPECIFIC PROGRAMMED EXPENSE	100,000	100,000	100,000
NET PROFIT CONTRIBUTION	$ 50,000	$ 60,000	$ 40,000
% TO SALES	10.0%	13.6%	6.5%

Exhibit 11–7. Effect of alternative prices on profit.

prices and of the present price is shown in Exhibit 11–7. Although this analysis indicates that the higher price offers the most profitable alternative, management may well decide that the difference (and the possible errors in the estimates on which the difference is based) does not justify the risk inherent in a price change.

Management might ask essentially the same questions in a somewhat different way. They might first calculate the new higher volume required with the 10% lower price in order to produce the same amount of profit contribution as at present. This would require about a 50% increase in volume. Similarly, a 25% reduction from present volume would exactly offset a 10% increase in price. Management could then ask the market analysts whether the volumes at each of the new prices were likely to be significantly larger than those which would leave the present level of profit contribution unchanged. This question of whether the volumes at each of several different prices will exceed the volumes which produce identical profit contribution may also be asked for a desired level of profit contribution which is higher than the existing level.

Frequently, the type of profit contribution analysis described above is more meaningful to businessmen if performed graphically. Exhibit 11–8(1) displays graphically the same comparative data as were shown in tabular form in Exhibit 11–7, while Exhibit 11–8(2) is a graphic representation of the volumes required to offset the price changes and maintain the existing level of profit

1. ESTIMATED DEMAND AND PROFIT CONTRIBUTION AT ALTERNATIVE PRICES

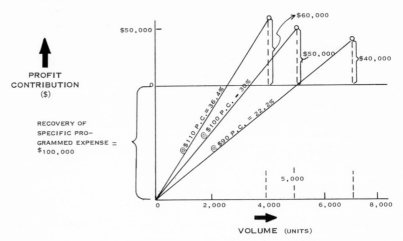

2. VOLUME CHANGES REQUIRED TO OFFSET EFFECT OF PRICE CHANGES ON PROFIT CONTRIBUTION

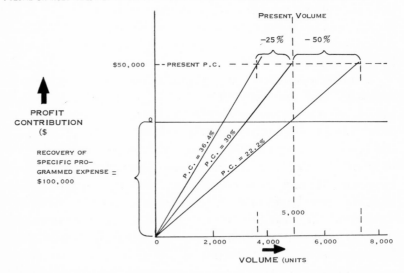

Exhibit 11–8. Graphic analysis of effect of price on profit contribution.

contribution. In both graphs, the slope of the slanting lines shows, for each price, the rate at which profit contribution dollars increase with the volume of units sold. The intersection of one of these lines with the heavy horizontal line at zero dollars indicates the break-even volume at which the profit contribution covers the specific programmed expenses of the product line. Vertical distances above the zero line indicate the profit contribution available to defray general programmed and standby expenses and to produce profit.

Graphs such as the above can also be used to compare alternatives with differing programmed expenses and may also show recovery of standby costs where these can be identified with the pricing problem under consideration. The point of this entire illustration is to indicate how profit contribution accounting assists management in reaching a decision on pricing problems. While the ultimate decision as to the price is made on the basis of market factors such as demand, supply, marginal competitors, substitutes, etc., the role of costs is to quantify the expected results of alternative decisions. There has been no attempt made here to work up from full costs to a "fair" price. The accountant has not determined the price; he has assisted in interpreting the price-volume-cost relationship so that management is fully informed of the possible effects on profits before making pricing decisions.

Selective Selling Based on Profit Contribution

Since profit contribution analysis directs attention to the relative profitability of different products, it is frequently used as the basis for a non-pricing decision which may have important repercussions in the pricing area. It is often used as a guide for allocating selling effort to products in a selective manner, with proportionately greater emphasis on the products with the higher rates of profit contribution. This may be done by focusing advertising and sales promotion effort on the most profitable products. It has also been done successfully in some instances by relating salesmen's compensation to the profitability of their sales rather than to sales volume alone.

For example, a tool and die manufacturer distributed its products through a number of regional manufacturer's representatives, paying them a flat 10% commission on sales. These representatives also sold products of other non-competitive manufacturers, and most of these sales yielded a 12% commission. In addition, other representatives were getting a 12% rate on competitive tool and die products. The representatives' sales of this company's products seemed to be unduly concentrated in items with low profit contribution.

This commission structure was revised as follows: The companies' products were grouped into a number of categories based on their rate of profit contribution. Sales quotas were set for each category, and the commission rate remained at 10% on sales up to these quotas. On additional sales above the quotas, the commission ranged from 12% in the category with the lowest rate of profit contribution to 20% for the highest category. In addition, the quotas were set higher in the categories with the lower profit contributions.

The revised commission structure was received favorably by the representatives and within a few months brought about a marked improvement in the over-all rate of profit contribution from these sales. Some representatives who had never before sold any of the items in the category with the highest profit contribution were selling them in significant amounts within three months.

In this case and in similar cases with other companies, acceptance by sales people of a sales incentive plan tied to profit contribution was only gained by ensuring that it did not reduce their compensation for the existing volume and mix of sales. Their concern on this point is one very good reason for limiting variations in commission rates to sales in excess of quotas. More importantly, their concern reflects a realistic appreciation of the probable effects of a selective discount structure. It will probably change the sales mix without necessarily increasing the sales volume. The tool and die manufacturer was able to actually increase his sales by increasing the effort that his part time salesmen expended on selling his products, but the more typical result is merely a shift in sales mix. Therefore, it is important that the discount structure be arranged carefully so that both the company and the sales people will benefit from a change in sales mix.

Before leaving the subject of selective selling, a word of caution is in order. Although the relative profit contribution percentages of various products do identify those products for which a volume increase is most desirable, this does not mean that they are an automatic guide to the allocation of selling effort. In the article by Mr. Devine that was referred to earlier in this chapter, he questioned the cost accountants' contention that selective selling effort should be concentrated on those products which have the largest mark-up over cost. This reasoning, he points out, is valid only under perfect competition. It ignores the demand schedules for various products and the extent to which a given amount of selective selling effort may influence the demand curve for a low-margin product much more than the demand for a high-margin product. In other words, a given amount of selective selling effort might result in the most profit, through increasing volumes or permitting increases in price, if applied to the products which currently show the lowest rate of profit contribution. As is usual in the marketing area, there are no automatic decision rules for selective selling which can be safely followed in all cases.

ESTABLISHING POOLS OF NON-VARIABLE COSTS

While analysis of profit contribution provides the most informative basis for evaluating the effect of pricing on profit, other measures should be taken to ensure that this does not lead to overlooking programmed and standby costs when making pricing decisions. Profit contribution data which do not reflect total costs can be readily misused in support of arguments for price reductions, particularly when there are strong competitive pressures for such reductions. For this reason, it is generally advisable to carry product profitability analysis below the level of profit contribution to amounts which approximate net profit by product.

Such amounts can only be determined by the use of some more or less arbitrary cost allocations. They should not, therefore, be interpreted as precise measures of the actual net profit from any individual product but rather as explicit reminders of the average relationship of the aggregate profit contribution from a group of products to the corresponding net profit. The costs which are considered in arriving at profit contribution by product are specifically identifiable with a particular product and directly variable with its volume. The remaining programmed and standby costs do not vary directly with volume and should be related to groups of products in lump sum amounts or pools of non-variable costs.

Specific and General Cost Pools

The term *non-variable costs* does not imply that certain costs are completely inflexible, but rather that the time required for a change in these costs is long relative to that required for a change in direct costs. The classification of these costs into programmed and standby amounts is based largely on a further distinction between costs that can be changed within a year or so and costs that are essentially fixed for an even longer period if the company intends to remain in operation. It is frequently desirable to subdivide the pools of programmed and standby costs further, into specific and general pools. The extent to which some of the programmed and standby costs can be identified specifically with certain groups of products, whereas others can only be generally related to all products, is the principal consideration in establishing these pools.

The general rule for classifying a cost pool as specific is that the cost could be eliminated if the group of products to which it is related were not produced. This definition of "specific" can encompass such diverse costs as depreciation, advertising, and salaries. The purpose of the classification is to focus attention on any significant and realistic differences in product profitability which are not reflected at the level of profit contribution, and thus provide additional information for decisions on pricing or on the discontinuance of certain products.

Exhibit 11–9 illustrates the establishment of specific and general pools of programmed and standby costs for a small paint company, which, as the exhibit shows, was not very profitable. The company produced a variety of products, usually to customer specifications and often in small orders. Prior to the adoption of the product line income statement shown here and the pricing formula mentioned in the next section of this chapter, the sales policy of pricing to meet competition had eliminated the profit in the operation. As a consequence of the variety of individual products, the number of small orders, and the nature of process-type manufacturing, the company lacked individual product costs which could serve as lower limits on prices. Because of the alternative methods by which a particular product might be made, depending on the size of the order and on the other products in process at the same time, attempts to allocate all labor costs to individual products had resulted in irrational cost differences which could not be reflected in the prices. The result was inadequate consideration of costs in the setting of prices.

	TOTAL	PRODUCT			GROUP	
		1	2		8	9
RAW MATERIAL COST PER GAL.		$.01 –$.30	$.31–$.45		$1.26–$1.50	$1.51 & OVER
GALLONS SOLD	100,000	21,000	12,000		9,000	8,000
SALES	$150,000	$12,000	$10,500		$22,500	$25,500
DEDUCT:						
SALES COMMISSIONS	3,000	240	210		450	510
RAW MATERIAL COSTS	90,000	6,300	5,400		14,400	15,300
DRUM EXPENSE	4,500	945	540		405	360
GROSS PROFIT CONTRIBUTION	$ 52,500	$ 4,515	$ 4,350		$ 7,245	$ 9,330
% TO SALES	35.0%	37.5%	41.6%		32.2%	36.6%
SPECIFIC PROGRAMMED :						
COOKING	1,800	600	320		60	– 0 –
TINTING	4,000	–0–	–0–		920	2,960
CHURNS	1,200	–0–	–0–		360	600
NET PROFIT CONTRIBUTION	$ 45,500	$ 3,915	$ 4,030		$ 5,905	$ 5,770
% TO SALES	30.3%	32.6%	38.4%		26.2%	22.3%
GENERAL PROGRAMMED	25,000	5,250	3,000		2,250	2,000
GENERAL STANDBY	26,500	1,855	1,590		4,240	4,505
NET PROFIT (LOSS)	($ 6,000)	($ 3,190)	($ 560)		($ 585)	($ 755)

allocated on gallons sold
allocated on raw materials

Exhibit 11–9. Paint company monthly income by product group, showing pools of non-variable costs.

Note that the gross profit contribution in Exhibit 11–9 does not reflect any deductions for labor cost, because the labor force was essentially a fixed number of people who shifted back and forth among operations as required. Their wages were included in the programmed and standby cost pools. The pools of specific programmed costs shown could be identified with particular operations, and these could be identified, in turn, with particular groups of products. Product groups 1 and 9 seem about equally profitable until consideration of these specific programmed costs indicates some significant differences.

The remaining costs were collected in two pools, general programmed and general standby. The allocation of these two pools of costs to product groupings is discussed in the next section, on pricing formulas.

The paint company provides a simple illustration of the use of specific cost pools. It is not an exhaustive or even a particularly dramatic example of their use, since only about 12% of the programmed and standby costs are classified as specific. Even this small proportion, however, provides some useful additional information about product profitability. Some additional insight on such cost pools is provided in the subsequent example of a pricing formula for a metal producer.

USING FORMULAS AS PRICING GUIDES

The fact that pressures in the market place will usually prevent rigid adherence to cost-plus pricing has been emphasized earlier in this chapter. On the other hand, the profit position of the paint company shown in the last exhibit is only one actual example of what happens all too frequently because costs are not given adequate consideration in price setting. In companies which have to make any large number of pricing decisions, consistent consideration of costs is only likely if pricing formulas are established as guides to pricing. These formulas should not only give effect to significant differences in costs among products, they may also provide the means for formally recognizing and systematically planning the different mark-ups obtainable from different products. The use of such formulas enables management to set target prices which reflect the varying upper limits imposed by the market on each product's profitability, as well as the lower limits which they consider acceptable under existing conditions. The prices established may have to differ from those calculated from the formulas, but this difference, or price variance, provides an explicit measure of the deviation of pricing practice from pricing policy and of the effect of such deviation on profit.

In the case of the paint company, it was possible to devise a simple, general formula which could be applied to all products on the basis of analysis of the data shown in Exhibit 11–9. The only items which were treated differently in the formulas for different products were the raw material costs, the largest single element of cost and the one which was known most accurately, and the specific programmed cost of cooking, tinting, and churns. The former were costed separately in the formula for each individual product, while the latter were applied at different rates per gallon for each product group on the basis of the relation of the pools of these costs to average volume. Drum expense was actually related directly to gallonage, and general programmed costs were allocated to all products on the basis of one average rate per gallon. Standby costs, on the other hand, were allocated on the basis of an over-all average rate per dollar of raw material cost. The sales commission, which was a fixed percentage of sales, and the desired profit, which was set at a fixed percentage of sales, could then be added on the basis of the corresponding percentage of costs. (For example, if commission and profit are 8% of sales, they equal about 8.7% of cost.)

The target prices that resulted from use of this formula could not be applied rigidly to all products and all customers, but the formula did provide a disciplined method of establishing standard selling prices in a pattern that conformed generally with market conditions. The benefits that accrued to the company from the use of this formula are illustrated graphically in Exhibit 11–11 later in this chapter.

Marking Up Conversion Costs vs. Total Variable Costs

The difference in the handling of general programmed costs and general standby costs at the paint company is worthy of a brief explanation, because it does not result from differences in the behavior of these costs. It indicates a compromise on a basic question that often faces management when setting pricing policies. Should they mark up total variable costs, including raw material costs, or should they mark up conversion costs only when trying to determine a price which will cover standby costs, programmed costs, and profit? The management of the paint company knew that any variability in its programmed and standby costs (which included some labor) was more related to gallons produced than to anything else. They also knew, however, that the market permitted proportionately higher mark-ups on the products with the higher material costs and the lower volumes. This was reflected in the pricing formula by marking up raw material costs to cover a portion of the non-variable costs.

As in the example above, the proper policy to be followed with respect to including or excluding raw material costs from the pricing base depends primarily on market conditions such as the prices of competitive products and the reaction of customers. In effect, the paint company's customers were willing to pay more for a given amount of work by the company if it were performed on a higher-priced raw material. Frequently, however, the company which attempts to apply fairly uniform mark-ups to total variable costs may price itself out of the market on those products where the proportion of raw material costs to total cost is relatively high. One company produced a line of electrical appliances with many small parts requiring a considerable amount of machining and assembly labor and a line of residential furnaces requiring relatively little labor to assemble a good deal of sheet metal and install a burner unit. The company could remain competitive while pricing appliances by marking up total costs. The same percentage of mark-up could only be applied to assembly labor and material-handling costs in pricing the furnace line, however, because of the ease with which small, low-overhead shops could go into the business of assembling furnaces. In many instances, market acceptance of product prices will indicate that the company's profits should vary more with the company's contribution to the finished product (with the company's conversion or processing costs) than with the total costs in the end product.

The last example of the use of pricing formulas happens to show the selection of one which is based on marking up total variable costs rather than variable conversion costs. More importantly, it shows a method of evaluating a number of alternative pricing policies, on the basis of differing arrangements of cost pools, which might be followed in attempting to meet a particular profit objective. The company produced extrusions from metal ingots and also fabricated extruded products for various industries from either their own or the customer's extrusions. To induce consistency into the pricing of numerous individual orders, management wanted a basic pricing formula within which prices could be set largely by clerical routine. Since the price of the extrusions was heavily influenced by a few large companies, the policy selected had to be generally consistent with industry pricing patterns and still accomplish some particular objectives of the company.

Exhibit 11–10 shows the comparative mark-up percentages which would have resulted under each of 12 basic pricing formulas. The mark-ups shown are those necessary under each formula in order to cover standby costs and produce a budgeted amount of profit based on forecast sales volume and mix. Under

	MAJOR OPERATIONS	SINGLE POOL FOR ALL STANDBY COSTS AND VARIANCES			SEPARATE STANDBY COST POOLS FOR MAJOR OPERATIONS			SEPARATE STANDBY PLUS VARIANCE POOLS FOR MAJOR OPERATIONS		
		AVERAGE ALL LINES	MAJOR LINE	OTHER LINES	AVERAGE ALL LINES	MAJOR LINE	OTHER LINES	AVERAGE ALL LINES	MAJOR LINE	OTHER LINES
MARK-UP ON TOTAL VARIABLE COSTS	EXTRUDE	141	134	144	139	132	142	135	128	138
	FABRICATE	141	134	144	145	138	148	154	147	157
	EXTRUDE	141	134	144	139	132	142	135	128	138
	FABRICATE	141	134	144	150	143	153	178	171	181
	ANODIZE	141	134	144	142	135	145	139	132	142
MARK-UP ON VARIABLE CONVERSION COSTS	EXTRUDE	156	147	159	119	116	120	117	114	118
	FABRICATE	156	147	159	193	177	198	198	182	203
	EXTRUDE	156	147	159	119	116	120	117	114	118
	FABRICATE	156	147	159	198	182	203	222	206	227
	ANODIZE	156	147	159	190	174	195	183	168	188

Exhibit 11–10. Comparison of "12" alternative pricing policies for a metal extruder and fabricator (figures are percentage mark-ups required on variable costs in order to provide planned profit contribution of $300,000).

both the policy of marking up total variable costs and the alternative policy of marking up only variable conversion costs, consideration was given to the alternatives of separately marking up the cost of the anodizing operation (which applied to only some products) or including it in the computation of an average mark-up on fabrication. For each of these 4 alternatives, the mark-ups were computed (1) for a single pool of total standby costs and variances, (2) for separate pools of standby costs for each major operation, and (3) for separate pools of variance plus standby costs for each operation. The resulting "12" alternative policies actually reduce to 10, since there is no point in distinguishing between operations if there is only a single pool of costs.

As indicated in Exhibit 11–10, the company selected a policy which marked up total variable costs, because prices under this method conformed more closely with industry pricing practice than did those from marking up conversion costs. They selected a policy which recognized separate pools of standby cost, because it gave higher mark-ups on the "fabricate only" business which they wanted to discourage in order to keep their extrusion presses busy. They did not include variances in these pools, because the resulting prices would probably have eliminated the "fabricate only" business. They used a separate pool for anodizing costs, because they believed they should and could recover the higher costs of anodized products.

The particular cost pools and pricing policies used in this case are not important in themselves. They are merely indicative of how cost pools can be set up to provide a pricing formula which reflects marketing considerations, recognizes total costs, and guides a company in deciding upon pricing policy and carrying out consistent pricing practices.

REPORTING SALES VARIANCES

The existence of basic pricing formulas enables a company to measure and report on the performance of its sales organization in carrying out its pricing policies. Pricing variances can be determined and interpreted in a manner similar to those developed for measuring performance in controlling costs. In fact, the combination of standard variable costs and formula pricing standards can be used to provide a detailed analysis of sales performance in terms of variances from planned profit because of individual deviations from the planned prices, volumes, and mix of sales. This is illustrated by an example later in this section.

First, it is worthwhile to emphasize the benefits that can accrue from the mere existence of pricing formulas and the reporting of selling price variances. The unprofitable picture of the paint company that was presented in Exhibit 11–9 is typical of the monthly losses which this company was incurring prior to establishing its pricing formulas. The company began double-pricing each order at the actual selling price and the price indicated by the formulas. The net selling price variance was reported monthly, beginning in April. Within a few months, as shown in Exhibit 11–11, an unfavorable variance of several thousand dollars a month changed to a favorable variance of a somewhat larger amount. The sales and profits for the same periods are also shown in this exhibit. Although the effect of price on profit is partially obscured by the effect of sales on the profit of a company which is operating near the break-even point, the fact remains that the annual dollar value

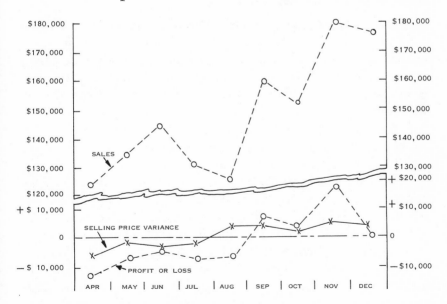

Exhibit 11–11. How reporting of price variance improved pricing and profits.

of the improvement in price variances exceeded the annual profits of the company.

The significance of the pricing formulas in this and similar cases is that they provide sales people with some explicit guides which help to counterbalance the market pressures for price reductions to which these people are continually exposed. The reporting of selling price variances not only provides another element in the analysis of variations from planned profit; it also reminds sales people that management is concerned with pricing performance and has a method for measuring it.

A final comment might be made in connection with the mechanical problems of computing selling price variances. Double-pricing of every sales order can be a tedious process. For reasons of administrative simplicity, however, a company will usually limit the number of different pricing formulas in use to correspond with a limited number of product groups. It may be possible to summarize cost data for each group and compute sales at standard selling prices in a single calculation.

Price, Volume, and Mix Variances

Price variance measures one of the three possible deviations from planned sales that can be measured in terms of their effect on planned profit. When sales forecasts are combined with standard variable costs in the profit plan, the effect of actual variations from the planned volume and the planned mix of sales can be measured separately in terms of the gain or loss in standard profit contribution. These three sales variances, along with the cost variances discussed previously, make possible a complete reconciliation between actual and planned profit.

The determination of sales volume and mix variances can be understood most readily by reference to an example. For this purpose, the standard profit contribution data in the profit plan of Exhibit 11–6 are reproduced and an example of actual performance against this plan is analyzed in Exhibit 11–12. This kind of comparison would ordinarily be done monthly and reported in trend statements of the type illustrated in Chapter 10. The first step in the analysis is to compute the *price variance* from the difference between actual sales at actual prices and actual sales at standard prices. The latter are used along with the standard vari-

( ) = unfavorable variance

PROFIT PLAN	PRODUCT LINE			
	A	B	C	TOTAL
Planned Sales	$500,000	$300,000	$200,000	$1,000,000
Std. Variable Cost	350,000	180,000	100,000	630,000
Std. Profit Contribution	$150,000	$120,000	$100,000	$ 370,000
% to Sales	30.0%	40.0%	50.0%	37.0%

ACTUAL RESULTS	PRODUCT LINE			
Price Variance:	A	B	C	TOTAL
Actual Sales - Actual Price	$465,000	$380,000	$225,000	$1,070,000
Actual Sales -Std.Price	450,000	400,000	250,000	1,100,000
Price Variance	$ 15,000	($20,000)	($ 25,000)	($ 30,000)

Profit Contribution:				
Actual Sales - Std. Price	$450,000	$400,000	$250,000	$1,100,000
Std. Variable Cost	292,500	238,800	137,500	668,800
Std. Profit Contribution	$157,500	$161,200	$112,500	$ 431,200
% to Sales	35.0%	40.3%	45.0%	39.2%

Volume Variance:				
Actual Sales - Std. Price	$450,000	$400,000	$250,000	
Planned Sales	500,000	300,000	200,000	
Difference in Sales	($ 50,000)	$100,000	$ 50,000	
x Planned Std.P.C.%	x30.0%	x40.0%	x50.0%	
Volume Variance	($ 15,000)	$ 40,000	$ 25,000	$ 50,000

Mix Variance:				
Actual P.C.%	35.0%	40.3%	45.0%	
Planned P.C.%	30.0	40.0	50.0	
Difference in P.C.%	5.0%	0.3%	(5.0%)	
x Actual Sales-Std.Price	x$450,000	x$400,000	x$250,000	
Mix Variance	$ 22,500	$ 1,200	($ 12,500)	$ 11,200

RECONCILIATION OF PLAN AND ACTUAL		
Planned Profit Contribution		$ 370,000
Add: Volume Variance		50,000
Mix Variance		11,200
Std. Profit Contribution at Std.Sales Prices		$ 431,200
Deduct: Price Variance		(30,000)
Standard Profit Contribution		$ 401,200

Exhibit 11–12. Computation of sales, price, volume, and mix variances.

able cost of these sales to compute the standard profit contribution at standard sales prices. The difference between this amount and the planned amount of standard profit contribution is made up of volume and mix variances.

Volume variance is defined as the difference between actual sales and planned sales, multiplied by the planned percentage of standard profit contribution. *Mix variance* is defined as the difference between the actual percentage of profit contribution and the planned percentage, multiplied by the actual sales. Note that these calculations are performed separately for each product line in Exhibit 11–12 so that the total mix variance for the company is the sum of the mix variances within each product line. This is usually done where there is considerable variation in the rate of profit contribution among different products within one line. In some cases where there is little such variation within each line, the company may prefer to report the mix variance between product lines. The calculations described above are then performed just once on the total sales rather than on the sales of each line. Use of this second method of calculation will result in changing the answers for the separate amounts of volume variance and mix variance, although the total of the two will remain the same. The mix variance in Exhibit 11–12, for example, would become $(39.2\% - 37.0\%) \times \$1,100,000 = \$24,200$ rather than the $11,200 shown. The corresponding volume variance would be changed to $37,000.

A number of companies that do not maintain standard selling prices use sales at actual prices to compute volume and mix variances from planned profit contribution. The effect of this is to bury any price variance in the mix variance reported. If this method were applied to the total sales at actual prices in Exhibit 11–12, the total of the mix and volume variances would be reduced from $61,200 to $31,200, and the mix variance would be $5,800 unfavorable.

The major point of this discussion of price, volume, and mix variances is not the absolute correctness of one particular method of calculating them, but the inherent advantages of reporting this kind of data, even if based on rather crude calculations. It focuses attention on the individual elements which make up total planned sales, and it permits variations from plan in each of these to be measured directly in terms of their effect on profit.

SUMMARY

Careful preparation of Profitability Accounting data can provide management with information which, if properly used, will greatly assist them in making pricing decisions. Although marketing considerations will frequently dominate cost considerations in the establishment of any particular price, the latter must be used to evaluate the effect on profits of individual pricing decisions and over-all pricing policies. Profit contribution data are most useful for such evaluations, because they avoid the confusing effect of volume fluctuations on unit amounts of programmed and standby costs. To ensure that these non-variable costs are not overlooked in pricing, however, it is desirable to carry product line reporting from the level of profit contribution down to a level which approximates net profit. This can best be done by establishing pools of programmed and standby costs which are related to groups of products and which distinguish between costs that are specifically identifiable with a group of products and costs that can only be allocated generally to all products. Pricing formulas based on these costs should be used as a guide to pricing. The development of them will ensure more explicit consideration of costs when establishing pricing policies, and their existence will induce greater consistency in pricing practice. The reporting of sales price, volume, and mix variances in terms of effect on profit contribution tends to increase the precision of sales planning and provides measures of sales performance which can be incorporated in a complete reconciliation of planned and actual profit.

Chapter 12

Foundation for Advanced Business Systems

INTRODUCTION

THE FIRST chapter of this book mentioned the trend in many companies toward a single automated and integrated system for management information and control, based upon combining analyses of management's functional needs for information with revised concepts of corporate organization, and taking advantage of the opportunities offered by advances in the three technical areas of Electronic Data Processing, Operations Research, and Profitability Accounting.

The conceptual goal of the many companies that are following this trend is a single information system (or more properly a network of sub-systems which are linked by automated data processing) into which each element of basic data need only be entered once. The system would then ensure that the data are used for all of their various purposes and would provide information tailored to the various particular needs of individual managers. The system would incorporate decision rules which enable it to take certain routine actions automatically and to provide certain information only on an exception basis. Where justified by the importance of access to the most current information, the system would summarize certain transactions continuously as they occur and provide certain data almost immediately upon request.

Few companies are anywhere near this goal of a totally integrated system, and no company will ever attain it completely, because the goal itself changes as different requirements for information arise and systems technology is improved. Many companies have made considerable progress toward such a goal, however, by uniting large and diverse segments of their information processing within one integrated system. The term *advanced business systems* is used here to include those systems which represent a significant step by a company toward this goal. This step may be the combination of techniques from two or three of the technical areas mentioned above within a single information system; it may be the installation of one fully integrated process which supplies all of the information needs related to a particular set of basic data; or it may be the establishment of continuously updated files which can provide critical information within a few seconds of its being requested.

The three technical areas which provide the components for building an advanced business system have one important characteristic in common. Each is a collection of disciplines, where a *discipline* is defined as a system of formal and explicit rules. The body of disciplines which make up *Profitability Accounting* have been discussed at length. The term *Operations Research* is used generally to cover the application of various mathematical disciplines to business problems. *Electronic Data Processing* represents perhaps the ultimate discipline, since the equipment will do only what it has been programmed to do in step-by-step detail.

In contrast, the various business systems that co-exist within most companies are, in general, rather loosely knit and somewhat informal. There are exceptions of course—the usual formality of the custodial accounting system, the frequent integration of billing with sales analysis and accounts receivable, and some highly sophisticated systems for controlling production and inventories. Even a company with one or more fairly advanced systems will have other systems (in important areas such as sales forecasting, pricing, credit or cost accounting) which are quite unsophisticated and often completely implicit. That is to say, they lack clearly defined channels of information flow, written procedures, and explicit decision rules.

The development of an advanced business system usually requires greater formality and discipline than exist in the system which it supplants. To date, the greatest impetus to inducing such discipline into business systems has been provided by efforts to reduce costs through tranferring clerical data processing jobs onto computers. The expected reductions in clerical costs have not always materialized, but often the computer has paid for itself in another way. It has often enabled management to obtain information which was previously unavailable in a timely or an economic manner, and it has often enabled them to make decisions which were measurably better than in the past. This last improvement usually depends, not only on the speed and accuracy of Electronic Data Processing, but also on the application of Operations Research techniques and the availability of pertinent Profitability Accounting data. This chapter is intended to introduce briefly some of the developments in Electronic Data Processing and Operations Research that underlie the trend toward advanced business systems.

OPERATIONS RESEARCH

One of the three technical areas on which advanced business systems are founded is Operations Research, a body of technology which evolved out of World War II efforts to improve military operations through studies conducted by teams of people representing various scientific disciplines. The only definition of *Operations Research* on which all of its practitioners, with their diverse backgrounds, are likely to agree is that "it is what Operations Research people do." Since this is not very informative to the uninitiated, the following attempt at a definition is offered.

Operations Research is the study and quantitative evaluation of alternative systems for making decisions under conditions of complexity or uncertainty. In most business situations, the evaluation is made in terms of costs or profits which are not readily available from the traditional accounting system. Most successful applications of Operations Research require special arrangements of data of the Profitability Accounting type.

The term *Management Sciences* is frequently used to encompass most of the same activities that are included under the heading of *Operations Research*. The definition of *Management Sciences* as the study of the application of scientific techniques to the problems of business management does not serve to distinguish it clearly from *Operations Research*. One might say that *Management Sciences* includes more of the elements of designing actual business systems and is more empirically oriented, while *Operations Research* is more concerned with developing the mathematical models and is more theoretically oriented. Even this subtle distinction is an over-simplification, reflecting only some vague differences in emphasis between practitioners who tend to identify themselves with one term or the other. The distinction between the two terms is neither simple nor well defined, but that need not concern us here. Either term could be applied to the techniques that are presented in this section. *Operations Research* is used because it suggests a sharper separation between

344   PROFITABILITY ACCOUNTING

the mathematical and the data processing aspects of advanced business systems.

One concept is fundamental to all Operations Research activity. This is the concept of "making a model of the operation." A model is an explicit, idealized representation of the important relationships in an actual operation or system. A simple flow chart is a model, but we are more interested here in the use of a set of mathematical equations to describe an operation or a system for making decisions. Although a model is a simplified representation of an actual operation, it can be an adequate representation for the operation to be improvable as a result of experiments with the model. An accountant should have little difficulty in understanding the concept of a model, since his entire vocation is built on a very complex and useful model, i.e., the double entry system for recording both the flow of monies through a business and the financial position of the business.

Although much of the Operations Research activity is devoted to modeling the behavior of specific operations or systems within a particular company, this activity has produced a number of classes of models or mathematical techniques which are generally applicable to a variety of companies and business problems. A number of these are listed below along with a brief, non-technical description. Two of the most widely used techniques are then discussed at somewhat greater length with examples which point up the kinds of accounting data required in order to use them.

Some Operations Research Techniques

The classes listed below are neither exhaustive nor mutually exclusive. Statistical probability theory, for example, plays an important part in simulation, inventory theory, and queuing theory. Some are individual techniques for solving a particular class of problems, while others are bodies of mathematical theories or models. Some, such as network programming, are aids to planning and control, while others, such as linear programming, are aids to making specific decisions. Some are directed toward a particular business problem, while others are not. The classes that have been selected merely provide the layman with a somewhat orderly introduction to some of the technical terminology of Operations Research.

- *Dynamic programming* is a mathematical technique for systematically determining the best combination of decisions where a series of consecutive and interrelated decisions have to be made over a period of time.
- *Forecasting theory* is a collection of empirically derived rules for making systematic predictions (usually of future sales) based on analysis of historical data in terms of trends, seasonal patterns, and random variations.
- *Game theory* is the study of decision rules under competitive situations where the best decision for a company is dependent upon the decision made by a competitor.
- *Information theory* (or *communication theory*) is the study of the effects of the size, frequency, and timing of messages, and the capacity, noise level, and feedback mechanism of a communications network, upon the amount of information transmitted.
- *Inventory theory* is a collection of models of inventory behavior, from which are derived various sets of rules for deciding when and how much to order, so as to minimize costs and meet specified levels of protection against stockouts.
- *Linear programming* is a mathematical technique for determining the least costly (or most profitable) allocation of a number of limited resources among a number of specific tasks, where many allocations are possible, where each combination of a resource with a task affects the ability to make other combinations, and where all of the variable relationships are linear. This includes the *assignment method,* where a resource only has to be matched with a task; the *transportation method,* where the amount of each resource and each task can be expressed in terms of one common unit; and the *simplex method,* which can be applied to any linear programming problem but is usually restricted to those for which the two simpler methods are inapplicable.
- *Network analysis* is a formal method of diagramming all of the precedence relationships and estimating all of the times for a complex series of interdependent activities. It is used to determine potential bottlenecks for planning purposes, and to report on progress against plan which may shift the bottlenecks. It may be combined with cost data to facilitate trade-offs between time of completion and cost of completion. *PERT* (program evaluation and review technique) was originally directed toward research and development work where probabilistic esti-

mates of time were important, whereas *CPM* (critical path method) was directed at industrial work where time and cost trade-offs received more attention. These original distinctions disappeared as the two methods were refined.

- *Statistical probability theory* is a vast body of mathematics dealing with the "laws of chance" which enables uncertain events to be considered in an explicit, quantitative manner. It is the foundation of a number of extensive bodies of techniques. One of these is *statistical survey sampling* of large populations or masses of data in order to make estimates with a specific precision and reliability. Another is *statistical quality control* of manufacturing operations; this includes the use of control charts to indicate a significant change from the expected variation in a process, and the use of acceptance sampling for a yes or no decision on the quality of a production lot. A third is *regression analysis* (or *correlation analysis*) for expressing relationships between variables in an effort to predict one variable (often sales) on the basis of the information about one or more other variables.

- *Sequencing theory* is perhaps an overly formal title for the study of problems and priority rules concerning the order in which tasks should be performed so as to make the best use of available facilities and meet completion schedules. One specialized technique related to this general area of study is *assembly line balancing*, which is concerned with sequencing the elements of work along such a line and assigning them to individuals so as to minimize the total number of workers required.

- *Simulation* is a method of solving complex problems that cannot be solved analytically; that is to say, they cannot be completely formulated in a set of equations which can be solved for an exact answer. The method consists of making a model of a system or operation and then determining average expected results under particular operating conditions by repeated processing of data through the model. It is usually done on a high-speed computer. The term *Monte Carlo method* is applied to a simulation in which some variables are introduced into the model by randomly sampling a statistical distribution.

- *Queuing theory* (or *waiting line theory*) involves a collection of models for relating the number of facilities providing a service to the length of the queues waiting for that service under conditions of random arrivals in the queues and random times for performing the service.

The brief descriptions above provide a general idea of the kinds of business problems to which various Operations Research techniques can be applied. They do not, however, provide any real understanding of how these techniques are applied, except to a person who is already familiar with the techniques themselves. Two of the most widely used techniques, linear programming and scientific inventory management, are discussed briefly and simply below. The discussion should provide some insight into the workings of the techniques and the possibilities for their use. Equally important, it demonstrates how the use of these techniques imposes demands on the accounting system for special arrangements of accounting data.

Linear Programming Problems

The communication gap between the businessman with a problem and the technician with a potential method of solution is the greatest obstacle to more widespread use of Operations Research techniques. The precise statement of a complex allocation problem in the algebraic language of linear programming results in a series of equations which may seem incomprehensible to the non-mathematician. Yet the very complexity of the problem makes it very unlikely that a "cut and try" approach will produce the best solution. This point can be appreciated by considering a very simple allocation problem of a type that is amenable to solution by linear programming.

The first table in Exhibit 12–1 describes a problem in which the output of three plants is to be distributed to three warehouses. The requirement for each warehouse is shown along with the availability from each plant. The totals happen to be equal, but that is not a prerequisite for the application of linear programming. The body of the table shows the cost per ton to ship from each plant to each warehouse. The problem is to distribute the total tonnage at minimum cost.

The second table shows a feasible solution which supplies each warehouse's requirements without exceeding any plant's capacity, and results in a total cost of $675. Under linear programming, this solution would be evaluated by determining so-called shadow prices for all of the unused combinations of a plant with a warehouse. A shadow price can be thought of here as the cost of not

PROBLEM — How should plant production be distributed to warehouses?

COST PER TON SHIPPED TO FROM		WAREHOUSE			TONS AVAILABLE
		A	B	C	
PLANT	1	$3.00	$4.00	$5.00	30
	2	$6.00	$8.00	$9.00	50
	3	$7.00	$8.00	$10.00	20
TONS REQUIRED		40	35	25	100

A SOLUTION

TONS SHIPPED TO FROM		WAREHOUSE			TOTAL
		A	B	C	
PLANT	1	30			30
	2	10	35	5	50
	3			20	20
TTOAL		40	35	25	100

TOTAL COST

90 + 0 +   =$ 90

60 + 280 + 45 = 385

0 + 0 + 200   = 200

$675

A BEST SOLUTION *

TONS SHIPPED TO FROM		WAREHOUSE			TOTAL
		A	B	C	
PLANT	1		5	25	30
	2	40	10		50
	3		20		20
TOTAL		40	35	25	100

TOTAL COST

0 + 20 + 125   = $145

240 + 80 +0   = 320

0 + 160 + 0   = 160

$625

* THE SAME COST WOULD RESULT IF 10 TONS FROM PLANT 2 WERE SENT TO WAREHOUSE C RATHER THAN B WITH AN OFFSETTING CHANGE IN THE SHIPMENTS FROM PLANT 1.

Exhibit 12–1. A simple linear programming problem to determine the lowest-cost distribution plan.

using a particular combination. If any of these shadow prices exceeds the actual cost of using a particular combination, a better solution is possible. Such an evaluation of the first solution in Exhibit 12–1 indicates that three of the unused combinations should be used.

The third table shows a best solution which makes use of the three previously unused combinations and reduces the total cost of distribution to $625. One other solution, with a shipment from Plant 2 to Warehouse C, would result in the same minimum cost.

Neither of these best over-all solutions, however, makes use of the lowest cost shipping route, from Plant 1 to Warehouse A. The reason lies in the interdependence of each step in the allocation process. A decision to supply Warehouse A from Plant 1 forces us to supply the other two warehouses from Plants 2 and 3. It is the existence of this interdependence which complicates the problem and renders linear programming applicable. The simple problem of Exhibit 12–1 can be solved by trying, and costing, every possible solution, but the feasibility of this diminishes rapidly as the problem increases in size.

The solution of a problem much like the one above led to the use of the term *transportation problem* to describe a class of linear programming problems. A problem falls in this class, however, not because it deals with physical transportation, but because all of the supply and demand restrictions can be expressed in terms of one common unit. The tons in the above example could be shifted about between warehouses and plants on a one-for-one basis, which greatly simplifies the process of solution. The second of our two examples is introduced because it is not a transportation problem, and because it is a problem of maximizing profit rather than one of minimizing cost. In addition, it demonstrates the kind of problem which may not be solved for the best answer just because its full implications can be easily overlooked.

Exhibit 12–2 shows a simple problem of determining the most profitable mix of two products, where the combined demand for both exceeds the available production capacity. Each product requires production time in each of two departments. For simplicity, variable cost is assumed equal to $1 for each production hour. Thus the same numbers used for dollar costs can be divided into hours of capacity to determine upper limits on the production of each product. The fact that a unit of demand is not equal to an hour of capacity removes this problem from the transportation class. Some production-scheduling problems can be converted into problems in equivalent units, which are interchangeable, because of consistent proportional relationships between machine times for each product. The equivalent problem can then be solved by the transportation method. The required relationship does not exist in our simple problem.

A feasible solution to the problem is readily obtainable. Since

PROBLEM – WHAT TO PRODUCE?

	PRODUCT		CAPACITY
	A	B	(HOURS = $)
SALES PRICE PER UNIT	$15	$12	
VARIABLE COST @ $ 1 PER HOUR:			
DEPT. 1	5	2	‖ 240
DEPT. 2	3	4	‖ 240
PROFIT CONTRIBUTION PER UNIT	$7	$6	
SALES DEMAND (UNITS) ⟶	70	70	

A SOLUTION – MAKE AS MUCH OF A AS POSSIBLE (LIMITED BY DEPT. 1)
240 ÷ 5 = 48 UNITS: PROFIT CONTRIBUTION = $336

A BETTER SOLUTION – MAKE AS MUCH OF B AS POSSIBLE (LIMITED BY DEPT. 2)
240 ÷ 4 = 60 UNITS: PROFIT CONTRIBUTION = $360

THE BEST SOLUTION – MAXIMIZE PROFIT CONTRIBUTION WITHIN CONSTRAINTS
MAKE 34 UNITS OF EACH. PROFIT CONTRIBUTION = $442

ANALYSIS OF PROBLEM

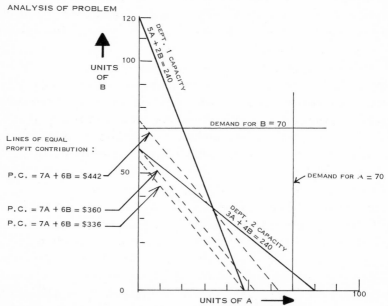

Exhibit 12–2. A simple linear programming problem to determine the most profitable product mix.

Product A provides the greatest profit contribution, we might make as much of it as possible. Production capacity in Department 1 restricts output to 48 units and $336 of profit contribution. Product B, which requires the same amount of total hours per unit, requires less of these hours in a single department. Therefore, 60 units of B can be produced for a contribution of $360. Neither of these solutions is the best possible, however.

The graph at the bottom of Exhibit 12–2 shows why the highest profit contribution of $442 can be obtained by producing 34 units of each product. It also depicts clearly the meaning of linear constraints on a problem which can be shown in two dimensions. The graph relates Product A to Product B, with the solid lines showing the restrictions imposed on the production of each by sales demand and departmental capacity. For instance, the product mix combinations under the capacity restrictions of Department 2 run from B = 60 units and A = 0 to A = 80 units and B = 0. Within these restrictions, the objective is to maximize profit contribution. Each broken line on the graph shows the various mixes of A and B that result in a single amount of profit contribution. All lines have the same slope, reflecting the $7 to $6 relation between products. The line farthest away from the origin of the graph, and containing one point which falls within all of the restrictions, represents the maximum profit contribution. That point represents the most profitable mix. Technically the point would fall at 34 and a fraction units of each product, and the best solution actually leaves two hours of idle capacity in each department. This merely means that a continuous straight line is a slightly idealized representation of a relation which is actually made up of many little discrete steps.

It should be apparent that a larger problem of this second type is even less amenable to solution by "cut and try" methods than one of the first type. It should also be apparent that the utility of linear programming is directly dependent on the availability of accurate variable cost and profit contribution data. In most companies, obtaining the data consumes much more time than applying the technique. In one application to a machine-scheduling problem, development of profit contribution data required many man-months, while formulation of the linear programming problem was a matter of weeks and solution was a matter of hours.

This discussion concludes by listing a few of the many and varied business problems to which linear programming has been successfully applied.

- Selecting the one of many potential new plant sites which minimizes the sum of inbound transportation costs from suppliers, outbound transportation costs to sales districts, and local labor and tax costs

- Scheduling products on machines so as to maximize profit contribution or minimize variable costs
- Minimizing the waste in cutting standard rolls of paper or metal into strips of varying widths and lengths
- Determining the lowest cost mix of raw materials to meet product specifications for grain processors, chemical processors, oil refineries, plywood producers, and foundries
- Determining which plants will supply which warehouses or sales territories at a minimum over-all cost

An Inventory Model

One other area of Operations Research techniques is worthy of a brief elaboration for several reasons: It has made a significant impact on business practices. It illustrates a simple model which has proved widely useful when incorporated into a working business system, often through the use of a computer. It is also concerned with an arrangement of costs which are not ordinarily available from the typical accounting systems.

Exhibit 12–3 depicts the essential features of a basic model of inventory behavior and the resulting rules for managing inventory. The model is based on the assumption that all variable costs of managing inventory can be related to order quantities in one of two ways. Ordering costs such as order-processing and set-up charges are assumed to vary directly with the number of orders placed. For a given level of sales, therefore, the annual cost of ordering decreases at a decreasing rate as the size of the order quantity increases. Carrying costs include the costs of physical storage and interest charges on the investment in inventory and are assumed to vary directly with the amount of inventory. Since the average inventory is assumed to increase by an amount equal to one-half of any increase in the order quantity, annual carrying costs are assumed to increase linearly with increases in order quantity. Based upon these assumptions, there is a most economic order quantity as is indicated in the top half of Exhibit 12–3. The formula for calculating this quantity is not important here, except to mention that it includes carrying cost in terms of unit cost multiplied by an annual percentage (such as 20% per year) and also includes annual unit sales as well as ordering cost. This gives a rule for how much to order.

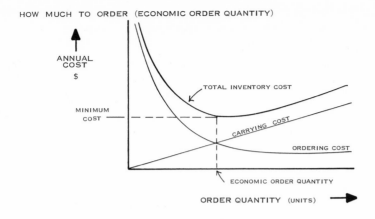

HOW MUCH TO ORDER (ECONOMIC ORDER QUANTITY)

ANNUAL
COST
$

TOTAL INVENTORY COST

MINIMUM
COST

CARRYING COST

ORDERING COST

ECONOMIC ORDER QUANTITY

ORDER QUANTITY (UNITS)

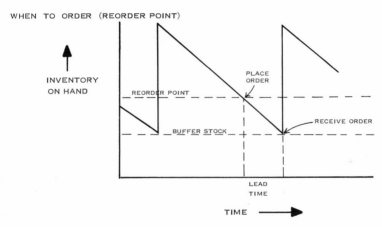

WHEN TO ORDER (REORDER POINT)

INVENTORY
ON HAND

REORDER POINT

PLACE
ORDER

RECEIVE ORDER

BUFFER STOCK

LEAD
TIME

TIME

Exhibit 12–3. A basic inventory model.

The bottom half of the exhibit illustrates the rule for determining when to place orders under a re-order point system.
When inventory level is decreased by usage to the re-order point
level, another order is placed. The re-order point is set so that
average sales during the lead time should reduce the inventory to
the level of buffer stock just as the order is received. The buffer
stock is set to cover variations from average sales and average
lead time, on the basis of statistical analyses of these variations
and the desired level of protection against stockouts.

It is not necessary to discuss the difficulties of determining
accurate ordering and carrying costs. However, the order quan-

tity can be permitted to vary over some range about the most economic quantity without much effect on total costs, as indicated by the flatness of the curve near that point. And an error of a particular size in the estimate of ordering or carrying cost does not introduce as large an error in the calculation of the order quantity, because of the mathematical formulation. Despite the simplicity of this model and the difficulties of cost estimation, its adoption has enabled many companies to reduce inventory levels by as much as 20% while maintaining or improving the stockout position. Its success lies in the ability of explicit rules, systematically applied, to induce consistency into the large number of inventory management decisions which have to be made continually in most companies. The results of using this and related models in inventory management systems have been documented for a variety of industries including department stores, supermarkets, wholesalers, and manufacturers of paper, paint, automobiles, and aircraft.[1]

ELECTRONIC DATA PROCESSING

Although Electronic Data Processing is the predominant technology of the three which make up advanced business systems, it is the most difficult one to describe briefly. Whereas much of Operations Research can be communicated by a brief description of the concept behind a technique or the problem at which the technique is directed, Electronic Data Processing involves a myriad of system details and a bewildering variety of hardware and software which are continually being updated or replaced.

One of the most remarkable things about this field is its great rate of growth. The dozen or so digital computer installations in existence prior to 1950 (none of them in use for business data processing) had grown to about 2,000 by the middle of 1958. As shown in Exhibit 12–4, which traces this growth separately for small, medium, and large computers, the total exceeded 8,800 by December, 1961. At that time, *Business Automation Newsletter*, which compiled the data shown, forecast an increased rate of growth to a total of almost 14,000 installations by December, 1962.

[1] Joseph Buchan and Ernest Koenigsberg, *Scientific Inventory Management* (Englewood Cliffs, N.J.: Prentice-Hall, Inc., 1963).

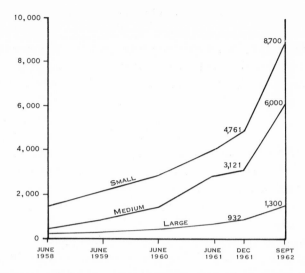

Exhibit 12–4. Growth in number of general-purpose digital computer installations (June, 1958, to September, 1962).

This figure was actually exceeded by September of that year. Similar growth occurred in the field of On-Line–Real-Time systems, a field which is discussed briefly in this chapter. The number of such systems installed or in the planning stage increased from about 12 at the beginning of 1960 to more than 70 two years later.

Technological Advances and Integrated Systems

A number of factors in addition to the intensive marketing efforts of the equipment manufacturers contributed to this rapid growth. Businessmen became more aware of what could be done with a computer, and could buy more computational power per dollar spent. This made it possible for more companies to justify the acquisition of a computer and for more complex applications to be put on a computer in a particular price range. A very rough indication of this increase in power is given by comparing the access time to the high-speed memory of the most popular medium size computer of 1958 and its counterpart of 1962. In the 1958 version, ten digits of information could be obtained in about .0024 second, while the 1962 version required about .00012 second, a twentyfold increase in speed. Improvements of a similar order of magnitude were made in input-output speeds and memory sizes.

In addition to significant improvements in the capabilities of the electronic equipment, or hardware, much progress was made in the so-called software, the body of techniques for instructing the equipment to perform various tasks. The problem of the great amount of time consumed in "programming" the computer to perform its step-by-step functions was alleviated to a considerable extent. More technicians were trained to program in "machine language," to formulate a complex problem in a lengthy and rigorously logical sequence of exact instructions which enable a particular computer to store, find, manipulate, and re-produce each datum. Libraries of "canned programs" were built for a variety of routine applications. "Compilers" were developed which enabled programs to be written more quickly in a formal type of problem-oriented, rather than machine-oriented, shorthand which could then be converted automatically into the many more detailed steps of a program in machine language.

The increased number of computers in business use had one type of immediate impact on the accounting area. It tended to reduce the number of people within an accounting department who were performing strictly clerical operations. Certain individual accounting functions such as payroll, customer billing, and inventory record keeping became almost automatic candidates for transfer onto a newly acquired computer. While the speed and accuracy of computing machinery reduced the amount of routine bookkeeping work to be performed by people at the bottom of an accounting organization, the evolution of advanced business systems began to have an impact on the functions performed by the people at the top.

In the mid 1950's, the phrase "Integrated Data Processing" became popular to describe a step forward in the evolution of business data processing. The concept of IDP was far reaching, namely, that basic information which was originated in one location should be recorded in a form suitable for mechanical transmission to any other location, so that it would never again have to be re-generated by human beings.

As a practical matter, the systems to which the phrase was applied were limited by existing technology to the mechanical linking of several operations into a semi-automatically integrated sub-system. For example, sales order processing, customer billing, sales analysis, and accounts receivable might be linked by punching cards or paper tape on a typewriter and transmitting the punched data over electrical wires to be reproduced by another typewriter. Typists could manually insert information at various physical locations. The cards or tapes were used for batch processing of calculations in a computer.

As a general rule, the various systems which were developed under the term *Integrated Data Processing* did not cross organizational lines within a company. The exceptions to this rule were more apparent than real. The example of sales order processing, cited above, was basically an accounting system which produced some information for the sales organization as a by-product. Because of the identification of *Integrated Data Processing* with semi-automated systems which stopped at organizational boundaries, the people in the computer field discontinued the use of this term when referring to the subsequent evolution of the more highly automated and integrated systems mentioned at the beginning of this chapter. The terms *total business system* and *advanced business system* came into use. Despite the terminological preferences of the practitioners in the field of Electronic Data Processing, one of the most notable features of the systems evolution was the tendency toward greater integration, particularly across organizational lines.

On-Line–Real-Time Systems

Before attempting to discuss the effect of the evolution of advanced business systems on the organization structure of a company, brief mention should be made of one of the most important innovations in the field of Electronic Data Processing. That is the emergence of the so-called On-Line–Real-Time (OLRT) systems in a variety of businesses.[2] A basic understanding of what is meant by an OLRT system can be obtained from reference to Exhibit 12–5. The system includes a central data processing complex made up of computers, storage devices, central communica-

---

[2] Richard E. Sprague, *Electronic Business Systems: Management Use of On-Line–Real-Time Computers* (New York: The Ronald Press Co., 1962).

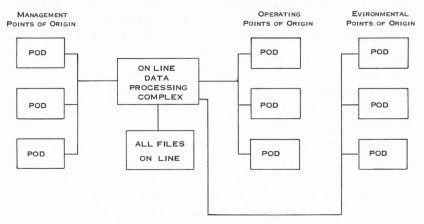

Exhibit 12–5. Total OLRT system diagram.

tions equipment, and various input-output devices such as punched card or punched tape readers and punches and high-speed printers. "Point of origin devices" (POD's) are connected directly and electrically to the central complex. *Point of origin* refers to the natural physical location at which information is needed or originated within a company.

The direct connections between the POD's and the data processing center permit a kind of two-way communication between a person at a POD and the system itself. A person at a POD can send information to the center, which then confirms to the sender that the information has been correctly received and entered into the system, or he may interrogate the system through the POD and receive an answer from the center. The elapsed time from activation of the POD to receipt of an acknowledgement or an answer depends on the speed of response required by the user. This may vary from milliseconds, where one machine is interrogating another, to seconds, in the case of a sales clerk asking for availability of stock while a customer is on the phone.

The term *Real Time* refers to this matching of the time of response of the system with the real-time response requirements of the user. The term *On-Line* has a significance beyond that of merely connecting the POD's directly to the computing center. It implies that information filed within the system is updated immediately upon the processing of each individual transaction.

This contrasts with the common method of "batch processing," where transaction data are collected and then processed at periodic intervals.

Although few, if any, companies can justify the cost of applying OLRT systems to every area of their data processing, many companies have decided that the value of almost immediate information does justify the cost in a number of areas. And frequently a system which is originally designed for one area within a company can be expanded to include other areas at little added cost. At the end of 1962, at least 70 companies were installing, or planning to install, an OLRT system for some phase of their information processing. The earliest example of an OLRT system in business was the one for airline reservations, where the high cost and extreme perishability of the inventory of available seats placed a high value on knowing the most current status of that inventory. The original system for reservations was then expanded to encompass ticketing, accounting, and sales analysis. Another industry which adopted an OLRT system early because of customer service requirements was that of savings banks, where the teller window functions were directly connected to a computing center which posted accounts on an immediate basis. Other industries which have started toward OLRT systems include stock brokers and the stock exchange itself, insurance companies, commercial banks, public utilities, and a variety of manufacturing and service businesses.

IMPACT ON CORPORATE ORGANIZATION

The foregoing introduction to developments in the areas of Management Sciences and Electronic Data Processing, although brief and sketchy, provides a basis for understanding the impact of the evolution of advanced business systems on the organization structure of companies. The primary force behind this evolution is the continuing improvement in the data processing capabilities which can be obtained for a given investment in electronic equipment. Thus more and more of the routine work previously done by people can be economically transferred onto a machine. Preoccupation with the immediate system details involved in each step of this evolution within an organization, and with the accompanying displacement of people in the lower levels of the organization, has tended to obscure the longer-range effect which this evolution is likely to have upon the top level of an organization.

In general, the development of advanced business systems tends to upset both of the two basically different types of corporate organization which are commonly encountered, the functional and the divisional. On the one hand, it reduces the significance of the traditional functional organization with its separate lines of reporting up through various levels to an executive with over-all responsibility for a function such as sales, production, or accounting. Not only do the evolving systems cross these lines and eliminate many of the clerical people within a functional area, but they frequently reduce the time spent by people on various activities considered more or less managerial in nature. The time required for supervision of clerical people is likely to decrease. Human review and interpretation of voluminous reports may be replaced by mechanical screening and exception reporting. Certain classes of routine decisions may require much less of people's time. Thus, some of the lower and middle management links in a functional chain of command tend to disappear. Functional organization, therefore, becomes less important as a means of reporting on the performance of people, at the same time that it becomes less representative of the flow of information within a company.

On the other hand, advanced business systems often make feasible and desirable the centralization of many functions which were previously performed separately at each division of a divisionally organized company. These systems may not only permit cost reductions through centralization of clerical data processing activities; they may also enable better over-all corporate planning through centralized integration of divisional planning decisions. The development of these systems also has the same tendency to eliminate certain lower- and middle-management functions in a divisional organization that it has in a functional organization. Divisional organization, therefore, becomes less of an economic necessity for processing information at widely separated locations, at the same time that it becomes less representative of the decision-making points within a company.

Although advanced business systems can and do work within both of the above types of organization, the development of these systems weakens the reason for strict adherence to either type. The type of organization that is most likely to evolve from the adoption of these systems is perhaps best indicated by the way companies have managed the development and installation of these systems. Because the systems cross existing organizational lines, the authority to make system changes has to be vested in an individual (or a committee) that is responsible only to top management, the president, or the board of directors. This "director of advanced business systems" supervises a group of specialists who devote full time to analyzing existing systems and designing and installing new ones. The specialists work directly with the people in each of the existing departments who are concerned with the system. With growth in the number of advanced systems installed, the group becomes a more or less permanent organization with some people responsible for operating the information processing center while others design new systems or program additional applications. The group (or groups) is usually made up largely of technical experts in systems analysis, computer programming, and operations research.

The technical orientation of the people composing the group should not be allowed to obscure the key fact about the establishment of such a group: It must become involved in decisions as to what information is to be provided for which decisions, to whom, and in what manner! The position of the person (or persons) directing this group is obviously quite important. Somehow he must resolve conflicting demands for information from various organizational areas within the company in the way which is in the best interests of the whole company. And the way in which these conflicts are resolved may vitally affect the status of the heads of the various areas concerned.

This would seem to indicate the fundamental impact of the evolution of advanced business systems on corporate organizational structure. A new function of "information control" will appear at the top level in the organization. It will encompass most of the routine work done anywhere in a company, including certain types of duties previously considered managerial. Management status in other functions will become less a matter of making many routine decisions or supervising much routine work and more a matter of evaluating and deciding and acting upon the more difficult problems.

The accounting function in a company is in a somewhat enviable position with respect to the impact of the evolution of advanced business systems. Accounting techniques form one of the three technological foundations of this evolution. Most of the information processed in a company is of an accounting nature. There is a tendency for the advanced business systems to find an administrative home in the accounting department, because that has been the most frequent location for the earlier punched card and computer installations. This position can be forfeited, however, unless the accountant has a basic appreciation of Electronic Data Processing and Operations Research and lends creative assistance to the development of advanced business systems which do more than merely process accounting data.

SUMMARY

The decade of the 1950's saw the introduction and widespread application in business of two important bodies of technology, Operations Research and Electronic Data Processing. The problem-solving capabilities of the first and the speed and accuracy of the second have opened new areas of approach to many business problems. The combination of techniques from these two areas with the techniques of Profitability Accounting makes possible the development of advanced business systems which will drastically change the processes of handling information and making decisions within a business. It may also cause radical change in the way in which a business is organized.

Index